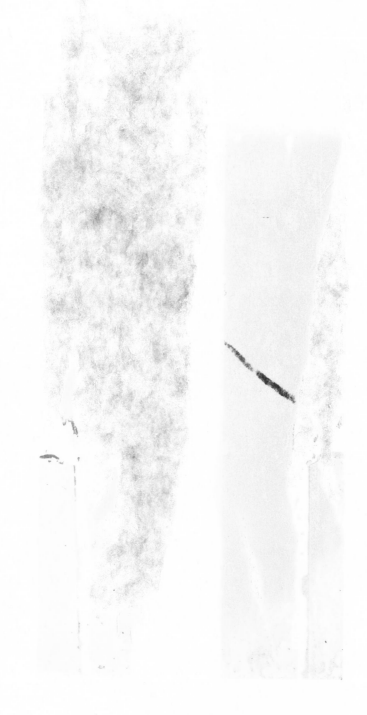

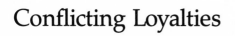

Conflicting Loyalties

Conflicting Loyalties

Law and Politics in the Attorney
General's Office, 1789–1990

Nancy V. Baker

University Press of Kansas

To
Dorothy Ellen Baker
and
the memory of Ray Gordon Baker

© 1992 by the University Press of Kansas
All rights reserved

Published by the University Press of Kansas (Lawrence, Kansas 66049), which was organized by the Kansas Board of Regents and is operated and funded by Emporia State University, Fort Hays State University, Kansas State University, Pittsburg State University, the University of Kansas, and Wichita State University

Library of Congress Cataloging-in-Publication Data

Baker, N. V.
    Conflicting loyalties : law and politics in the Attorney General's office, 1789–1990 / Nancy V. Baker.
        p.   cm.
    Includes bibliographical references (p.   ) and index.
    ISBN 0-7006-0530-4 (hardcover : alk. paper)
    1. United States. Dept. of Justice. Office of the Attorney General—History.   2. Political questions and judicial power—United States—History.   3. Law and politics.   I. Title.
    KF5107.B34 1992
    353.5—dc20   91-42344

British Library Cataloguing in Publication Data is available.

Printed in the United States of America
10 9 8 7 6 5 4 3 2 1

The paper used in this publication meets the minimum requirements of the American National Standard for Permanence of Paper for Printed Library Materials Z39.48-1984.

Contents

Preface

The question of the attorney general's advisory relationship with the president lies uncomfortably between presidential and legal studies and perhaps for this reason has been largely ignored by the political science community. Yet the question is one worth pursuing; the attorney general serves both as a presidential appointee and as an officer of the court. Many of the responsibilities are quasi-judicial, including the long-standing role as the president's legal adviser. The attorney general has a foot in both the political and legal worlds. This poses few problems when—as is usually the case—both worlds rotate in the same direction. However, balancing becomes difficult when they do not, and attorneys general have on occasion lost their equilibrium.

For the president and the executive officers to be under the law, they must rely on a chief legal adviser for guidance. The overriding importance of sound legal advice in the executive branch was illustrated as recently as 1986 when reports of arms sales to Iran and diversion of profits to Nicaraguan contras became public. Where was the attorney general during the planning and execution of these activities? There appears to have been a remarkable lack of legal review, one of the primary criticisms of the congressional committee that examined the Iran-contra affair.

In addition to the revelations of Iran-contra, Attorney General Edwin Meese's reversal of established legal positions and the reports of his unusual financial dealings served to resurrect questions that seemed to have been beaten to death just fifteen years ago after Watergate. Again we are asking: Is there something fundamentally wrong in the structure of the attorney generalship? Who is the attorney general's client? How may an incumbent resolve a potential conflict between loyalty to the law and loyalty to the president? Can one ascertain the kinds of qualities an attorney general nominee ought to have?

This study attempts to explore these issues. It draws heavily on original sources, such as congressional hearings and Department of Justice reports. I also had the opportunity to use the archival holdings of four presidential libraries—those of John Kennedy, Lyndon Johnson, Gerald Ford, and Jimmy Carter—and I appreciate the time and attention of their excellent staffs. Former attorneys general Elliot Richardson of the Nixon administration and Griffin Bell of the Carter administration were gracious in granting me interviews, and I am grateful to both men for their insights. Thomas Kauper of the Nixon/Ford Justice Department also shared his experiences and reflections, as did Charles Cooper, Terry Eastland, and Gary McDowell of the Reagan Justice Department. I wish to thank all of them for their thoughtful analyses of the office.

My research was aided by travel grants from the Gerald R. Ford Foundation, the John F. Kennedy Library Foundation, and the Tulane University Graduate School and Department of Political Science. I thank those organizations for their timely support.

I particularly wish to thank Dr. William B. Gwyn of Tulane University and Dr. Robert A. Strong of Washington and Lee University for their patient and intelligent reviews of the work-in-progress. I, however, remain completely responsible for any errors in the book. In conclusion, I appreciate the good humor, encouragement, and professional commitment of my colleagues in the Department of Government at New Mexico State University.

A brief note about gender in my choice of language: I have used the traditional "he" and "his" for the sake of flow and as a reflection of the fact that there have been no women attorneys general or presidents to date. That situation, I hope, will not long continue.

Nancy V. Baker
Las Cruces, New Mexico
August 1991

Chapter One

The Attorney General
of the United States

Two hundred years since its founding, the office of attorney general remains a key one within an administration. In some respects, it is a unique institution, unlike its peers in the executive branch, because the incumbent (sometimes uncomfortably) straddles two worlds: the legal and the political. An examination of the tensions that this may cause, and the responses of various attorneys general, may enable us to clarify our expectations of the office and reject those that are unrealistic or problematic.

Seventy-five men have sat at that figurative desk since 1789.[1] The burdens on the incumbent have increased heavily since Edmund Randolph took the first oath of office, significantly so over the past fifty years. The attorney general now administers the large bureaucracy of the Department of Justice and in that capacity supervises much of the investigative and courtroom work of the U.S. government. Beneath him, six divisions handle specific issues relating to criminal and civil law, tax law, antitrust, civil rights, and land and natural resources. He has responsibilities before the Supreme Court that are delegated to the solicitor general. In addition, he oversees U.S. attorneys and marshals, the Federal Bureau of Investigation, and the Immigration and Naturalization Service. Federal prisons, parole, pardons, and other law enforcement programs fall within his administrative jurisdiction.[2]

But before he became an administrator, the attorney general assumed the role of the adviser to the president. Second in seniority only to his role before the courts (which dates from the fourteenth century), his responsibility to advise the chief executive has antecedents in seventeenth-century England and the American colonies. Despite the tremen-

1

dous expansion of his official duties, the attorney general remains remarkably like his predecessors in this traditional advisory role. Admittedly, all department heads are constitutionally mandated to advise the president, but the attorney general is specifically charged with the statutory responsibility to "give his advice and opinion upon questions of law when required by the President of the United States, or when requested by the heads of any of the departments, touching any matters that may concern their departments."[3]

Unlike colleagues in the executive branch, the attorney general has responsibilities that are distinctly legal in character. He is the chief law officer of the nation, legal adviser, and officer of the court.[4] Yet he is also a political adviser, an appointed official in the executive branch, a member of the cabinet. Throughout, he is accountable to a political chief executive. His position is singular because he is, as one scholar has written, a "unique bridge between the executive and the judicial branches."[5] It is the dual nature of the office, in particular as it impinges on the advisory role, that is the central subject of this study.

Serving Two Masters

The legal/political duality has been noted by many scholars. Daniel Meador writes that the attorney general is both a law officer and an "executive officer who must act consistently with the policies of the Administration of which he is a part."[6] Robert Palmer argues that this "schizophrenic" condition has become more acute with the rise of the imperial presidency and the growth of executive power.[7] The most evocative phrasing comes from Whitney North Seymour, Jr., who writes that the law officer is compelled to serve two masters—the president and the law. To the president, he is a personal and political adviser; yet he also is responsible for "the ideal of nonpartisan, evenhanded Justice. Time and time again, these two functions collide with each other head on."[8] Seymour had experienced some of this tension during his tenure as a U.S. attorney. Others in public office have noted these joint obligations on the attorney general, including former special counsel Theodore Sorensen in the Kennedy administration[9] and Sen. Robert Byrd of West Virginia.[10] Late in life, Robert Jackson, who had been attorney general under Franklin Roosevelt, described the office as a dual one, encompassing responsibilities to the president and the country. As legal officer of the United States, he noted, the attorney general is not as free "to advocate an untenable position" for his client as a private attorney is.[11]

The attorney general's responsibilities can and do collide, as Seymour points out, yet they are not necessarily antagonistic. They coexist in an inherent tension. For some incumbents, the coexistence is uneasy and occasionally forces a difficult choice between competing loyalties: to the president and to the law. Obligated to serve the president, who is, in a sense, his client, the attorney general also must exhibit what former attorney general and legal scholar Edward Levi calls "a proper loyalty which we all recognize as lawyers to the idea of law itself."[12]

The case of Edward Bates, Abraham Lincoln's attorney general, illustrates the tension at work. Bates is credited with this idealistic conception of his responsibilities: "The office I hold is not properly *political*, but strictly *legal*; and it is my duty, above all other ministers of state, to uphold the law and to resist all encroachments, from whatever quarter, of mere will and power."[13] He also blasted his successor, James Speed, for supporting the legality of a military trial for Lincoln's assassins, calling him a mere tool of political forces.[14] A review of some of his advice, however, suggests that Bates himself often was concerned with expediency, military utility, and political repercussions as well as legality.[15] His justification of Lincoln's suspension of the writ of habeas corpus shows that he was not immune to the political exigencies of the time. Military authorities in May 1861 arrested John Merryman and other active secessionists in Maryland and then refused to obey a writ of habeas corpus issued by Chief Justice Roger Taney. Taney argued that the executive had exceeded its limits because the constitutional provision permitting a suspension was in the article dealing with Congress. As of early June, Attorney General Bates said the government had not yet decided its official policy. But the next month, the day after Lincoln defended his actions before a special session of Congress, Bates wrote a lengthy official opinion justifying the act.[16] Arguing that the constitutional language was unclear, Bates characterized the whole issue as political, not judicial. Insurrection itself is purely political, he wrote, and no court or judge can reverse the president's political decisions.[17] This is a conception of broad executive power similar to that expressed by Taney himself when he served as attorney general under Andrew Jackson.[18]

The tension stems from two roots. One, to be considered briefly in the conclusion, has to do with the nature of American law in general. A variation of this tension affects the Supreme Court in its role as interpreter of the law. We consider this a twentieth-century phenomenon, but de Tocqueville commented on it one hundred and fifty years ago. The prescient French writer observed: "An American judge, armed with the right to declare laws unconstitutional, is constantly intervening in political affairs. . . . There is hardly a political question in the United States which does not sooner or later turn into a judicial one."[19] One might speculate that the inverse is true as well, that many legal issues have inescapable policy implications. Even though there are obvious and important differences between an attorney general and a justice, this lack of a clear delineation between law and politics in our system plagues every officer who is charged with the task of legal interpretation.

The other root, the focus of much of this book, involves the structure of the office itself. The tension stems from the dual obligations imposed on the attorney general, who is charged with both quasi-judicial and executive/political responsibilities. Various incumbents have responded to this structural duality differently.

The Attorney General as a Legal Adviser

As the chief legal adviser of the government, the attorney general assists the president in fulfilling his constitutional obligation to "take care that the laws be faithfully executed." Before the president can "take care," he must first ascertain what those laws mean in concrete terms. For this, he "must have the counsel of those skilled in legal interpretation and legal institutions," to clearly define the scope and meaning of the law.[20] The attorney general (or his subordinates) often provides that counsel by writing a legal opinion.[21] Opinions also may be written to guide others in the executive branch who need legal advice, "as a check on executive conduct that may not be in accord with the law," writes former attorney general Griffin Bell, who adds, "In this complex society, the need for sound legal advice in advance of governmental action has become particularly acute."[22] In the drafting of legislation, a certain amount of imprecision is inescapable, which increases the need for legal interpretation. Levi, a legal scholar and former attorney general, explains, "It is only folklore which holds that a statute if clearly written can be completely unambiguous and applied as intended to a specific case. Fortunately or otherwise, ambiguity is inevitable in both statute and constitution as well as with case law."[23] Because of the broad language that characterizes much of modern lawmaking, Edward Corwin argues that executive interpretation of the law "frequently amounts today to a species of subordinate legislation."[24] For these reasons, the attorney general's opinions can affect both the administration and the development of the law. Clear-cut questions do not need his review; many of those that come to him could be decided either way and, presumably, his opinion will influence the outcome.

Further enhancing the importance of the opinion function is the fact that many of these questions never go to court. As Caleb Cushing explained in his famous treatise on the office in 1856, an opinion "is in practice final and conclusive,—not only as respects the action of public officers in administrative matters . . . but also in questions of private right, inasmuch as parties, having concerns with the government, possess in general no means of bringing a controverted matter before the courts of law."[25] Without the means to seek redress in the courts, individual parties are bound by the attorney general's interpretation as the definitive one. In fact, one legal scholar notes that "the answers [that the opinion] provides make up a considerable portion of the layman's version of the law."[26]

The opinion function has been widely regarded as quasi-judicial for more than a century. Legal articles referred to it as such as early as 1905.[27] Cushing considered it the *only* quasi-judicial function of the office. He denied that the attorney general's role in the courts required as much independence, because in the courts the attorney general serves as an advocate of the United States. In contrast, when he gives legal advice, "he is not a counsel giving advice to the government as his client, but a public officer, acting judicially, under all the solemn responsibilities of conscience and legal obligation."[28] Writing opinions relates directly to our system of law. It has been described as "legal in essence, administrative in its character and quasi-judicial in its effect."[29]

Attorneys general themselves vary in the amount of importance that they attach to the task. To recent attorney general Edwin Meese, for example, the courtroom role was of the greatest importance, because the subsequent ruling could change the course of the law.[30] Elliot Richardson, who has held several cabinet posts, including Justice, considers the administrative work the most interesting.[31] But some law officers assign the paramount position to the advisory function. For example, Richard Olney in the Cleveland administration considered "his duty in the attorney generalship was that he must be prepared before all else to assist the President as his legal adviser." He saw this as his first and foremost responsibility.[32]

The president is not bound by this legal advice. He may choose not to seek advice in the first place or ignore it once it has been rendered. The president retains the ultimate constitutional authority to decide a legal issue for the executive branch. Even so, if the president has enough doubts about the law that he requests advice, the presumption is that he will follow it. Presidents ignore legal advice at their own risk. President Nixon, for example, was publicly embarrassed when he announced a policy change without consulting his attorneys in the Justice Department. Wanting to demonstrate his seriousness about cutting the budget, Nixon informed Congress that he had abolished the U.S. Board of Tea Tasters. Unfortunately, the abolition order had not been cleared through the Office of Legal Counsel. One Justice Department attorney explains:

> We sent back an opinion that you cannot eliminate the Board of Tea Tasters because it was created by statute. This made the president look silly. His staff pleaded with the OLC to find some way to permit the president to eliminate it. But there was no way. The White House tried to eliminate [the board] through the reorganization powers, but this would have left tea locked up in warehouses. The tea could only be released on the approval of the Board of Tea Tasters, which would no longer exist. This is trivial but typical of what happens when advice is not solicited.[33]

There are occasions when a president has waited for an attorney general's advice before acting, or chosen not to act when told that his powers were in doubt. In 1939, for example, FDR heeded Frank Murphy's advice when he flatly told the president that he could not seize German and Italian vessels in American waters as a precaution against sabotage. Murphy also successfully countered the assertions of Interior Secretary Harold Ickes that Roosevelt should ignore the Neutrality Act as an invasion of his constitutional authority as commander-in-chief.[34] However, there are other examples of a president deciding to act contrary to the legal advice of his attorney general. The advice that Attorney General Cushing gave President Pierce on the Clayton-Bulwer Treaty was not followed, nor was Bates's advice against the admission of West Virginia into the union.[35] A president who is unhappy with an unfavorable opinion also has the option of resubmitting the question to a new attorney general. When Roosevelt wanted to lift the Spanish arms embargo in 1938, his then attorney general, Homer Cummings, advised him that he did not have the authority to do so without congressional action. Soon thereafter, Cummings resigned. Murphy, the new attorney general, was believed to be opposed to the embargo, so Ickes suggested that Roosevelt resubmit the question to Murphy, on the good chance that Murphy would rule favorably on the arms embargo issue. The president agreed, but the plan was aborted after Drew Pearson publicized Murphy's opposition to the embargo in his newspaper column. The story brought such strong pro-embargo pressure from Catholics on Murphy, himself a Catholic, that he had to deny his opposition. Roosevelt, in turn, was not able to receive from Murphy the advice that he had hoped for.[36]

In addition to the possibility that presidents will not seek or will not follow their advice, attorneys general also must be cognizant of the courts; they do not operate in a legal vacuum. Admittedly, these opinions serve as the expression of the law unless and until they are refuted by the courts; even so, they are subject to judicial review and have been overturned by the Supreme Court.[37] For example, as an associate justice, Robert Jackson concurred in two decisions that overruled his earlier attorney general opinions.[38] This, however, is not usual. While not feeling bound by these opinions, the judiciary does treat them with deference, occasionally adopting the law officer's reasoning or wording. The Court of Appeals of Maryland, for example, wrote that the Maryland attorney general's opinions, while not binding, were due careful consideration.[39] The courts generally recognize the maxim that executive interpretation, if it has been uniform and long-standing, ought to be accorded great weight by the justices and should not be ignored without strong and urgent reasons.[40] Mr. Justice Woodbury of the Supreme Court described this approach in 1850: "The opinions of [two] law officers of the government at different periods coincide. . . . Their opinions likewise have without doubt been adopted by the government, and our consuls instructed to conform to them, and this furnishes an additional consideration for not disturbing what is in operation under them."[41] Because of this deference, executive interpretation may influence subsequent judicial interpretation of the law.

While opinions are not binding on presidents or courts, they have occasionally been considered binding on other political actors in the executive branch. Some attorneys general have demanded adherence to their legal advice, as when Cummings wrote to Roosevelt: "The opinions of the Attorney General as chief law officer of the Government should be respected and followed in the administration of the executive branch of the Government."[42] Attorneys General Olney and William Moody, who served under Cleveland and Theodore Roosevelt, respectively, also considered opinions rendered to executive departments to be conclusive.[43] This view that advice is binding was evident as early as 1834, when a cabinet colleague eulogized on the death of Attorney General William Wirt that his "opinions, too, are official; not merely persuasive upon the judgment of officers, but, so far as the construction of the law is concerned, regarded as binding."[44]

But because courts have held themselves not bound by attorney general opinions, executive branch officers on occasion have made a similar claim.[45] During debates over the Department of Justice Act in 1870, the framers of the statute implied that officers are under a normative, not a legal, requirement to abide by formal opinions. Rep. Thomas A. Jenckes of Rhode Island, for example, said that executive officers should follow advice but were not legally bound to do so. He added, "Whether the opinion of the attorney general be right or wrong, it is an opinion which ought to be followed by all officers of the government until it is reversed by some competent court."[46] Other early attorneys general, with less exalted notions of their opinions, tended to agree. They considered them advisory only, although they cautioned executive officers to heed their advice in legal matters. Reverdy Johnson informed President Taylor's secretary of the Treasury that while his advice was not binding, department heads would be wise to follow it.[47] President Buchanan's attorney general, Jeremiah S. Black, wrote to a department head: "The duty of the Attorney General is to advise, not to decide. . . . He aids you in forming a judgment on questions of law; but still the judgment is yours, not his. You are not bound to see with his eyes, but only to use the light which he furnishes, in order to see the better with your own."[48] John Crittenden, Benjamin Butler, and Benjamin Brewster, also nineteenth-century law officers, agreed with the view that their opinions were only advisory and could be ignored by the department head requesting them.[49]

The federal courts have supported the view that an attorney general's opinion imposes certain obligations on executive officers. In the 1918 case of *Smith v. Jackson,* the Supreme Court ruled that an auditor for the Panama Canal Zone should have heeded the attorney general's opinion issued to the secretary of War.[50] Two legal scholars go so far as to cite this case as evidence that the court holds the binding view.[51] But in fact the case does not seem to present a clear and definitive statement that opinions are legally binding.[52]

Presidents have sometimes instructed subordinates to accede to official legal opinions, as Andrew Jackson did when he told his Treasury secretary "to take the atto. Genls. opinion and pursue it, he being our legal adviser, his opinion of the law, where there were doubts, ought to govern the heads of Departments as it did the President."[53] Woodrow Wilson, alarmed at the chaos in the nation's legal business during the war, also sought to compel compliance with his attorney general's opinions. His Executive Order No. 2877 (1918) read in part that "any opinion or ruling by the Attorney General upon any question of law arising in any department, executive bureau, agency or office shall be treated as binding upon all departments, bureaus or offices therewith concerned."[54]

The possibility of litigation involving legal liability also may affect a department's willingness to comply with advice. Following the attorney general's advice may show that an official acted in good faith and so help to protect him from liability for damages resulting from his discretionary acts.[55] The attorney general's control of government litigation provides a strong inducement for departments to seek and then follow advice. "The ultimate club that the Department of Justice has is the position it takes in litigation," Thomas Kauper explains. "I said to one agency that we would confess error when it came to court if they continued [to refuse to comply with the Freedom of Information Act] and litigation was brought."[56] Most executive officers must rely on the attorney general's office to defend their actions if a case comes before the courts. The law officer is in an untenable position if he must defend departmental action that he had advised against; his own earlier opinion may be turned against him by the opposition in court. One legal scholar writes that an attorney general cannot refuse to represent a government client who has ignored his advice, as a private attorney may.[57] But Kauper argues that Justice Department attorneys do not have to support an agency in court if they believe the agency is wrong. Furthermore, Justice has a policy of refusing to give opinions on issues already in litigation or about to go into litigation.[58]

There are occasions when an opinion has not been followed by executive officers, although it may be impossible to determine the precise extent to which this might be so.[59] Furthermore, an official may choose not to ask advice when he suspects a disagreement with the attorney general. There is no method to compel a department head to seek advice from outside his departmental attorneys. The general rule that has developed is that an opinion ought to be followed if the department head has requested it.

Not every scholar agrees with this normative approach—the notion that executive officers should feel obligated to follow the attorney general's advice. In her critical analysis of the office in Kentucky, Dee Ashley Akers argues that an opinion "is not law, so it should not be treated as law. . . . There is no persuasive reason why an administrator, who is responsible for the administration of his department, and often himself a lawyer, should blindly pursue a course deemed best by an advisor neither connected nor familiar with [his department]. Judicial viewpoints . . . roam the range from liberal to conservative. Attorneys general are no less susceptible to variation."[60] The function is useful and probably essential in modern government, she concedes, but it can assume an importance out of proportion with the rest of government. When official opinions receive absolute deference (as she said they did in a few agencies in Kentucky), the result is "attorney general legislation," a kind of unadjudicated law, that can create confusion at the very least and raise questions about democratic process.[61]

Attorneys general experience other limitations on their advisory role than the generally held notion that their opinions are not binding. One substantial limit is the law officer's enormous workload. His daily agenda is full of activities that compete for his limited time and attention. Increasingly, incumbents have delegated the advisory duty to the Office of Legal Counsel. Created in 1933, the OLC is headed by an assistant attorney general who has a staff of twenty lawyers.[62] They prepare formal and informal legal opinions for government agencies and departments. "Our mission is to assist the attorney general in his advice-giving role. The president, usually through the White House counsel, is our biggest client," the recent head of the OLC, Charles Cooper, explains.[63] Essentially, the office is an arm of the attorney general. Cooper defined his role as the attorney general's attorney. As such, the office has assumed a larger role in issuing formal opinions, some involving important issues. In 1974, for example, the OLC considered the applicability of the Congressional Budget and Impoundment Control Act to prior executive impoundments and ruled on the ownership of presidential papers in the possession of the White House.[64] Both of these were highly controversial at the time. But although subordinate to the attorney general, the office operates with autonomy under some law officers. Under John Mitchell, for example, the OLC cleared very little of its advice with the attorney general. "Requests for opinions did not come through Mitchell, and they were never routed back through unless they were quite spectacular. They generally were sent to the White House without the attorney general's input," Kauper explains. He believes that the same practice continued during the Johnson years. "During the transition, I did not get the impression from [the outgoing people at OLC] that very much went through Ramsey Clark [LBJ's attorney general], possibly because he was never a very popular figure with the White House." Kauper speculates, for example, that John Mitchell was completely unaware of the Tea Tasters incident involving the OLC and President Nixon.[65]

The opinion function is also hampered by the fact that the attorney general and his staff have no monopoly on legal advice; other sources, especially in the executive branch, are available to the president and department heads. Before the first attorney general arrived in the capital, the president relied on the New York Bar for legal opinions.[66] Later, the Supreme Court, in particular Chief Justice John Jay, briefly fulfilled the role of adviser. Even after the responsibility for providing legal advice devolved onto the law officer, President Washington continued to look to his other department heads, including Thomas Jefferson, Alexander Hamilton and Henry Knox. On occasion, he also drew on the expertise of Madison in the House of Representatives.[67] While presidents no longer seem to seek legal advice from sources in other branches, they continue to depend on lawyers elsewhere in the executive branch. Each department maintains its own legal staff to advise on strictly departmental matters. In matters of international law, the State Department's legal adviser is recognized for expertise. That officer testified to Congress in 1954 that "we do not depend upon the Attorney General to advise us," although their relations were close and cooperative.[68] In budgetary matters, the White House relies on the general counsel of the Office of Management and Budget for legal advice. "It is a whole body of law that no one else on the face of God's earth has ever heard of," Kauper says. While formally these officers are subordinate to the attorney general, in practice they operate autonomously. "Sometimes I wondered whether the attorney general had any idea what legal advice the president was relying on, or the president, where it [the advice] came from. He may assume it comes from the attorney general, but ninety-nine out of one hundred times, it does not."[69]

The attorney general's advice also occasionally conflicts with that rendered by government advisers outside the executive branch, in particular the comptroller general of the General Accounting Office. The GAO, an independent auditing agency, assists congressmen in a variety of ways, including issuing legal opinions on the implementation of legislation. In the fifteen years ending in 1976, more than five hundred legal opinions were issued by the comptroller general in response to congressional requests. Some conflicted with the attorney general's. In 1966, disagreement arose between the GAO and Justice over the legality of a shipment of medical supplies to Yugoslavia.[70] Three years later, a more serious confrontation occurred involving an affirmative action program in the awarding of government contracts. The GAO ruled that the Labor Department's proposed implementation, called the Philadelphia Plan, was a violation of the ban on racial quotas in the Civil Rights Act of 1964. Attorney General John Mitchell, however, upheld the plan's legality and the Labor secretary put the plan into effect. Then, before a Senate subcommittee, the comptroller general testified against the notion that "the executive branch of the government has the right to act upon its own interpretation of the laws enacted by Congress, and to expend and obligate funds . . . in a manner which my office . . . has found to be contrary to law."[71] This is an interesting assertion of legal preeminence by an officer closely identified with Congress. The Senate passed a rider to enforce his authority in approving any federal monies spent by contractors. The House rejected the rider. While Nixon tried to conciliate the comptroller general, a federal district court upheld Mitchell's view.[72] The immediate source of conflict was resolved; however, the potential for future confrontation between the legal advisers in the two branches remains.

The attorney general faces his most constant and genuine competitor in the White House counsel. The counsel, a post created by Franklin Roosevelt, provides the president with advice on a gamut of legal and nonlegal issues. As a member of the staff, this lawyer is not coequal with the cabinet-level attorney general, and his advice does not carry the same weight before the courts. But his placement in the White House gives him a proximity to the president that enhances his advisory role. Justice Felix Frankfurter expressed his concern regarding the special counsel to the president, as it was then called, in an indirect communication to Eisenhower's attorney general nominee, Herbert Brownell. The justice wrote: "I do not think this subordination of the Department of Justice, as the President's legal advisor, to the legal shop of the White House has been a conspicuous success." He blamed the special counsel for Truman's bad decision to seize and operate the nation's steel mills in 1952,[73] an action later ruled unconstitutional by the Supreme Court in the case *Youngstown Sheet & Tube Co. v. Sawyer*. Griffin Bell, who served as Carter's attorney general, considers the White House counsel's office a competing power center. "At times, the counsel has been more of a general presidential assistant than a lawyer, but in recent years the job has taken on increasing amounts of legal work."[74] Bell describes several instances when the counsel's office attempted to usurp Justice Department authority in judicial nominations, in legal policy, and in government positions in litigation.[75] Other examples to be explored in a later chapter include the active advisory role played by Gerald Ford's White House counsel in the *Mayaguez* incident, when the attorney general evidently was not consulted.[76]

Under different administrations, the White House counsel does not seem to play as active of a role in legal, as opposed to policy, advice. Former Attorney General Elliot Richardson believes that the White House counsel's staff does not play a major role in the average administration. "They address issues peculiar to the White House," he notes, and do not replace the attorney general as legal adviser.[77] Terry Eastland, chief spokesman in the Meese Justice Department of the Reagan administration, agrees: "The White House is not a pure lawyer shop." Because that office is more preoccupied with policy concerns, it cannot duplicate the legal advice role.[78] His colleague at Justice, Charles Cooper, also said that there are important differences between the White House counsel's office and the attorney general's, with the latter encompassing the principal legal advisers in the executive branch. While the counsel's office may spot the legal issues, the important and controversial questions go to Justice.[79] Theodore C. Sorensen, John Kennedy's special counsel, also asserted that his duties did not overlap with the attorney general's. He was involved "as a policy adviser to the President with respect to legislation, with respect to his programs and messages, with respect to Executive orders, and with respect to those few formally legal problems, which come to the White House."[80] Nicholas Katzenbach, Johnson's law officer, warned of the danger to a president who depends on his White House staff for legal advice, "because they simply don't have the time and experience and the files on some of this that are absolutely essential to giving good advice to the president. There are files in the Office of Legal Counsel that go back through the years; you know what other presidents have been advised; you know where other presidents have gotten in trouble."[81]

Another potential competitor in the giving of advice could be the president himself. On rare occasions, presidents have assumed the legal advisory role. The practice is perfectly constitutional given that the "take care" duty rests with the president. Taft presided over a presidential court to determine the legal meaning of the word "whiskey" raised under the pure food laws, since his attorney general and solicitor general disagreed on the scope of the definition. The president summoned Attorney General Charles Bonaparte and the secretary of Agriculture to sit with him while he heard two days of argument by distinguished counsel. After that, he read the 1,200 pages of testimony taken earlier by the solicitor general. Then Taft wrote his own opinion in the appropriate judicial manner and directed the secretaries of Agriculture, Commerce, Labor, and Treasury to use it in preparing regulations under the pure food law. His definition was broader than that suggested by either of his law officers.[82] Taft, who genuinely enjoyed judicial activities, later served on the Supreme Court as Chief Justice.

Franklin Roosevelt also issued his own legal opinion, in an incident recorded years later by Robert Jackson when he sat on the bench. Jackson wrote in 1953, "The document probably is the only one of its kind in our history—it is extraordinary for the President to render a legal opinion to the Attorney General." In 1941, Roosevelt was in a dilemma over the Lend-Lease Act, which he badly wanted. Congress had attached a provision that he thought unconstitutional. It provided for the repeal of the legislation by concurrent resolution of both houses, without any presidential action; FDR worried about its long-term effect on the president's veto power. (As attorney general, Jackson was less convinced that the provision was unconstitutional.) Roosevelt did not want to veto the bill, or to express his disapproval of the provision publicly, because the bill's opponents had used these same arguments in Congress. Instead, he signed the bill and then secretly sent to the attorney general his own official memorandum objecting to the provision. Jackson received the document, dated April 7, 1941, and was puzzled as to its status. He wrote: "While it was referred to as an 'official' opinion, it neither required nor prohibited any departmental official action, and bound no one officially. Despite the high official position of its author, it is not an official act but a personal explanation and opinion of Franklin D. Roosevelt on a smouldering issue between the Executive and Congress."[83] Satisfied that this opinion protected the presidency from a dangerous precedent, Roosevelt thereafter approved other acts with the same offending provision and thus was able to secure passage of much wartime legislation.

The final group of restrictions placed on an attorney general's ability to render legal advice are the self-imposed restraints. Through the years, incumbents have developed informal guidelines, many of them borrowed from judicial traditions. One rule prohibits the attorney general from giving advice to Congress, except in his capacity as a department head called to testify. Initially, the attorney general provided the legislature with legal advice; in fact, the task accounted for a large portion of his business in the first thirty years of the office, even though many congressmen were themselves skilled lawyers.[84] Until the appointment of William Wirt, attorneys general did not question their responsibility to advise Congress, on issues ranging from the judiciary to individual claims against the government. Wirt was the first law officer to respond to a congressional request with the assertion that he was limited by statute to the executive branch. In January 1820 the House asked his opinion on a petition of Maj. Joseph Wheaton; Wirt wrote back that his duties were specified by law and did not include advising Congress. "The Attorney General is sworn to discharge the duties of his office according to law. To be instrumental in enlarging the sphere of his official duties beyond that which is prescribed by law would, in my opinion, be a violation of this oath," he wrote. He had intimated in a similar incident in 1818 that the House could legally enlarge his duties if it wished his advice, but the House had not done so. He concluded, "Believing as I do that, in a government purely of laws, it would be incalculably dangerous to permit an officer to act, under color of his office, beyond the pale of the law, I trust that I shall be excused from making any *official* report on the order with which the House has honored me."[85] For some time, the Congress continued to make its requests for advice. Lincoln's attorney general, Edward Bates, responded to a Senate query on much the same grounds more than forty years later.[86] While attorneys general no longer serve as congressional legal advisers, they do continue the practice of appearing before committees to testify on proposed legislation dealing with their department, criminal justice, or the courts; in this sense they continue to contribute their expertise to the Congress.

Attorneys general also have limited the scope of legal advice that they may render to the heads of the executive departments. Unlike their broad advisory relationship with the president, they advise departments only on questions of law, and only on those that pertain to that particular department.[87] The request must come from the department head, not a subordinate officer.[88] Furthermore, many law officers have refused to give opinions on questions that are really judicial, preferring to have the courts decide.[89] The departments also must give the attorney general a full brief of the facts and pose real, not abstract, questions, although increasingly law officers render advice on contemplated action as well as on actual cases.[90] As Robert Kennedy advised his brother in 1960, the attorney general "will not answer questions which are hypothetical in nature or the solution of which depends upon facts which have not been made available to him."[91]

Law officers also tend to bind themselves to such common law judicial traditions as the principle of *stare decisis*, abiding by decisions of predecessors when deciding analogous cases. For example, Katzenbach responded to a departmental request that he reexamine a 1934 opinion by writing: "Even if the question were more doubtful as an original matter, I would nevertheless adhere to the opinion rendered by Attorney General Cummings. That opinion has been outstanding for over thirty years and the . . . policy developed in reliance on it has had a significant impact on worldwide shipping practices."[92] The principle is not as binding on them as it is on the judiciary, and law officers on occasion do change earlier opinions, although when opinions are changed, the tradition is that they are "overruled much like cases, instead of being merely withdrawn."[93] Such niceties are not always followed, however. Some changes have been made with little deference for the earlier opinion. For example, in 1831, Attorney General John Berrien overturned an earlier opinion by William Wirt that found Negro seamen laws to be unconstitutional. These laws, prevalent in the Antebellum South, required that black seamen be imprisoned while their ships were in Southern ports. Berrien felt that such laws were part of state police powers and protected by the Tenth Amendment, so he overruled Wirt's 1823 opinion.[94]

Attorneys general also attempt to avoid ruling on the constitutionality of legislation. Attorney General Francis Biddle told Franklin Roosevelt that he should not give opinions to executive officers on the constitutionality of laws they were appointed to administer. Biddle wrote, "There can rarely be proper occasion for an opinion by the attorney general upon the constitutionality of a measure after it has become law, and it is not within his province to declare an act of the Congress unconstitutional—at least where it does not involve conflict between the prerogatives of the legislature and executive departments."[95] Mitchell Palmer earlier expressed this view as well, arguing that "it is the duty of the executive department to administer it until it is declared unconstitutional by the courts."[96] The same does not seem to be the case when the legislation is still pending. George Washington sought advice from his law officer on the constitutionality of the bank bill before signing it into law.[97] Taft vetoed the Webb-Kenyon Act of 1913 after his attorney general, George Wickersham, advised him that it would probably be found unconstitutional by the Supreme Court. As it turned out, Wickersham had misread the Court and was chided four years later by the Chief Justice. Homer Cummings and Carl McFarland cite this rebuke as the reason that their contemporaries in the Justice Department were more circumspect in questioning a bill's constitutionality,[98] but they fail to make the important distinction between legislation already enacted and legislation awaiting presidential signature. Pending legislation often has been the subject of attorney general advice. In fact, even enacted legislation is facing an erosion of this traditional presumption of constitutionality. Two recent attorneys general have challenged the constitutionality of certain laws and court decisions. Edwin Meese consistently called the independent counsel law unconstitutional, a charge he also leveled at the *Roe v. Wade* Supreme Court ruling, as has Attorney General Richard Thornburgh.[99] It is too early to tell if this constitutes a break from tradition or is peculiar to these particular incumbents.

The attorney general's opinion function is not narrow and restricted, despite the foregoing restraints on it. The enabling legislation is so open-ended that attorneys general and their presidents have found plenty of room to maneuver in their efforts to determine the legal advisability of particular courses of action.

The Attorney General as a Policy Adviser

The attorney general has another advisory role in addition to that of legal counsel: that of political adviser. This function, which is paramount in some administrations, stems from his position as an appointed official in the administration of an elected chief executive. Luther A. Huston writes that

> men who have held the office of attorney general have woven binding threads into the fabric of history and have participated as statesmen or as counselors of statesmen in events that have shaped the policies and destinies of the nation. . . . The law, however, has not always been their primary interest. Some have been more interested and better qualified for diplomacy, politics, or even other administrative positions in the executive department.[100]

The attorney general offers policy/political advice in three of his capacities. First of all, he is the head of the Department of Justice in the executive branch. Article II, Section 2 of the Constitution provides that the president "may require the opinion, in writing, of the principal officer in each of the executive departments, upon any subject relating to the duties of their respective offices." As an administrator (formally since 1870 but *de facto* much earlier), the attorney general furnishes the chief executive with policy advice relating to his departmental responsibilities. He defines priorities, develops policy, submits budgetary requests, and participates in formulating legislation related to justice and the federal court system. He assists in selecting and screening nominees to the federal bench. In addition, he testifies before Congress, explaining policy, supporting or opposing legislation, and defending his budget. Many of these responsibilities date from the first term of George Washington. His attorney general, Edmund Randolph, sent to the House of Representatives at their request an analysis of the faults of the Judiciary Act of 1789 and a bill to rectify those faults.[101]

In his second capacity, as a member of the cabinet, a law officer may be involved in policy-making, depending on the administration's use of the cabinet. As Biddle and others note, the cabinet can make policy, although often incrementally, through small decisions.[102] The attorney general, like all cabinet members, may advise on matters not connected to his department at all, participating in decisions affecting foreign or domestic affairs, such as education or national security. He may be required to lobby Congress on measures that are only tangentially related, if that, to his department.[103] A political cost may be attached to his cabinet membership because of the danger that "his inevitable involvement in [policy] discussions contributes to the appearance in the eyes of his cabinet colleagues and the White House staff that he is simply another political appointee."[104] The practice of presidents consulting executive officers on issues outside of their jurisdiction also has a long history. Washington relied on Randolph's counsel and not that of Secretary of State Jefferson when confronted with France's demand that Ambassador Gouverneur Morris be replaced.[105]

Many attorneys general operate in a third capacity as well, as a friend and political ally of the president. As such, they may help plan campaign strategy or articulate broad administration policy goals. With few exceptions, law officers maintain warm personal relations with their chief executives. Of that number, a handful are trusted advisers on whom their presidents depend for a wide range of advice. Historically, "presidents have relied heavily on selected advisors, regardless of their bureaucratic status, in whom they had great confidence and trust."[106] Randolph, who had been Washington's personal lawyer, undertook many unofficial missions for the president, including one to assess domestic political reactions to the French Revolution and the president's

Neutrality Proclamation.[107] Robert Kennedy filled a similar role in his brother's administration; his influence during the Cuban Missile Crisis indicates the trust in which he was held by John Kennedy. Reagan and Attorney General Edwin Meese had such a close personal and political friendship that Meese would have been an intimate adviser regardless of official title. As one colleague explained, Reagan would have relied on him on a whole range of issues even if he had been the secretary of the Interior.[108]

Other law officers have engaged in the same pattern of combining legal and political functions. Judge Ebenezer Hoar, who served under Grant, "took exclusive charge of the political business of the office," in particular, relations with Great Britain. Relations were deteriorating in large part because of U.S. claims that Britain should pay for damages done by the *Alabama* and other Confederate ships, which Britain had accorded belligerency status. Hoar served as the administration's liaison with several opposition senators who urged a hard-line approach to England. He also was influential in convincing the eager president not to grant belligerency status to insurgents in Cuba—as Britain had done to the Confederates—because it was not justified by international law and because it weakened the U.S. position on the *Alabama* claims.[109]

Cleveland's attorney general, Richard Olney, also mixed his political and legal duties. He actively sought advice on the national financial crisis of 1893 and assisted in drafting economic legislation. He became involved in foreign affairs as well, especially in developing the administration's negative response to the overthrow of Queen Liliuokalani of Hawaii, which had been aided and abetted by the State Department of the previous administration.[110]

Most attorneys general have had politically active pasts, a phenomenon evident as early as the Jefferson administration; his attorneys general—Levi Lincoln, John Breckenridge, and Caesar Rodney—were all active in politics before appointment.[111] Some have even been pivotal in the election of their chief executives. Buchanan's law officer, Jeremiah Black, has been described as "an important wheel in the machine which elevated that elderly functionary to the Presidency."[112] Among the twentieth-century presidents who chose former campaign managers for the post are Warren G. Harding (Harry Daugherty), Dwight Eisenhower (Herbert Brownell), John Kennedy (Robert Kennedy), and Richard Nixon (John Mitchell). Franklin Roosevelt's first attorney general, Homer Cummings, had been the chair of the Democratic National Committee for many years.[113] J. Howard McGrath was national party chair during Truman's difficult 1948 race; he joined Justice the next year.[114] Theodore Roosevelt, Woodrow Wilson, and Ronald Reagan also selected active campaigners to be attorney general, and Calvin Coolidge attempted to do so.[115] In fact, every president since 1933—with the exception of Johnson, Ford, and Carter—named either a campaign manager or national party chairman as attorney general sometime during his administration.[116] Nonpolitical law officers have been appointed on occasion, but they are the exception. Instead, "most Presidents have appointed men who have worked closely with them on political matters."[117] Speculation that the days of politically active law officers are gone has proven to be premature or unrealistic. In 1980, Harold Tyler predicted on the basis of the Ford and Carter experience that "it is likely that Presidents in the future, when considering an appointment for Attorney General, will turn to men and women who did not play a prominent role in presidential election campaigns."[118] Just five years later, Reagan nominated for the post Edwin Meese, a man who had played an active part in his previous campaigns.

Before and after their service in the Justice Department, many incumbents have held elective office. Fifteen have served in the Senate; fifteen in the House of Representatives. Ten have been governors.[119] A few have had presidential ambitions,[120] although no attorney general has yet become president or vice-president.[121] They often have been assigned other cabinet posts.[122] The attorney generalship also has served as a stepping stone to the Supreme Court; seven have been confirmed, with three others nominated but rejected by the Senate. This trend seemed the rule in the 1940s, when three of the decade's four attorneys general became justices.[123] None has been named since that time, however.

The issue of politics influencing the law is complicated by the fact that so many law officers have had political pasts and even may owe their appointments to politics. But an attorney general's background, of itself, is not at the heart of the tension. Nor is the fact that, under some of his many hats, he engages in policy-making. Rather, the fundamental tension between law and politics may emerge out of the intertwined nature of the two in the American political system.

The Tradition of Law and Politics

Because so many legal issues have inescapable policy/political aspects, it may not be possible for opinions to be politically neutral. Furthermore, law officers themselves, because they are appointees of a political chief executive, are considered by some scholars as unavoidably predisposed to favor politics over legalities. This view is reflected in the 1950 report of the International Law Commission, which suggested caution in using opinions of national legal advisers to determine customary international law, "for the efforts of legal advisers are necessarily directed to the implementation of policy."[124] In his study of state attorneys general, Peter Heiser notes that "some attorneys general will be more likely to 'adjust' their legal conclusions to reflect political predilections."[125] The attorney general's advisory role has been criticized for being especially susceptible to executive branch politicization. As a presidential adviser, he is unable "to act in a politically neutral fashion, free from the influence of the executive, [which] casts further doubt upon his ability to act on behalf of the public."[126] The contention that attorneys general render legally questionable opinions to support their presidents' policies has a long tradition. It was raised in a Senate debate in 1866, for example, when legislators sought to overturn an interpretation that Attorney General Wirt had given a clause in the Constitution more than forty years earlier. The issue involved the presidential appointment power, which the Senate was seeking to restrict. Sen. Jacob Howard of Michigan complained that Wirt and subsequent attorneys general "took very great liberties with this [constitutional] language . . . [even though the language] is too plain to be mistaken." In an impassioned reply, Sen. Reverdy Johnson, who had himself been an attorney general in 1849, reminded the Senate that eminent men had long served in that office:

As far as I am advised, without any exception, from the time of their appointment to the present hour, there never has been an opinion given by any incumbent of that office upon any question which he did not believe to be in itself sound. It is possible that party may have unconsciously influenced his judgment; but if it be true that officers of that kind might be influenced by party considerations, I suppose it is equally true that Senators of the United States may unconsciously be influenced by like motives.

He went on to assert that the opinion in question had been supported not only by a succession of law officers, but also by all of the presidents under whom they had served, and even by congressional sanction.[127]

The issue resurfaced a few years later, during the House debate over the act creating the Department of Justice. Arguing that law officers throughout government should be accountable to the attorney general, Representative Jenckes said that otherwise they "give advice which seems to have been instigated by the heads of the Department, or at least advice which seems designed to strengthen the resolution" of the department head. Rep. Horace Maynard responded:

Does the gentlemen think it peculiar in this country for a law officer to give an opinion to sustain the attitude of his superior? Has it not been done more than once in the office of the Attorney General of the United States? . . . I remind him of the anecdote of a former President who sent word to his Attorney General that if he could not find law for a particular policy he (the President) would find an Attorney General who could find law for it.

In his lengthy reply, Jenckes conceded that a president or department head might "act on his own responsibility," but he never really addressed the issue that Maynard raised.[128]

The anecdote to which Maynard referred is the quintessential myth dealing with the issue of adjusting legal opinions to suit political needs. It continues to be cited as an example of presidents pressuring their law officers for favorable legal interpretations,[129] but there is ample evidence undermining its historical veracity. The tradition is that President Andrew Jackson, determined to destroy the U.S. Bank by withdrawing federal deposits, instructed his reluctant attorney general to find a legal means to withdraw the funds, or he would find an attorney general who could. But a study of his then attorney general, Roger Taney, forces one to challenge the accuracy of the tale. Taney was a more avid opponent of the bank than Jackson and, far from being restrained and legalistic, favored an activist application of the law. While it is true that Taney, as a state senator in 1818, opposed the Maryland law taxing the bank, he generally supported state banking interests and even became an attorney and director for the Union Bank of Maryland.[130] Six years before becoming attorney general, Taney was counsel in a suit against the U.S. Bank, charging its officers with misappropriating $3.5 million in bank stock.[131] Further discrediting the myth are the remarks made by Reverdy Johnson, Taney's longtime friend and occasional political foe, after Chief Justice Taney's death. Johnson repudiated the allegation "that Mr. Taney was appointed to be the mere instrument . . . of the President's will" in the bank affair. Well before he joined Jackson's cabinet, Taney had confided in Johnson that the bank was dangerous because it was used for partisan political ends: "He therefore considered it to be the duty and interest of the Government . . . to remove the public money from its custody, and said that if the authority was with him he would lose no time in exercising it. If influence, therefore, was exerted at all . . . it was the influence of *Taney* on Jackson, and not Jackson on Taney."[132] Far from being a servile attorney general intimidated by Jackson's threats, Taney originated the plan to withdraw the funds, at a time when John Berrien was still the attorney general.[133] Jackson's alleged threat may have been made instead to William J. Duane, who as Treasury secretary refused the presidential order to withdraw the deposits. Jackson responded by shifting his cabinet personnel, moving Taney into the Treasury post. Believing that the bank's charter gave the president the power to withdraw the funds, Taney executed the order. Reverdy Johnson noted that even the bank never questioned the legal right of the executive to pass the order.[134]

The suspicion that opinions are fixed to support legally questionable actions continues. In his account of the Watergate investigation, Sam Ervin writes that "the Department of Justice . . . all too often makes its ruling on constitutional and legal questions harmonize with the political desires of the White House."[135] Griffin Bell also notes that the independent deliberations of attorneys general occasionally conflict with the policy preferences of their presidents. He recounted a historical incident involving a previous attorney general from Georgia: "A. T. Akerman, who was in office in 1870 when the Department of Justice was created, lost his job over independence. Akerman . . . refused President Ulysses Grant's request that he execute the deed conveying western lands to the railroads. The signatures of both the President and the Attorney General are needed to convey public lands. Grant fired Akerman."[136] In the view of some, policy preferences of either president or attorney general should not influence the drafting of a legal opinion. "The Attorney General is responsible for giving the President his legal opinion rather than an opinion that would meet the chief executive's policy views or needs."[137]

Another accusation leveled at attorneys general is that they use their legal opinions to buttress presidential authority in relation to the other branches. This is the thesis of Martin Sheffer, who considers Robert Jackson's opinion on the legality of the bases-for-destroyers exchange to be a blatant attempt to aggrandize executive power.[138] This case will be examined in depth later, but other incidents reinforce Sheffer's basic argument. For example, Jackson gave two other opinions that expanded executive power. One supported Roosevelt's authorizing British pilots to receive flight instructions from the Army Air Corps.[139] Another informed the Agriculture secretary that he had authority to purchase land to construct a migratory labor camp without explicit statutory provision.[140] Jackson's successor, Francis Biddle, interpreted presidential power broadly when he recognized the president's authority to direct the Commerce secretary to take possession of Montgomery Ward.[141] The company had refused to comply with the War Labor Board's orders regarding union rights. The issue was potentially explosive because of the threat of strikes during wartime.[142] Lyndon Johnson's law officer, Ramsey Clark, advised that the executive branch was not compelled to spend funds authorized by congressional appropriations. He justified the impoundment of $3 billion in federal expenditures as a necessary act because of the inflationary economy.[143]

Contrary to Sheffer's theory, examples of opinions limiting presidential action do exist. Both Hugh Legare in the Tyler administration and Reverdy Johnson in the Taylor administration advised their presidents against acts that could violate neutrality laws.[144] Benjamin Brewster in the Arthur administration was especially scrupulous in limiting the legal scope of executive authority, which is consistent with the rest of his tenure, to be examined in chapter five.[145] Opinions restricting executive power are evident throughout FDR's first term. Palmer in 1920, Daugherty in 1922 and 1923, and Cummings in 1935 and 1936 all rendered opinions that restricted some action by the executive branch until Congress had acted.[146] Attorneys general have often advised their presidents that they may not intervene in departmental responsibilities that are statutorily imposed on their subordinate executive officials. When performing these statutory duties, officials are not agents of the president.[147] Few examples can be found in contemporary records; attorneys general in the modern era seem to be less restrictive in defining the scope of presidential power. However, a large number of current opinions are not published, so examples may exist but are not in the official compilations.

For other attorneys general, the record is mixed. Attorney General Philander Knox, for example, ruled against executive authority and his own preferences in 1901 when he advised that game refuges in the national forests could only be established through legislation. He told McKinley that he regretted having to make that decision: "I would be glad to find authority for the intervention by the secretary [of Interior] for the preservation of what is left of the game. . . . But it would seem that whatever is done in that direction must be done by Congress, which alone has the power."[148] Yet Knox is also responsible for the 300-page opinion validating a French company's questionable title to a canal concession across the Isthmus of Panama.[149] The opinion opened the way for the United States to purchase the concession and build a canal, which Theodore Roosevelt badly wanted. The incident has been cited as an example of the law being manipulated for policy ends. One version of the tale has Knox reportedly saying afterward that the great plan was not marred by the slightest "taint of legality."[150]

If legal opinions are adjusted to support presidential policy choices, the result does not necessarily expand presidential power. It depends, of course, on the president's preferences. James Buchanan, for example, did not want to be told he had the power to send federal reinforcements to forts in Charleston, South Carolina. Although South Carolina had seceded, he balked at the use of force, still believing that war could be averted through compromise. He asked his law officer, Jeremiah Black, if he could send in troops when no federal officials there had requested them (all federal officials in that state had resigned, including judges, U.S. attorneys, and marshals). Black, who agreed with the conciliatory Buchanan, replied that troops could not be dispatched to aid the courts and marshals if there were no courts or marshals to be aided. The president could use force only defensively, to repel an assault on U.S. public property; to use force offensively would negate the Constitution and absolve all states of their federal obligations.[151] Black soon left to become secretary of State. In that position, under the influence of the new attorney general, Edwin Stanton, Black reversed himself and became one of the stronger cabinet voices in favor of federal action.[152]

There is a political atmosphere around the attorney general, stemming from the fact that many law officers have led active public and political lives, coupled with the policy-oriented roles imbedded in the structure of the office. While "exhortations concerning integrity, independence, and the rule of law" are helpful, politics and the danger of improper political influences are ever present.[153] Even if an attorney general consciously adopts a politically neutral approach, his actions in office, including in the area of legal advice, will affect policy and in that sense are political. The influence of politics may be indirect; there are few instances of a law officer being browbeaten by a president to render a politically motivated opinion. Instead, an attorney general may share the president's policy commitments and view the law as a tool for their accomplishment. This is especially evident in areas of the law—such as antitrust and civil rights—that have distinct policy repercussions. While attorneys general vary in the degree to which they embrace their political roles (and presidents vary in their political dependence on them), the function seems to be a legitimate aspect of the office. Theodore Sorensen, who served as Kennedy's special counsel, argues that "politics is necessarily tied up with policy, with one's concept of the public interest and response to public will. . . . An attorney general never elected by the people [should not] be allowed to make policy with regard to the administration of justice in any way he sees fit, without regard to the policies and standards of a popularly elected president."[154] Furthermore, Elliot Richardson notes, policy concerns inevitably inform legal interpretation to some extent. "Laws afterall are instruments of policy. They are not self-executing." He goes on to explain that "the attorney general has often been someone who is not just a legal adviser but a personal adviser" to his president. "The role of a lawyer in private life is often that of a counsellor as well as a technically qualified person. Advice to a president needs to have the political dimension clearly in view, without a regard for any pejorative attached to the word political. The presidency is by definition a political job."[155] And the attorney general is a political appointee, "a responsible member of a partisan administration which has been placed in power ostensibly for the purpose of carrying out a popularly approved policy."[156]

Defining the Appropriate Relationship

The appropriate relationship between the attorney general and the president—the balance between law and politics—has been debated extensively over the years in the political arena. Congress argued about it during hearings on the 1870 Judiciary Act creating the Department of Justice, and again in 1924 and 1953, when—in the wake of administration scandal—Congress rediscovered the unresolved issue. Perhaps the relationship was examined most thoroughly during a Senate subcommittee investigation in 1974, when the Senate considered two bills that would have removed the attorney general and the Department of Justice from presidential control. Chairman Sam Ervin, Jr., who was author of one of the bills, sought to reassert the principle of rule of law, which had been badly damaged in the preceding years. The author of the other bill, Alan Cranston, noted that "even our best attorneys general have never been free from suspicions that because they are political appointees of the president, they will be loyal to him over any other call of duty."[157]

Despite this periodic reassessment, the nature of this relationship—in both descriptive and normative terms—remains unclear. Our own expectations of the office are ill defined and contradictory. "The Attorney General's duties as the President's advisor are both important and legitimate. Nevertheless, the breadth and scope of this role in modern government are not clearly defined. Thus, it is not surprising to find confusion about, and criticism of, close ties between a President and his Attorney General."[158] Of all the confusion associated with the office, perhaps the most serious is the lack of understanding about the relationship between president and attorney general. Unfortunately, the scandals that marked the office during the early 1970s stirred up an overreaction that tends to cloud thinking about the proper relations between chief executive and chief legal officer; all politics is an anathema. Such a response, Meador writes, is "an oversimplification of a subtle and complex relationship. There is a failure to appreciate the appropriate political setting within which the laws are executed."[159] Presidents contribute to the confusion by insisting that they want "the qualities of legal acumen and political suitability"[160] in their attorneys general. While not mutually exclusive, these characteristics make different and occasionally conflicting demands on an incumbent.

One approach to studying this relationship may be to identify the attorney general's client. The attorney general, as a lawyer, is "expected to act as an advocate on behalf of his client's best interests, within the limits of legal ethics."[161] His client may be the president, a department, the executive branch, or some concept of the people or the nation. How the client question is answered can have a profound effect on an attorney general's service, because it resolves for him the disturbing question of where his ultimate loyalties lie. This dilemma is illustrated in the way Edwin Stanton resolved the issue of loyalty facing him in the final months of the ineffectual Buchanan presidency. Despairing of Buchanan's wavering after South Carolina's secession, yet unwilling to resign and lose all influence in the administration, Stanton began to work behind the president's back, leaking information to Sen. William Seward and other opposition Republicans in Congress. He decided "that his brief was from the Union" and not from a particular president.[162] The nation, not Buchanan, was his client, and he felt his first obligation lay there. In public, Stanton kept up the official Buchanan policy of conciliation with the South. His actions seem uncomfortably close to disloyalty; one contemporary, Caleb Cushing, accused him later of being a duplex character.[163] According to one biography, he approached that "thin line separating patriotism in the nation's cause from betrayal of his official trust as a cabinet officer."[164] His balance on that thin line depended on his own understanding of where his loyalties belonged.

Contrary to Stanton's view, many scholars and attorneys general consider the client to be the president. One proponent of this view, Stuart Eizenstat of the Carter White House, explains:

The attorney general's client is the president. After giving his advice, the attorney general must support the president's policies. The department should not act as an impartial court but should advocate the legality of the president's decision within the bounds of responsible and honest argument. This does not politicize the administration of justice but recognizes the president's constitutional power to establish policies to execute the laws faithfully.[165]

This understanding of the relationship is shared by Charles Cooper and Terry Eastland of the Meese Justice Department. Eastland said that the president is the ultimate client; the other executive officers whom the attorney general may advise are merely his instrumentalities.[166] Also expressing this view is Archibald Cox, former solicitor general and Watergate special prosecutor, although he adds that "there are times when it is every lawyer's duty to give his client advice that the client may not like to hear, to tell him what his obligations are under the law."[167] Arthur S. Miller, although critical, acknowledges that "since at least the days of Andrew Jackson, the Attorney General has been regarded as the President's lawyer."[168]

Not everyone is satisfied with the answer that the attorney general is the president's lawyer. Homer Cummings suggested that the national government is the client: "The Attorney General, together with the available machinery of the Department of Justice, is at the disposal of the government of the United States in performing the functions of attorney and counsellor at law. The client is the United States of America."[169] The courts tend to be more specific, identifying the client of federal attorneys to be the agency in government that employs them, or in some cases the agency to which they have been assigned. Once the client is identified, then the courts may recognize a confidential privilege in certain circumstances, as long as that agency acts within the public interest.[170] Even if a department is the client, the attorney general is expected to advance a position that is fair and just, not merely the narrow position of the bureaucracy.[171] Kauper agrees that the executive branch often is the client, but he argues that on occasion, as in writing a brief for the White House, he considers the president the client. Kauper rejects the answer that the country as a whole could be the client.[172]

Like Stanton, others do answer "the country" or "the people" when identifying the client. Tom Clark, while noting that he was also the president's lawyer, remarked to a gathering of private attorneys that "I am the people's lawyer. I am not the lawyer to prosecute; I am the lawyer to represent all the people."[173] Both Richardson and Bell, also former attorneys general, considered their first client to be the people. Richardson said, "The attorney general is the people's lawyer. I think in dealing with citizens, for example, the Department is not an ordinary litigant. I think it has a responsibility to decide what is right."[174] Bell agrees: "Although our client is the government, in the end we serve a more important constituency: the American people."[175] This view is shared by some in Congress as well. At Edwin Meese's confirmation hearings in 1984, Sen. Charles Mathias commented, "The first client of the first lawyer is the American people. The Committee will want to be satisfied that the nominee is ready, willing, and able to serve that first client without any reservation whatever."[176]

Those who believe that the people are the client will expect attorneys general to act differently than those who believe that the president is the client. On rare occasions, loyalty to one requires disloyalty to the other. Arguing that the client, by statute, is the United States, Palmer writes that "any conflict of interest concerning his loyalty towards the executive and the United States must ultimately be resolved in favor of the broader duty owed to his principal client, the United States." The law officer has a duty to the nation first, then a loyalty to the president second.[177] Sen. Alan Cranston agrees, adding that "an important part of his job as the Attorney General is to see to it that the government remains within the boundaries of the law."[178] This view is based on the notion that the attorney general, because he is charged with assisting the president in fulfilling his constitutional obligations, owes his final duty to the Constitution.

Yet few would argue that the attorney general should be the president's judge. Bell, who sat on the federal bench for fifteen years, distinguished between his judicial role and his role as a law officer. At his confirmation hearings he said, "I will be an advocate attorney general, not an arbiter as I was as a judge."[179] Theodore Sorensen notes that "the Attorney General is not intended and could not by statute be required to serve as the President's judge instead of his lawyer."[180] The most famous exposition of the distinction between judge and attorney general is found in the concurring opinion of Supreme Court Justice Robert Jackson in the *Youngstown Sheet and Tube Co. v. Sawyer* case of 1952. Harry Truman's seizure of the nation's steel mills was challenged in the courts as an unconstitutional exercise of his commander-in-chief powers. Government counsel cited as precedent Roosevelt's seizure of a North American Aviation Corporation plant in June 1941. Jackson's defense of the 1941 seizure (he was then FDR's attorney general) was used by the government to justify Truman's actions.[181] But Associate Justice Jackson rejected both the argument that the 1941 seizure was a precedent (he distinguished between the two instances) and the assertion that he should be consistent with his own earlier opinion. He wrote, "I do not regard it as a precedent for this, but even if I did, I should not bind present judicial judgment by earlier partisan advocacy."[182] He recognized that he had a different responsibility as a justice than he had had as a law officer. Responding to the solicitor general's mention of his 1941 opinion, Jackson said, "I claimed everything, of course, like every other Attorney General does. It was a custom that did not leave the Department of Justice when I did."[183] Jackson's phrase "partisan advocacy," describing his role as attorney general, is an interesting choice of words; Elliot Richardson philosophized on Jackson's meaning:

> An attorney general is not an advocate very often. In the bases-for-destroyers case, [Jackson] was not an advocate in the ordinary sense of dealing with a case in a court of law but as counsel for the chief executive who needed a legal rationale for what he was doing. He needed somebody to defend his action. Jackson was like a general counsel of a corporation who says to the CEO, "This is not free of doubt, boss, and we may get taken to court, but I think we have a strong foundation of justification for taking this position."[184]

This statement conceding the advocacy relationship with the president seems to contradict Richardson's earlier argument that the nation is his client, but in fact a law officer can be both the president's advocate and the nation's attorney. This is the usual pattern, and it is consistent with the president's goal of combining legal acumen and political suitability in the office. But it still does not address those few instances when the two roles cannot be reconciled, bringing us again to the inherent tension within the office of attorney general.

Another possible approach to understanding the attorney general vis-à-vis the president is through role theory. Role theory recognizes that certain established rules exist in each profession that alert practitioners to the possibility of compromising situations.[185] Beyond the codes that apply to all members of the bar, few formal rules exist to guide the attorney general. According to the originating legislation, he must be a lawyer who is a "meet" (or suitably fit) person,[186] an ambiguous job description at best. Statutory lists of his duties also provide little insight. However, three norms of behavior seem to apply to the attorney generalship, and a review of them may provide some resolution to the dilemma of the attorney general's dual obligations.

The first is the norm of independence from intrusive executive control, which has colonial antecedents. One early incident involved Peyton Randolph, attorney general in the colony of Virginia. In 1752, he challenged the "unlawful" orders of the colonial governor and received enthusiastic public approval for his independence. He also lost his appointment.[187] Independence became salient in the wake of Watergate, especially in confirmation hearings.[188] For example, Edward Levi in 1975 was grilled by five senators on the issue of independence; his views on such justice issues as law enforcement, antitrust, the death penalty, and the Voting Rights Act received much less attention.[189]

The second norm is that of nonpartisanship. While many appointees have had politically active pasts, they are expected to adhere to a partisan neutrality while in office. Like independence, this norm assumes a prominent role in postscandal periods. Political activity was prohibited in 1886 and 1926,[190] conceivably in response to the scandals of the early 1880s and 1920s. A similar sensitivity to partisanship is evident in the recent administrations of Gerald Ford and Jimmy Carter. Ford even went so far as to limit the 1976 election activity of all cabinet members.[191] Bell, Carter's law officer, retired a full year before the 1980 race to maintain the perception as well as the reality of nonpartisanship.[192]

The third important norm is that of loyalty. The cabinet system in the United States reinforces the sense of loyalty that all department heads feel toward the president.[193] Because the cabinet is a creature of custom rather than statute, "it lives in a state of institutional dependency to promote the effective exercise of the President's authority."[194] The cabinet is the president's tool, to be used as he decides.

Yet these norms are not intrinsically compatible either. Fidelity to the norm of loyalty will sometimes violate the norms of independence and nonpartisanship, and vice versa. This conflict further illustrates the fundamental and recurring duality in the office of attorney general. In a sense, norms are an expression of obligation; predictably, then, potentially contradictory norms develop as a consequence of potentially contradictory obligations. Underlying each one is some concept of client and loyalty.

A deep personal conflict may occur when a law officer is genuinely torn by both loyalties, both sets of norms, both characteristics. Finding a balance between these dual claims may not be possible, forcing the incumbent into an unhappy choice. Such a dilemma faced Francis Biddle, Franklin Roosevelt's last attorney general. His feelings for his chief were strong. "I admired him enormously," he writes in his autobiography.[195] Yet the former circuit court judge was committed to civil liberties as well.[196] For example, he expanded the recently formed Civil Liberties Unit in the Justice Department and used Reconstruction era statutes to prosecute state officials for lynchings, police brutality and election discrimination. The conflict came in 1942, when Biddle learned of the administration's plans to intern Japanese Americans on the grounds of military necessity.[197] He opposed the program as "ill advised, unnecessary and unnecessarily cruel." He was determined to avoid the hysteria and mass internment that had characterized the nation during World War I. Furthermore, he questioned the constitutionality of interning those who were U.S. citizens; after all, there was no evidence of any subversive activity to justify their detention. Ignoring the attorney general, Roosevelt signed Executive Order No. 9066 and Public Law 503 instructing the War Department to proceed with the wholesale relocation of people of Japanese ancestry, including citizens. Civil liberties, FDR thought, should yield to the necessities of war. With the president's decision, Biddle acquiesced. "I did not think I should oppose it any further." But twenty years later, he struggled with the memory of his acquiescence, wondering if he should have protested directly to Secretary of War Henry Stimson, rather than to his subordinates, because Stimson could have influenced Roosevelt. Then Biddle justifies himself by noting, "I was new to the cabinet, and disinclined to insist on my view to an elder statesman."[198] He felt the tug of dual loyalties in another case as well, involving eight German saboteurs who had been court-martialed. Roosevelt had informed Biddle that he would not give them up to any U.S. marshal armed with a writ of habeas corpus. Biddle recalled that "his words did not make things any easier for his Attorney General, who was under a very special obligation to obey the law."[199]

While Biddle's experience is not unique, it would be inaccurate to suggest that all attorneys general feel, at some time, a conflict between their loyalty to the president and to the law. The conflictual tendencies of these two roles may be minimized and even eliminated in either of these situations: when the attorney general's commitment to the law is so clear and absolute that he is excluded from a political or policy-oriented role; or when his loyalty to the president and/or sympathy with his policies is so thorough that he cannot help viewing the law through this lens. In either case—where the law officer is distinctly legal or political—no internal conflict may occur.

This discovery suggests that a more useful approach to studying an attorney general's response to the dualism of the office may be in terms of a continuum. Anchoring each end is an "ideal type"—one primarily legal, the other political. Those clustered at these poles, as noted, face a minimum of personal conflict. Background, activity in office, and relations with the president may provide the clues by which each incumbent can be classified and located.[200]

At the political end of this continuum is the Advocate type. With a politically activist conception of the office, the Advocate promotes both the president's and his own policy agenda while in office. Attorneys general of this type tend to be more responsive to the desires of the electorate or the president than to the niceties of rule of law. By being flexible and responsive to societal pressures, this type may help the chief executive deal with simmering issues before they reach the boiling point. A close friend or political ally of the president before appointment, the Advocate becomes an intimate and trusted adviser, counseling on a broad range of nonlegal as well as legal subjects, including domestic politics and foreign affairs. In legal terminology, an Advocate is one who "renders legal advice and aid and pleads the cause of another before a court or a tribunal." He is an assistant, an adviser, a pleader of causes.[201] He owes his loyalty to the president, and by extension to the people who have elected him and the administrators who serve under him.

The Neutral lies at the other pole. He is the eminent professional—capable, cautious, thoughtful, legalistic, nonpolitical. He seeks to expound the law in a neutral manner and stresses rule of law over majoritarian principles. He is a newcomer to politics, something of an outsider, not a close personal friend or political associate of the president. Perceived as independent, a Neutral attorney general has high credibility in times of national scandal. His advisory role centers almost exclusively on domestic legal issues, and policy-making is restricted to his departmental responsibilities. The term neutral in the legal definition signifies someone who is "unbiased, impartial, not engaged on either side."[202] In the final analysis, he is loyal to the law.

Most of this book will test the validity of these two ideal types against the actual experiences of several attorneys general. Although the case study method will be used to illustrate my findings, this work also draws on an empirical examination of almost forty attorneys general. A short detour in chapter two will trace the history and development of the modern U.S. attorney general. Chapter three returns to the Advocate type, assessing it in terms of several nineteenth- and twentieth-century incumbents. Chapter four examines the possibility of abuse in the Advocate officer. Chapter five will consider the Neutral type and test the hypothesis that such law officers are most evident in postscandal periods. The final chapter will consider the need for institutional change and offer a few normative conclusions regarding the types. It then will struggle to answer the study's underlying question on the proper balance between law and politics in a democracy.

Chapter Two

The Emergence of
the Modern Law Officer

The attorney general is one of the institutions of American government consciously drawn from an ancient English office. An attorney has represented the British government's interests in court for at least five hundred years and rendered legal advice for the past three hundred. In the United States, too, the office is venerable. Colonial law officers predate the Constitution by more than a century. They provided much needed legal advice and courtroom advocacy for such pioneer governments as Virginia, Rhode Island, Pennsylvania, and Maryland.

The functions of the American officer, James Norton-Kyshe wrote in 1900, are "on a somewhat similar footing to that held by the same high official in England," a view shared by other early scholars of the office.[1] This assertion seems unjustified to us now, in light of the important differences between the American and British legal systems. England, for example, has no judicial review or centralized justice ministry, factors that have affected the development of the American attorney generalship. Neither is the English officer a member of the cabinet nor the American officer a member of the legislature. Even at the turn of the century, Norton-Kyshe recognized that the office in the United States had branched in a distinctly different direction, in response to the American environment and constitutional terrain.

Despite these differences, the fact that the modern American office is a relatively recent outgrowth of the long taproot of English constitutional history justifies a brief historical examination, especially on the salient questions of law, politics, and independence from the executive.

The Development of the English Office

A history of the king's law officers is essentially a history of English law. Through centuries of evolutionary growth, the modern attorney general and solicitor general have emerged. British scholars remind us that they are not medieval officers, but their development did depend on important preliminary occurrences in the Middle Ages. Before there could be an attorney general, there had to be a king's attorney; and before there could be a king's attorney, there had to be an attorney.

Since the thirteenth century, an attorney has appeared on behalf of the king in the courts. The development of some type of royal law officer was necessary, given the English conception of the monarchy. The king embodied the law and the rights and liberties of the people; yet there were occasions when he was concerned as a litigant in his own courts, subject to the decisions of the judges. It was inconceivable that the king would appear in person as a plaintiff or defendant.[2]

The actual title "attorneys general" was first used in 1398 in reference to general attorneys appointed by noblemen to act in any and all future suits in any of the various English courts.[3] The king, in time, followed this example and broadened the jurisdiction of his attorneys as well. Initially, there was little difference between a king's attorney and an ordinary attorney. But by the fifteenth century, the office of the king's attorney was unique, endowed with exceptional privileges and powers.[4]

Medieval law officers differed dramatically from modern attorneys general, who did not emerge until the seventeenth century. They did not offer legal advice to the government, nor did they participate in any political functions such as drafting legislation. They were not members of Parliament nor ministers of the Crown. But in one respect they were modern: they had the exclusive responsibility to appear in court for the king's interests, and their responsibilities included preparing briefs and arguing cases. In their prosecution of important state trials, attorneys general such as Edward Coke, Francis Bacon, and Francis North essentially did the same work as that done by contemporary attorneys general.

For a short time during the fifteenth century, kings appointed attorneys general for life or on condition of good behavior. But in an interesting development, their tenures became more precarious as their powers continued to grow. Henry VIII began the practice of appointing them to serve only during the Crown's pleasure. This tied law officers more closely to the chief executive, undercutting any claim that their office was judicial in nature.[5] This was an important step in the development of the office toward its modern form.

The year 1461 seems to be of particular significance in the development of the office. It was the first time that the official title of attorney general for the king was used.[6] For the first time, a solicitor general was appointed to assist the attorney general. And it was the first time that the king's attorney was called to advise the House of Lords. The Lords also requested legal advice from judges and the king's serjeants, evidence that the attorney's rank had risen to a level on par with these other legal actors, although the king's serjeants remained the elite legal officers for two more centuries.[7]

Economic and political changes in the sixteenth and seventeenth centuries brought the attorney generalship into its modern form and contributed to the emergence of the office as the preeminent legal adviser of the Crown. Commerce, trade, and colonization rapidly accelerated under the Tudors and Stuarts, so that the Crown's litigation became more important and government administration more complex. Positive law began to replace common law, which was the specialty of the king's serjeants. The attorney general's centralized control of royal legal affairs proved to be an advantage in dealing with changing economic realities.[8] Political changes in those tumultuous centuries also made the preeminence of the attorney general inevitable. Initially, his position was enhanced because the Crown found him to be a more reliable ally than the king's serjeant, "more useful and subservient to the royal cause."[9] But in the wake of the constitutional struggles between king and Parliament, the attorney general's role underwent an important shift. No longer did he serve the king alone; instead, he became the chief legal adviser to the government. When the dust of the civil war century settled, the House of Commons was the primary policy-making organ, and the attorney general a member and legal adviser. "The attorney general thus ceased to be a royal agent and became an adviser to the government as a whole."[10]

Through centuries of gradual change, then, the government's legal office became increasingly centralized and single. By the end of the seventeenth century, the modern English attorney general had emerged.

No longer simply a law officer, he was a political participant as well, active in policy-making in the House of Commons and advising the government in power. This emergence occurred simultaneously with the settlement of the American colonies. The colonists, therefore, were acquainted with an attorney general's office that was single, centralized, and quasi-political. It was this office that they sought to transplant in the New World, along with other English governmental arrangements.[11]

The American Colonial Experience

American colonial law officers were not independent in any formal sense. Their authority was delegated to them by the English attorney general, who remained the *de jure* law officer of the colonies.[12] But because of the great distances involved, this dependence was more nominal than real. Some of the colonial officials had even broader responsibilities than their English superior. New York's attorney general, for example, handled land transactions and letters patent for corporations; in England, a different officer was responsible for these tasks.[13] In addition, colonial attorneys general came to monopolize all criminal prosecutions. The English attorney general, in contrast, conducted only those criminal prosecutions that were considered important to the Crown, leaving routine prosecutions up to the victims.[14] In sum, when Norton-Kyshe concludes that colonial attorneys general were subservient to the English office, he is reflecting nineteenth- and not eighteenth-century reality.[15] In the seventeenth and eighteenth centuries, before the development of adequate transportation and communication technologies, American colonial law officers seem to have been able to operate with a degree of autonomy denied later colonial officers.

   The office of attorney general was established early in the New World. The earliest recorded appointment was in Virginia in 1643, just thirty-six years after the first settlement at Jamestown. In Rhode Island, a colonial law officer was appointed in 1650, fourteen years after the first settlement and six years after Roger Williams had received a royal patent. In Pennsylvania also, the attorney general was one of the first public offices created. William Penn had received a charter for the former Swedish settlement in 1681; by 1683, the attorney general was presenting an indictment to a petit jury. Another early attorney general appeared in Maryland in 1660. By the end of the seventeenth century, most of the thirteen colonies had attorneys general, although in a few cases, neighboring colonies shared legal officers.[16]

While colonial attorneys general were more preoccupied with arguing cases and collecting court fines than giving advice to the government, their role as legal advisers was well established in England by this time and continued in America. Some of their legal advisory duties focused strictly on judicial issues. In Maryland, for example, the attorney general advised the court on technical legal questions and advised the governor and council on creating new courts and appointing additional attorneys. On other occasions, their advice more clearly had policy overtones, especially when rendered to colonial governors, councils, and legislatures. North Carolina's law officer "maintained a close relation to the Governor and Council" as a legal adviser. In New York, the attorney general advised the governor on such topics as the difficulty of enforcing the colony's revenue laws and the desirability of making a town a free port. The Pennsylvania officer, like his English prototype, had a seat on the council and frequently advised both it and the governor; records indicate that at least once he was required to give his approval on a piece of legislation. South Carolina's commission to Nicholas Trott in 1697 charged him "to peruse any acts of Assembly before confirmation, and see if there be ought repugnant to the laws of England, and report upon the same to the lords proprietors," a type of royal review of legislation. In Virginia and Rhode Island, the colonial attorney general counseled the House of Burgesses and the General Assembly, respectively.[17]

Colonial chief executives were not always receptive to advice. New York's Governor Benjamin Fletcher excluded his attorney general from the colonial council's deliberations on land grant applications. This ran counter to the widespread colonial practice of having the attorney general review land grants to ensure that they would not be prejudicial to the king's interest. Because of this lack of royal review, the next governor, the Earl of Bellomont, had to direct the attorney general to take action to rescind some of Fletcher's land grants.[18] Bellomont, however, was no more responsive to legal advice from his attorney general than was Fletcher. On one occasion he asked his attorney general, James Graham, and the chief justice if he had the authority from the king to establish a court system, which the general assembly had not done. Bellomont believed he had been delegated the necessary authority in his commission, but both men advised him that the king could establish courts only through the legislature and therefore could not delegate the power to his governor. Criticizing the attorney general, Bellomont rejected the advice and went ahead with his order creating the courts.[19] The governor continued to criticize Graham, complaining to the Council of Trade and Plantations in a letter of May 1699 that he lacked "a good Attorney General to advise me in behalf of the king." Because Graham was "bred to a trade," the governor said, his legal advice was so lame that many opportunities to seize ships and unlawful goods were lost. In a letter of 1701 Bellomont said of the same attorney general that "ten pieces of eight would bribe him at any time."[20]

Changes in the colonial attorney generalship were suggested by Edward Randolph, Surveyor General of His Majesty's Customs for North America, in his report sent to England in the late seventeenth century. Primarily concerned with the enforcement of the navigation acts, he reported that the current law officers were either too corrupt or too ignorant to vigorously enforce the law. His report targeted Anthony Checkley of Massachusetts, who "combined ignorance of the law with skill in its violation"; William Randolph of Virginia, who knew nothing of the law; George Plater of Maryland, also a customs collector, who had failed to prevent illicit trade with Scotland; and David Lloyd of Pennsylvania, who had refused to sue on forfeited bonds and thus had ignored the Acts of Trade. Randolph argued that centralized authority and supervision were needed if the king was to have able and loyal advocacy. He proposed that America be divided into districts, with an advocate general in each, appointed by the king and not by colonial governors, who were sometimes unsympathetic toward English law. If the office of advocate general was combined with that of attorney general, he wrote, the king's interests would be loyally served in admiralty as well as regular courts. The plan was partially implemented; the king directly appointed attorneys general to the royal colonies. However, he did not appoint attorneys to the corporate or proprietary colonies, as Randolph had proposed, instead empowering attorneys general of royal colonies to act as advocates general in those other colonies.[21]

While Sewall Key calls Randolph's report a conscientious response to complaints about the attorney general's office,[22] one could argue that Randolph, who complained often of colonial maladministration, was more concerned with reining in colonial independence and circumventing colonial antipathy to unpopular English laws, especially the navigation acts. For example, Lloyd of Pennsylvania, one of Randolph's targets, was considered by Cummings and McFarland to be one of the outstanding colonial attorneys general.[23] Repeatedly in his report, Randolph stressed the need for loyal advocacy and enforcement of the king's laws by the sometimes recalcitrant colonial governments. From the beginning, it seems, American law officers have struggled with dual loyalties.

Besides Lloyd, there were other very capable colonial attorneys general. They were men of substance and genuine ability, some of whom had studied law in England, but most without formal training. Among the eighteenth-century law officers were such outstanding men as James Otis, Jr., of Massachusetts, the man "who became a link in the chain between Coke and the post-revolutionary exponents of judicial review,"[24] and Andrew Hamilton of Pennsylvania, who late in life defended John Peter Zenger in the famous free press trial of 1735. Serving in Virginia were George Wythe, Benjamin Harrison, Peyton Randolph and John Randolph, some of whom were pivotal in the later formation of the new nation.[25]

It is unclear to whom the attorney general answered, whether it was the king, the English attorney general, or the colonial governor. Edward Randolph clearly saw the law officer as the representative of the Crown. But colonial understandings sometimes differed. Maryland's attorney general was considered a public servant, according to one historian: "His actions, although primarily taken in the interest of the Lord Proprietor, were also considered to be 'for the Publick' when 'relating to the Liberty of the Inhabitants or their Possessions.'"[26] The colonists seemed to have had this expectation as well, as illustrated in one incident in 1752, when Peyton Randolph, colonial attorney general for Virginia, was removed from office when he challenged the governor's "unlawful orders." Randolph had widespread public support for his position, however, and when the governor replaced him with George Wythe, Wythe promptly relinquished the seat to his predecessor. The controversy involved a pistole fee for the signing of land grants, which the governor had imposed without colonial legislative approval. Colonists and Randolph considered the fee unconstitutional.[27] This tradition that the colonial attorney general worked for the public continued in the new states. For example, New York's first state constitution calls the attorney general the representative of the people, not the government, and says he is the only officer who could represent the people in prosecutions because of his common law powers.[28]

By the time of the Declaration of Independence, a fairly coherent system of law officers and courts had been established in the colonies, in existence in some of them for more than a century. The system of attorneys general, solicitors general, and deputy or local attorneys was so well established that it continued without interruption as each new state government replaced the colonial apparatus. Royal incumbents were simply replaced with Americans. Every state except Connecticut made express provision for the office: five in their state constitutions and the others by statute. The attorney general's duties remained largely undefined, with powers stemming from common law, colonial custom, and legislation. No definition was thought necessary, any more than a definition was needed to describe the functions of a judge.[29]

The Office in the Confederacy

Although extant on the state level, no national attorney general operated under the Articles of Confederation. The issue was not completely dormant. The Continental Congress considered establishing the office on February 16, 1781, when a committee reporting on the proceedings of the Hartford convention presented this resolution: "That an Attorney General for the United States be appointed by Congress, whose duty shall be to prosecute all suits in behalf of the United States. To give his advice on all such matters as shall be referred to him by Congress. And when any case shall arise in any of these states, where his personal attendance is rendered impracticable, he shall be authorized to appoint a Deputy or Deputies to prosecute the said suit."[30] No action was taken on the report that day. The issue was considered again a week later, but, after debate and amendments, the entire report was recommitted. No further movement was taken to establish a national law office during the confederation.[31]

But while a national attorney general remained eight years away, the Continental Congress found it necessary to appoint attorneys to prosecute on its behalf in the state courts, generally over debts incurred during the ongoing war. To these attorneys they gave the title *procura-*

tors, the same title given the earliest king's attorneys of the Middle Ages. One such procurator was assigned in 1781 to New York, at the request of the New York delegation, to prosecute for debts or frauds committed against the United States.[32]

Congressionally appointed procurators in the various states were considered sufficient in the early days of the Republic, when the fear of a strong centralized government was prevalent. The decentralization of the office was related to the general political attitude of the time. "Having just paid the price of war to snap the bond of a government which they considered tyrannical, the States were fiercely protective of their independence and sovereignty. . . . They tolerated an ineffective legal administration rather than submit to a national Attorney Generalship."[33] In time, however, this tolerance faded as many came to recognize the dangers of a weak and decentralized government, which led to the convening of the Constitutional Convention in 1787.

Neither the U.S. Constitution nor the contemporary debates of the framers mentioned an attorney general, but the office is as much a result of the Constitution as are expressly created institutions. By constituting a national government, based on the people and not on the states, the framers prepared the way for a national law office. National institutions, not existing state machinery, were to handle national functions.[34]

Certain types of litigation are, by definition, the prerogative of the National Government as a sovereign nation, and the Congress is empowered to provide a system for the national administration of justice. Both of these factors imply the existence of a national attorney. The authors of the Constitution did not explicitly establish an Attorney General for the United States, but they clearly anticipated the office and included provisions allowing for its creation.[35]

A review of the founding document buttresses this assertion. For one thing, the powers granted by the Constitution to the president imply a need for an attorney general to provide advice. A president may require legal assistance to draft legislation (his Constitutional responsibility to "recommend to [Congress's] consideration such measures as he shall judge necessary and expedient") and to interpret legislation in order to execute it (his duty to "take care that the laws be faithfully executed").[36]

He is given the power to grant reprieves and pardons; the power, with the Senate's advice and consent, to make treaties; and the power to appoint Supreme Court judges, which also suggest a role for legal counsel. The framers foresaw his need for advice by granting him the power to require written opinions of his principal executive officers, which anticipated the formal opinions issued by attorneys general.[37] In addition, the Constitution's division of power between branches and between national and state governments meant that certain cases would arise requiring national adjudication, and for this a lawyer representing the U.S. government would be necessary.

The fact that the convention delegates did not consider an attorney general in 1787 is not remarkable; it was one of many offices to be created later by statute, along with other executive offices and the lower federal courts. As one nineteenth-century attorney general wrote, the Constitution does not specify any subordinate ministers or administrators, although it does imply their existence.[38] The attorney general's inclusion in the Constitution would have been inappropriately specific in a general outline of government. In addition, other important features of American government were not included, such as judicial review and the cabinet. One may deduce that the framers intended to create a national law officer from the fact that the office was mentioned in the first Senate bill in the first Congress, where many of the framers sat.

The Judiciary Act of 1789

The primary purpose of Senate Bill No. 1 was to create a federal judiciary, but it was here that the office of the U.S. Attorney General was created, not in legislation dealing with the executive branch. This may have been in recognition of the fact that the attorney general was a quasi-judicial officer of the court. At this time, of course, the attorney general did not head an executive department; the Department of Justice was not created until eighty years later.

Although the issue of a federal judiciary and an attorney general was assigned to a Senate committee on the second day of business, other executive offices received congressional and presidential approval more quickly. The Department of War was the first, created August 7, 1789, followed by the Department of Treasury and the Department of

State. Only later did the bill creating the federal judiciary and attorney general pass both houses.

Draft versions have enabled legal historians to recreate the legislative history of the bill. Thus we discover that the attorney general initially was to have been appointed by the Supreme Court, with U.S. district attorneys appointed by district courts. This provision suggests that the attorney general was viewed as a quasi-judicial officer. One reason this proposal may have failed was the fear of some senators that it was an effort by federalists "to draw by degrees all law business into the Federal Courts."[39] Complicating the debate at this time was a concurrent congressional debate on the Bill of Rights, which served to reinvigorate the antifederalists' commitment to state sovereignty.[40] This sensitivity to state interests also may have slowed the judiciary bill's progress through Congress, because a federal judicial system represented a more direct challenge to the states than did the legislation creating executive departments for foreign affairs and defense.

The ten senators who worked on the bill included two who had served as their states' attorneys general: Oliver Ellsworth of Connecticut and William Paterson of New Jersey. Another had served as county attorney. These three men, according to the handwriting of the original draft, dominated the writing. Seven of the ten had practiced law; four had been judges; five had been members of the Constitutional Convention.[41] But this homogeneity did not mean committee members worked comfortably together; bitter political differences divided them. Just eighteen months before, for example, committee member Richard Henry Lee had engaged in a vituperative newspaper debate with Ellsworth over the Constitution's ratification. Nevertheless, after two months of hard work, the committee reported the bill to the full Senate on June 12, 1789.[42] Weeks of debate followed, with the bill finally passing the Senate.[43] In the House of Representatives, the bill was altered by a number of amendments unrelated to Section 35, which deals with the attorney general. The two chambers then worked out their differences and sent the bill to the president, who approved it in late September, the same day that the House and Senate "finally agreed on the final form of the twelve Amendments to the Constitution to be submitted to the States."[44] The attorney general was the fourth executive office created, so recognized in the order of presidential succession outlined in the Act of January 19, 1886.[45] The final version of section 35 reads:

And there shall also be appointed a meet person, learned in the law, to act as attorney general for the United States, who shall be sworn or affirmed to a faithful execution of the office; whose duty it shall be to prosecute and conduct all suits in the Supreme Court in which the United States shall be concerned, and to give his advice and opinion upon questions of law when required by the President of the United States, or when requested by the heads of any of the departments, touching any matters that may concern their departments, and shall receive such compensation for his services as shall by law be provided.[46]

The Judiciary Act gave the attorney general two primary responsibilities: handling litigation for the federal government and giving legal advice to the chief executive and, in certain cases, his department heads. These are two of the oldest functions of the office. The provision's vagueness regarding the attorney general's duties attests to the long tradition of the office in both England and the colonies. Specific grants of power were not thought necessary for an office of such longevity. One historian writes that the drafters intended to create an office similar to that with which they were familiar in colonial and state governments.[47] The brevity of this section also stems from the immaturity of the central government's administrative and judicial systems at the time.[48] The lack of detail may reflect as well the concern of some congressmen that a strong federal officer could infringe on state prerogatives.[49]

The final version does not mention the method of appointment. By not specifying, the act was understood to provide for presidential appointment, with the advice and consent of the Senate.[50] This was a meaningful change from the first proposal that the attorney general be a court-appointed official, because it signified that he was an officer of the United States, not one of the "inferior offices."[51] In addition, this method of appointment brought the attorney general solidly into the executive branch. State attorneys general, by contrast, often are closely tied with the judicial and legislative branches.[52]

The Judiciary Act was not a universally popular measure at the time nor in following years, although the criticism was aimed at the federal judicial system it created and not the office of attorney general per se.[53] Some senators claimed the bill would alarm the states; others, that it dangerously weakened the federal government. Such contradictory reactions may have been inevitable, because the bill was an uneasy compromise that did not satisfy either side of the debate. On one hand, it created a federal court system and a national attorney general; on the other, it imposed significant restrictions on each. The law officer, for example, was given no authority over U.S. district attorneys, who were responsible for federal litigation in the lower courts.[54] Because of this, the attorney general could not supervise federal cases unless and until they reached the Supreme Court. Each U.S. attorney could independently decide which cases to pursue and on what grounds—a situation that soon resulted in a morass of contradictory federal government legal positions.[55] The decentralization of the legal system continued, despite the presence of centralized machinery.

Congress itself was dissatisfied with the act and almost immediately ordered the first attorney general to report on possible improvements. At the same time, the legislature continued to create lower-level legal officers who were not answerable to the attorney general. The result was near anarchy in the nation's legal affairs.[56]

This was the unenviable reality facing Washington's new attorney general, Edmund Randolph. The lack of both centralized authority and institutionalized arrangements created problems that plagued the attorney general's office through the nineteenth century. Incumbents and Congress have managed to address the office's most demanding needs, yet some issues—foreshadowed in colonial times—remain unresolved today, in particular the nature of the relationship between the law officer and the chief executive.

"Mongrel" or "Chameleon":
The First Attorney General

Edmund Randolph acceded reluctantly to George Washington's request that he serve as the nation's first attorney general, contingent on the content of the Judiciary Act.[57] He was 36 years old, with a prestigious record of public service already behind him, having served as Washington's aide-de-camp in 1775, a member of Virginia's convention of 1776 where he helped draft a declaration of rights and plan of government, Virginia's first state attorney general, the mayor of Williamsburg, the governor of Virginia, a delegate to the Continental Congress, a

member of the Annapolis Convention, and a delegate to the Philadelphia Convention, which he persuaded General Washington to attend
and where he introduced the Virginia Plan.[58]

Since the siege of Boston, he had had close personal relations with
Washington. For years, even during his tenure as attorney general, he
handled without payment the general's complex personal legal affairs.
Even so, it was not clear that he would accept the new assignment when
Washington tendered it. He was busy revising the law code in the Virginia Assembly, his wife was ill, and he was heavily in debt, because of
his long years in public service, inherited debt, and his own unwise
land speculations. But Washington countered these complaints by as-
suring Randolph that the post would confer such status that his private
professional business would flourish. Randolph accepted, arriving just
in time for the opening ceremonies of the Supreme Court.[59]

He was an appropriate choice, according to Cummings and Mc-
Farland, acquainted with both the law and the responsibilities of the attorney generalship. Not only had he served in the Virginia post, but his
father and uncle had been king's attorneys.[60] In another sense, however,
he was a curious choice, because he had been an opponent of the new
federal Constitution that he was now bound to interpret. He believed
that the states should have had another convention before ratification to
discuss possible amendments. While he felt the Articles of Confederation were too democratic, the new form of government did not seem republican enough, even tending toward monarchy in the executive
branch. But Randolph changed his mind on ratification when he realized that the Union would not survive without Virginia's support. This
reversal has led some scholars, as well as some of his peers, to consider
Randolph irresolute and cautious and to question his commitment to
principle.[61]

Randolph encountered many problems when he assumed office in
February 1790. Federal litigation was decentralized and somewhat chaotic. His salary was low, half that of other cabinet officers. The Senate
had set the salary at $2,000, but the House lowered it to $1,500, perhaps
to penalize Randolph for his vacillation on the ratification issue.[62] He
had no clerk, no files, no furniture, and no office space. He had to write
out his own opinions, letters, and briefs. An office was not considered
essential since he and most of the early attorneys general were absent
from the capital a good bit of time, attending to their private business.[63]

In his first year, he wrote to a friend: "I am a sort of mongrel between the State and the U.S.; called an officer of some rank under the latter, and yet thrust out to get a livelihood in the former,—perhaps in a petty mayor's or county court. . . . Could I have foreseen it, [it] would have kept me at home to encounter pecuniary difficulties there, rather than add to them here."[64] After two years in office, he sent a long letter to Washington outlining problems with the handling of the nation's legal business, and the president sent the letter to Congress. In it, Randolph proposed two reforms in his office: first, that he be given authority over the U.S. district attorneys, and second, that he be given a transcribing clerk to record his many lengthy opinions. He justified the first request by pointing out that he could not help department heads when they asked him to direct the prosecution of certain suits in the lower courts. If he could supervise U.S. attorneys, he would be involved in litigation at the earliest stage, and government interests would be better served. He added that, under the current arrangement, he could not provide the president with an adequate review of the nation's law business for his State of the Union message.[65] Congress responded to his plea with legislation, which was favorably reported out of committee and then killed. It was the first of many attempts by various attorneys general to secure a more centralized operation, but even the relatively innocuous request for a clerk went unheeded for twenty-seven years.

During his first year in office Randolph was occupied almost exclusively with giving advice. He had no duties before the Supreme Court because there were few federal cases, and they had not yet traveled up the appellate process to the highest court. Federal prosecution in the inferior courts was left to subordinate attorneys over whom he had little control. Instead, he was occupied preparing official opinions for the secretaries of the Treasury, State, and War, as well as for the president.[66] He also regularly advised Congress on questions of private claims as well as on legislation, especially pertaining to the judiciary.[67] Leonard White notes, however, that despite the attorney general's advisory activities, Hamilton and Jefferson contributed the most important state papers of the time, "indeed, overshadowing the opinions of Randolph." But on lesser domestic and foreign matters, the attorney general contributed a growing number of opinions.[68]

Because of his closeness to Washington and his tepid partisanship, Randolph was occasionally used by the president as a private counselor "in matters of State not properly within the Attorney General's department."[69] For example, Washington relied on Randolph when French revolutionaries protested Ambassador Morris's support for the recently executed king; the president reportedly considered Secretary of State Jefferson too partisan to render impartial advice. The president also followed Randolph's advice over that of his other cabinet officers when the British government demanded restitution of a prize ship taken by a French privateer that had been fitted out in South Carolina and partly manned by Americans. Basing his advice both on legal interpretations of treaty obligations and on the foreign policy implications of angering France, the attorney general argued that the president should not attempt restitution to Britain, although the American citizens on board the French ship were subject to prosecution.[70] Randolph also advised Washington to veto a congressional apportionment bill that, he argued, violated the language of the Constitution. After consulting with Jefferson on the political angles, Washington did veto the measure, the first exercise of the veto power.[71] The president also utilized his attorney general for sensitive foreign affairs when they involved legal issues as well as policy considerations. Randolph assisted in the drafting of a presidential state paper that is considered the foundation of the international law of neutrality. Secretary of State Jefferson, who would normally have handled many of those tasks, was not considered to be the president's man. As Moncure Daniel Conway writes, "Jefferson was not the man to burn his mouth with the President's porridge."[72] Evidently Randolph was.

Washington did not always defer to Randolph's legal judgment. On the constitutionality of a United States bank, Washington sided with Treasury Secretary Hamilton, rejecting Randolph's assertion that Congress had exceeded its implied powers. The Constitution, however, was open to different interpretations on this issue; Jefferson, although he agreed with Randolph, advised Washington to sign the bank bill unless the president was reasonably certain that it was unconstitutional. Washington, torn between opposing interpretations, chose to give the benefit of the doubt to Congress.[73]

These incidents illustrate the attorney general's role as a legal adviser, but he fulfilled many other duties that were clearly divorced from his legal responsibilities. The president turned to him for what was essentially political advice when Jefferson challenged Hamilton's management of the Treasury. Randolph advised Washington to wait until Congress completed its investigation before acting against Hamilton, lest he look too partisan.[74] Also on Washington's request, the attorney general traveled through Delaware and Maryland in 1793 to ascertain and report back the feelings of leading citizens toward the French revolution and the president's proclamation of neutrality.[75] He served his president as well as a sort of executive secretary, one time negotiating room and board for Washington in Philadelphia, where the Congress was to meet. In addition, he began to collect materials for a history of Washington's administration.[76]

Randolph inaugurated another important precedent for attorneys general by attending cabinet meetings. Neither Washington nor Randolph attended the initial meeting of the cabinet. The president, away on a tour of the South, had asked his three department heads and vice-president to meet in 1791. The attorney general, who did not yet head a department, was busy with his own affairs, according to a letter he wrote to Madison. In addition, his exclusion was in keeping with English tradition, where the law officer is not a member of the cabinet. But the issues confronting the fledgling executive branch increasingly involved questions of law, and Randolph's attendance became essential. He joined the body on March 31, 1792.[77]

The creation of a cabinet satisfied the objection of some framers that the Constitution had failed to provide an executive council to give the president the advice and information he needed to govern effectively. Washington took the cabinet idea even further; he believed that the chief executive generally should defer to a cabinet majority. He also believed in staffing the cabinet with men of widely divergent political viewpoints, which meant that cabinet consensus was difficult to achieve. Randolph was often in the position of casting the tie-breaking vote between the diametrically opposed secretaries of State and Treasury, a fact that did not endear him to either Jefferson or Hamilton.[78] In time, Jefferson, who had been Randolph's friend, called him "the poorest cameleon I ever saw, having no color of his own, and reflecting that nearest him. . . . His opinion always makes the majority, and . . . the President acquiesces always in the majority; consequently that the government is now solely directed by him. . . . But he is in a station infinitely too important for his understanding, his firmness, or his circumstances."[79] With this cabinet spot and the pivotal role that he assumed between political extremes, the attorney general "played a role of substantial importance in the general policy of the Federalist era," White writes.[80]

Even before the first formal cabinet meeting, the president had periodically requested written advice from his executive officers, drawing on his constitutional authority. He also asked Chief Justice Jay of the Supreme Court for advisory opinions, although most of the advice dealt with foreign policy and not legal matters. Jay was invaluable because he had served as ambassador to Great Britain before ascending the bench; he also proffered advice on the judiciary at the request of the president. But when Washington, through his secretary of State, turned to the Supreme Court for advice on the nature of U.S. treaty obligations with France—a question that could not readily be raised in trial courts—Jay and the other justices demurred. They replied directly to the president that the questions were beyond their judicial province and belonged instead in the executive branch. Jefferson in the State Department then proposed to establish an executive board to give international legal advice. When Randolph countered that such a board should be attached to the attorney general's office, Jefferson was angry.[81] He wrote to his friend Judge Henry St. George Tucker: "I asked E. R. [Randolph] if we could not prepare a bill for Congress to appoint a board or some other body of advice for the Executive on such questions. He said he should propose to annex it to his office. In plain language, this would be to make him the sole arbiter of the line of conduct for the U.S. towards foreign nations."[82] Jefferson's criticism of Randolph, according to Cummings and McFarland, seemed to stem more from the attorney general's nonlegal than legal advice.[83] His complaints that the attorney general was usurping authority set a precedent of sorts. Parallel criticisms have been leveled at other attorneys general, up through the twentieth century.

By the time of Randolph's departure on January 2, 1794, when he left to become secretary of State, the broad characteristics of the office had been established and its strengths and vulnerabilities delineated. Many features of the modern attorney generalship were missing, of course. There was no bureaucracy to manage, not even a transcribing clerk. There still were no offices to occupy, no budget to administer. These features developed only gradually as the federal government was forced to respond to increased legal needs due to civil war, territorial expansion, and economic depression. But already some of the basic questions about the relationship between the attorney general and the president were evident, such as the attorney general's advisory independence and the extent to which party or president influenced his advice. Randolph expressed his view of the advisory duty in this telling passage to Washington in 1794: "My opinions, not containing any systematic adherence to party, but arising solely from my views of right, fall sometimes on one side and sometimes on the other. . . . I have often indeed expressed sentiments contrary to yours. This was my duty; because they were my sentiments. But, Sir, they were never tinctured by any other motive, than to present to your reflection the misconstructions which wicked men might make of your views."[84] The argument over the proper advisory role of the attorney general had already begun and would echo with startling similarity through the next two hundred years in very different administrations.

The Institutionalization of the Office

The office of attorney general expanded slowly during its first sixty years. The salary remained far below that of the other cabinet members because the post was considered part-time; the U.S. government was simply one client, paying an annual retainer for legal services. Attorneys general were expected to supplement their incomes with private practice.[85]

Little changed during the first thirty years. Describing the attorney generalship just before becoming president, James Monroe wrote in 1817, "The office has no apartment for business, nor clerks, nor a messenger, nor stationery, nor fuel allowed. These have been supplied by the officer himself, at his own expense."[86] Lacking these simple amenities made the work arduous. But Monroe's new attorney general, William Wirt, found something even more important missing when he arrived in Washington: the previous eight law officers had not kept records of their opinions. Wirt was shocked that he found "no books, documents or papers of any kind to inform me of what has been done by any one of my predecessors, since the establishment of the Federal Government."[87] Having no precedents to guide him, he pondered over the very real possibility that one of his opinions might conflict with earlier ones, resulting in an inconsistent executive interpretation of the law.

Brilliant attorneys had served in the post before, but Wirt was the first attorney general to comprehend the need for an administrative structure. He proceeded to establish a system of recordkeeping, filing copies of his correspondence and official opinions—copying the earliest ones himself—and soliciting from the departments any relevant documents pertaining to his opinions. He petitioned Congress for a clerk, stationery, office fuel, and a reference library of state laws, then suggested that they make the attorney general's post full-time, because of the "vast load of duties" involved.[88]

The legislature was slow to respond to these administrative demands, but, after much prodding, Congress in 1819 provided $1,000 for a clerk and $500 for contingent expenses. Later the clerk's salary was lowered to $800 and the $500 eliminated. A year after that, the attorney general was granted the service of a messenger and an annual sum of $500; the next year, he finally had an office. His salary, which Wirt described in a letter to a friend as "very low, only three thousand dollars,"[89] was increased to $3,500, still far below the salaries of other cabinet members, which meant the attorney general had to continue his private practice. For the next decade, the law officer had to run his office on $500 annually. Albert Langellutig writes, "It was not until 1831 that Congress finally realized that an efficient lawyer needs more than one $800 clerk and quarters in which to conduct the affairs of a great government." His salary was raised to $4,000, and he was given another $500 for contingencies, $500 for a messenger, $733 for office furniture, and $500 for books. Appropriations did not increase again for twenty years, when in 1853 the salary was raised to $8,000, finally on par with other cabinet members.[90] It remained at this level until the end of the nineteenth century.[91]

Throughout this period, the attorney general was not required to live in the capital. In the Jefferson administration, for example, Levi Lincoln took the office with him to Massachusetts; later, Caesar Rodney moved it to Delaware. As Leonard White notes, "Until 1814 the office of Attorney General was where the Attorney General happened to be."[92] In that year, the House passed a residency requirement aimed at keeping the attorney general close at hand in case Congress needed his legal advice; the bill, however, failed in the Senate.[93] President Madison, who favored the legislation, was disturbed to discover that his attorney general, William Pinkney, planned to resign rather than move from Baltimore, where he maintained a large private practice. Pinkney resigned even before the bill's fate was known. His replacement, Richard Rush, had to promise Madison that he would reside in the capital as long as Congress was in session.[94] The next president, Monroe, agreed that the attorney general "should reside at the seat of Government," because

> the Attorney General has been always, since the adoption of our Government, a member of the executive council or cabinet. . . . His duties in attending the cabinet deliberations are equal to those of any other member. Being at the seat of Government throughout the year, his labors are increased by giving opinions to the different Departments and public offices. . . . Being on the spot, it may be supposed that he will often be resorted to verbally in the progress of current business.[95]

The man he named to replace Rush, the remarkable Wirt, accepted without hesitation the residency terms of the office, moving his family to Washington and only occasionally leaving town to continue his private practice in Baltimore and Philadelphia courts. Once in the capital, the attorney general was available for frequent consultation with the rest of the cabinet, which in time gave the office a stronger identification with the cabinet and a more distinctly political character.[96]

Subsequent attorneys general followed Wirt's example, but the issue of residency was not completely resolved. They and other cabinet officers still left Washington for long periods of time, a practice that President Polk criticized in a letter to his cabinet appointees in 1845. Polk extracted a pledge from at least two of his three attorneys general to stay in Washington except for short absences. Eight years later, Caleb Cushing became the first attorney general to strictly adhere to the residency obligation.[97]

Unlike earlier law officers, Cushing had no need to travel out of town on his own business. When Cushing joined the Pierce administration in 1853, Congress increased the salary to that of other cabinet officers, which Cushing interpreted as a mandate to relinquish his private practice and serve as attorney general full-time. His decision had important repercussions on the status of the office. As a full-time officer, he had the time (as well as the personal inclination) to become active in a broad range of governmental activities, assuming responsibility for several areas previously under the secretary of State, such as pardons, legal and judicial appointments, and extradition cases. Historian Claude Fuess notes that these new duties made the position of attorney general under Pierce more important than it had been before. With his functions virtually doubled, "Cushing had a part in nearly every matter of significance arising during the next four years in Washington."[98] Before Cushing, the pay inequity and part-time status of the office had kept attorneys general from becoming full and equal participants in the cabinet or the administration.

Cushing's decision to abandon his private practice was not universally lauded. The tradition of maintaining an active professional life was believed to have positive effects on the office, by keeping the attorney general abreast of the law and sharpening his legal skills and intellectual prowess. It had long been the established practice of English law officers.[99] In addition, it provided a strong inducement to public service for attorneys who were well established professionally, because the job was thought to contribute to their careers. The promise of professional rewards enticed Randolph to accept the appointment, as it did Wirt, who explained: "My single motive for accepting the office was the calculation of being able to pursue my profession on a more advantageous ground," including appearing before the Supreme Court.[100] While in office, attorneys general participated as private counsel in some of the most famous constitutional cases of the Supreme Court: *Gibbons v. Ogden, Luther v. Borden, Dartmouth College v. Woodward, Barron v. Baltimore,* and *Chisholm v. Georgia.*[101] Their work before the Supreme Court enhanced their professional prestige. Furthermore, once the position was made full-time, accepting it could mean significant financial sacrifice. For example, in 1859, the year before he joined President Buchanan's administration, Edwin Stanton earned a handsome income of $40,000, plus bonuses and expenses.[102] As attorney general, his annual salary dropped to $8,000.

There were early voices warning that the system of private practice invited abuse. The primary concern was that private practice meant limited time devoted to the government's business. Monroe, for example, noted that "the Attorney General cannot well engage in the causes of private clients in this court [the Supreme Court] consistently with a diligent execution of the public business."[103] Yet when Wirt joined his cabinet, the new attorney general wrote to his wife, "They assure me that there is nothing in the duties of the office to prevent the general practice of my profession in this place."[104] While active in his private practice, Wirt also believed that the public office should be full-time, not because of conflict of interest but because of the heavy demands on his time.

Concern with an increased workload and lack of time also influenced Cushing. The events of the 1850s brought a rapid increase in government business. He wrote:

> Within the last few years . . . the condition of the country has undergone changes, occasioning a vast augmentation in the amount of administrative business . . . and it would not be possible now . . . for the Attorney General, compatibly with performing well the duties of his office, to be frequently absent from the seat of government, attending to private professional pursuits, nor could he find much leisure to prepare and argue private causes even before the Supreme Court.[105]

By the start of the Civil War, then, the attorney general had become a full-time cabinet member residing in the capital and readily available for advice on a wide variety of subjects. These changes, while not dramatic in themselves, had the cumulative effect of creating an institutionalized office. With the act of January 19, 1886, the attorney general also became part of the line of possible succession to the presidency, following those secretaries whose departments were established earlier. This was the final step in officially acknowledging the officer as a peer among his cabinet colleagues.[106]

Also indicative of the growing institutionalization of the office is the fact that incumbents began to refer to themselves (and were referred to by others) as heading a law department, decades before one was formally established.[107] Cushing described his office in 1856 as the administrative head of the government's legal business, adding, "So far, the administrative power and the correspondent administrative responsibility exist, and they require modification in details only in order to be completely adapted to the theory of departmental organization."[108]

Although law officers themselves seemed to recognize the need to adjust to the changing nature of the nation's law business, the office remained relatively unaltered. Under Cushing, sixty years after the Judiciary Act, it still claimed only four staff members: the attorney general, two clerks, and a messenger. In the 1860s, Congress provided for two assistant attorneys general, to be appointed by the president and confirmed by the Senate, and a law clerk. There were, in addition, a solicitor of the Court of Claims and a solicitor of the Treasury (who served under the attorney general for certain purposes). Beginning in 1861, the large number of scattered U.S. attorneys also were made subordinate to the attorney general, but the nation's legal system, Henry Barrett Learned writes, remained "very loosely knit and disjointed."[109] For example, it was Lincoln's secretary of State, William Seward, who sent instructions to the U.S. marshals and attorneys on how to proceed under the Act of August 2, 1861. When Attorney General Edward Bates read in the newspaper about Seward's actions, he protested that the general superintendence of those judicial officers was his responsibility and not the secretary of State's.[110] The jurisdiction over U.S. marshals and attorneys remained contested into the early twentieth century.

The Coming of the Department of Justice

Debates over the establishment of a law department began as early as 1829, when Jackson sent a proposal to Congress that would have increased the attorney general's responsibilities and salary. The bill's supporters claimed that the current system allowed incompetent U.S. district attorneys to injure the financial interests of the country, because they operated without federal supervision.

There was considerable congressional resistance to the legislation, led by the famous orator Daniel Webster. Webster asserted that the bill would have made the attorney general into "a half accountant, a half lawyer, a half clerk, in fine, a half everything and not much of any thing." The attorney general should be solely concerned with Supreme Court cases, he argued, with a Home Department dealing with the rest of the nation's domestic affairs. Countering the president, Webster introduced his own legislation, which created the post of solicitor of the Treasury.[111] In 1830, his bill passed and Jackson's failed, further splintering the nation's legal affairs.

The highly politicized atmosphere obscured the rationale behind the proposal for a Department of Justice. Sewall Key writes that the nation's legal affairs had been "tossed into the turbulent sea of politics . . . [and] became not a matter of efficiency but a pawn in the intrigues by which Jackson, Webster, and Vice-President John C. Calhoun were fighting for supremacy." He speculates on the reasons behind Webster's bitter opposition. One historical tradition is that Webster disliked the attorney general; another is that he wanted a particular person in the Treasury post. Webster at this time also began to harbor presidential ambitions and may have sought ways to present himself as the leading contender to Jackson. In any event, his bill "made the Government's legal forces distinctly two-headed and left them in much the same condition as England's in the fourteenth and fifteenth centuries," Key writes. With the precedent it created, other departments soon agitated for legal staffs of their own and for the right to supervise their own litigation.[112]

Presidents Madison, Polk, and Pierce also battled Congress in an effort to extend the attorney general's authority and to increase his salary and staff. Polk recommended the establishment of a justice department in 1845, but Congress did not respond. Pierce won a salary increase for his attorney general but little else. Instead, the legislature followed Treasury's example and created law posts in the Internal Revenue and the War Departments. Solicitors also were added to the Navy Department and the Post Office.[113] This tendency to fragment the nation's law business derived from Congress's fear of a strong attorney general. While Congress occasionally added to his duties through the years, it "refused to authorize any enlargement of his legal domain." His staff was just large enough to ensure that he would have no spare time to augment his power.[114]

Congressional action to create a consolidated law department was not taken until the post–Civil War years, when the move became essential because of the monumental increase in government litigation. The nation had to be represented in courts all across the country and in cases that ranged from property titles to personal rights. The attorney general's office, composed only of the attorney general and two assistants, did not have the manpower to oversee the government's business in the courts, nor did it have adequate supervision over the U.S. district attorneys. Outside counsel was hired by the various executive departments at prevailing professional rates. The enormous costs incurred—estimated at close to half a million dollars over four years—came to the notice of the Joint Committee on Retrenchments in the thirty-ninth Congress. In the following two Congresses, Thomas A. Jenckes, a representative from Rhode Island, introduced a bill to consolidate the nation's legal affairs in a single law department. Despite the need to economize, the bill faced opposition from those who continued to fear a central law department. In the debate before the Forty-first Congress, Jenckes assured opponents that the bill would not create a new department but simply transfer "to an existing Department some things properly belonging to it, but which are now scattered through other Departments." The bill, he argued, was necessary not simply as a cost-cutting measure, but as a resolution to a problem that had long plagued the nation's legal affairs: that of contradictory opinions being issued by the law officers of the different departments. The result, Jenckes said, "is that no citizen, no lawyer, can ever learn what has been decided, what are the rules governing any Department, bureau or officer. . . . So great is the confusion and conflict that we might as well attempt to read the whirlwind."[115]

The high cost of hiring outside legal assistance evidently impressed the Congress, and the bill was finally passed in June 1870. In the act is a prohibition on department secretaries employing outside counsel unless the attorney general certifies that his own legal staff is unable to perform such services.[116]

The Department of Justice came into existence on July 1, 1870, with the addition of two assistants and a solicitor general to share with the attorney general the duty to conduct cases for the United States.[117] The act also permitted the attorney general to refer questions of law to a subordinate, "except questions involving a construction of the Constitution." Once the subordinate's opinion was endorsed by the attorney general, it would have the same force and effect.[118] Huston notes that the act did little to change the statutory duties of the attorney general,[119] but the nature of the attorney general's work did change. No longer was he, in effect, "a counselor to the cabinet and barrister in the Supreme Court"; no longer was he simply the nation's lawyer. Now he administered an official bureaucracy, and he would become increasingly absorbed in complex administrative detail and national litigation.[120] This piece of legislation, according to one researcher, marks "the culmination of the evolutionary process through which the Attorney Generalship

. . . developed its essential nature."[121] Subsequent developments have been only variations.

Legislative fiat alone, however, could not create a Department of Justice, especially given two seemingly minor congressional oversights. The first was the failure to provide a centralized office space. Without it, the law officers in the Treasury, Internal Revenue, Navy, and State departments—nominally transferred to the attorney general's office—remained located with their respective departments, where they continued in much the same manner as before.[122] The other oversight was the failure to repeal the old statutes that had originally established and defined these solicitors. The attorney general strongly urged legislation remedying this anomaly, but Congress simply enacted the Revised Statutes of 1874, which reaffirmed the old laws.[123] Government lawyers were not appointed by the attorney general or housed with his staff. These actions signaled "a curious ambivalence about the role of the Attorney General."[124]

Further pleas to Congress in 1903 and 1909 did not alter this system of divided control and responsibility in the nation's legal system. By 1915, solicitors who were independent of Justice operated in the Departments of State, Treasury, Interior, Commerce, Labor, Agriculture, Navy, Post Office, and Internal Revenue. Each solicitor claimed the right to conduct litigation; each rendered legal advice to his department. The resulting chaotic legal conditions were reminiscent of the Civil War period. Another national crisis—this time a world war—made the situation so intolerable that change was essential. With the war had come a proliferation of governmental agencies and bureaus, each with its own legal counsel and the right to conduct its own cases. The mounting confusion finally caught President Woodrow Wilson's attention, and he responded with an executive order. Using his emergency war powers, he required all government law officers to operate under the supervision and control of the Department of Justice. He also reiterated the binding nature of the attorney general's opinions on executive officers. Throughout the war, departmental law officers were limited to rendering advice for their departments, leaving litigation to the Department of Justice, but as the emergency ended, and the authority of the executive order lapsed, they reasserted their right to control their litigation.[125]

Chaos had returned by the 1920s. Albert Langeluttig writes in his 1927 history that the law officers of the various departments "have long since ceased to be in fact members of the Department of Justice."[126] In the 1928 annual report, the attorney general listed only 115 of the 900 legal positions in the executive branch as even nominally under his control,[127] less than 13 percent of the total number of federal civilian attorneys. Once again, Congress contributed to the decentralization by permitting several executive boards to handle their own court cases, including the Interstate Commerce Commission and the Veterans' Bureau. Consolidation of legal work began again in 1933 under Attorney General Cummings with another executive order, but department heads continued to resist, as illustrated in the diary of Ickes, Roosevelt's outspoken Interior secretary. In response to Cumming's proposals to eliminate many of the departmental solicitors, Ickes asserted that he would fight. "I could not function without my legal staff. . . . I would be helpless if I had to wait for an opinion from the Department of Justice in the many matters on which I want legal opinions before making decisions. Moreover, I would not have any confidence in decisions from the Department of Justice. That Department is simply loaded with political appointees."[128] The practice of executive departments maintaining their own formal law offices continues today. Department attorneys generally are restricted to rendering legal advice on matters of concern to that department alone. Most of the government's litigation now is placed under Justice Department control,[129] except in the case of independent agencies, such as the Tennessee Valley Authority, which maintain their right to conduct their own litigation, although they may choose not to do so.

Congress may have been reluctant to centralize legal business, but the courts were not. They were the ones who suffered under the fractured system long in existence. As early as 1866, the justices demanded that the government present a unified legal position through the office of the attorney general. That year, in *The Gray Jacket* case, the Supreme Court ruled that when the attorney general represented the government in court, no counsel could be heard in opposition on behalf of another department.[130] The Supreme Court upheld the authority of the attorney general in later cases as well, recognizing in one 1888 case his plenary power over all government litigation.[131] This decision did not bury the issue once and for all; throughout the twentieth century, it has continued to resurface. In the 1930s, Interior Secretary Ickes objected to Justice handling of certain cases originating in his department, in particular those dealing with oil matters. He told Roosevelt that he opposed giving Cummings any supervision over regulations his department might issue, despite the president's argument that the attorney general would be responsible for any ensuing litigation. Ickes thought his department should handle any litigation, complaining that the government's only loss in an oil case resulted from the ignorance of Justice Department attorneys. Writing in his diary, Ickes said he told the president that he had "an exceedingly able legal staff that I would not trade man for man with members of the Attorney General's staff. . . . We have several lawyers who don't do anything except handle oil matters."[132] Despite his generally low opinion of Justice Department attorneys, however, Ickes lobbied only for his department's inclusion in litigation, not actual control.

While the Justice Department is widely recognized as the legitimate representative for the government in court, tensions occasionally arise when executive departments take contradictory stands on an issue in litigation. The solicitor general and attorney general must decide which departmental position will be defended. Occasionally, departments challenge the attorney general's authority to make this determination; during the Carter administration, the Interior Department and White House staff disagreed with the attorney general's position on litigation involving the Tellico Dam, to be discussed at length in chapter five.

This historical survey illustrates that attorneys general have assumed dual obligations since the early eighteenth century at least, both in their relations with the king and Parliament in Britain, and with colonial governors and councils in the New World. In the past two centuries, with the emergence of the modern office, the tension has grown greater as attorneys general have seen their authority extend into more and more policy areas. These expanded tasks not only exacerbate the old division between law and politics, they also consume much of the law officer's time and energy. In his efforts to satisfy the administrative demands of the modern bureaucracy, the attorney general may find himself giving less attention to the traditional lawyering roles. Meador notes: "Given the difficulties of performing the lawyering role with integrity, in light of the subtle interplay of law, policy, and politics, there is a limit to the number of distractions and other concerns with which an Attorney General can be expected to cope and still have time to deal wisely and sensitively with the lawyer's job."[133] This returns us to the theme of duality and the ways in which various incumbents have related to their presidents and their political tasks. The next chapter begins our analysis of the validity of the two types outlined in chapter one as it addresses those politically active attorneys general classified as Advocates.

Chapter Three

The Advocate Attorney General

Many law officers have been politically or personally close to their presidents. William Rehnquist argued in 1970 that "any President, and any Attorney General, wants his immediate underlings to be not only competent attorneys, but to be politically and philosophically attuned to the policies of the administration."[1] The average president "expects his attorney general . . . to be his advocate rather than an impartial arbiter, a judge of the legality of his action."[2] Because of a president's desire for loyalty, support, and compatibility, Advocate traits tend to be the norm among attorneys general.

Prior party work often plays a role in the selection; a large percentage of those to serve in this century have been party managers. The statutory requirement that the attorney general be "learned in the law" usually is no barrier to such an appointment because many party leaders are lawyers.[3] With a partisan background and/or close political or personal ties to the chief executive, the Advocate acts in distinctive ways once he is in office. Embracing an expansive view of legal interpretation, he uses the law as a tool for advancing administration—or his own—policy goals. He may become a trusted counselor on whom the president relies for a broad range of nonlegal as well as legal advice, including domestic politics or foreign affairs.

His strong bond of loyalty to the president does not mean that he merely acquiesces; he may pursue the president's political agenda because he shares it, not because he is ordered to do so. In fact, some Advocates have been noted for their independence of the White House, which may be enhanced when they have their own political base of support. Theodore Sorensen, a member of the Kennedy White House, writes that a background in politics can be a useful attribute for advisers. Not only are they more aware of the president's needs, but "those with a political base of their own are also more secure in case of attack."[4]

An independently minded Advocate attorney general may even use his political skills to pursue a policy that differs from his president's. In a more recent example, Herbert Brownell in 1956 was able to shepherd through Congress a much tougher civil rights bill than President Eisenhower wanted. Brownell had many traits of the Advocate model; he had been campaign manager for Thomas Dewey in 1944 and 1948, chair of the Republican National Committee, and an adviser in Eisenhower's 1952 race. When the president had a heart attack that kept him away from government for almost four months, Brownell quietly began to lobby the cabinet for a strong civil rights measure. Later, the politically adept attorney general was able to have the bill introduced in Congress with the implication that it was backed by the administration. Eisenhower, to keep from looking out of touch with his own branch, especially during an election year, found himself forced to go on record in its favor.[5]

The tradition of appointing allies to the post is a long one. The first law officer, Edmund Randolph, was an old friend of President Washington's; he filled many nonlegal responsibilities while in office. The nineteenth century saw other appointments of political and personal associates. The careers of two of the most outstanding—Roger Brooke Taney and Caleb Cushing—will be examined in this chapter, followed by a review of the law officers of Franklin Roosevelt and John Kennedy.

Roger Taney: The General's General

One of the earliest examples of an Advocate attorney general is Roger Brooke Taney, who served from 1831 to 1833 under Andrew Jackson. Taney, best known for his authorship of the *Dred Scott* ruling during his tenure as Chief Justice, first gained political notoriety for his opposition to the U.S. Bank while a member of the Jackson cabinet. He was no mere foot soldier in Jackson's war with the "monster"; he was the chief theoretician and strategist. He became General Jackson's general in the battle with the U.S. Bank.

Taney was not a close friend when Jackson asked him to become attorney general, but he had been an avid and longtime political supporter. A former Federalist office holder—he had served as a representative and then a senator in the Maryland state legislature—he split with the party over the War of 1812. In 1824, when Jackson made his first bid for the presidency, Taney abandoned the dying Federalist party and supported him.[6] Like many Federalists, he found Jackson an attractive candidate because Jackson many years before had urged Monroe to appoint Federalists to public office.[7] In addition, virtually all of the other contenders in 1824 were members of Monroe's cabinet, which led Taney to complain that he was "sick of all Secretary candidates [for the presidency], and would be glad to see it understood that a man might be elected without the patronage of the President for the time being, or the power of members of Congress, or a combination of mercenary presses, or local interests."[8] Jackson looked to be independent of special interests, a quality Taney admired. Initially lukewarm in his assessment, Taney became an ardent Jacksonian by the end of the 1924 campaign. When that election was thrown into the House of Representatives, he urged Maryland congressmen to support Jackson. After the defeat, Taney continued to work on Jackson's behalf, becoming chair of his central committee in Maryland and helping to organize a political convention in Baltimore to build support for the 1828 race.[9]

Scholars disagree on how well known Taney was to Jackson at the time of his appointment to the attorney generalship. Some write that "Taney was probably not well known" to the president then,[10] but others argue that that view is incorrect. "Taney had been one of his early supporters and they probably met when the General visited Baltimore in 1825. . . . No one as politically astute as General Jackson could have been ignorant of one who had taken such a prominent part on his behalf."[11] Furthermore, Taney's brother-in-law was Francis Scott Key, a strong Jacksonian; it was Key who approached Taney, then Maryland attorney general, about joining the administration. Twenty years afterward, Taney himself described his feelings toward Jackson at the time of his appointment:

I can say most truly that I did not desire the office and accepted it with reluctance. . . . But when General Jackson offered me this appointment, his first cabinet had been just dissolved. He was at that time vehemently assailed not only by his old enemies but by new ones who had before been his friends. I had scarcely any personal acquaintance with him, and knew him only from his public acts and the history of his life. But yet my feelings toward him were warmer than mere political confidence.[12]

Once in office, Taney became one of Jackson's most trusted advisers, probably closer than all other advisers on the issue of the U.S. Bank.[13] The myth of Taney being intimidated by Jackson on the bank issue was critically examined in chapter one. Far from being manipulated by a demanding president, Taney seems to have been the one who orchestrated administration policy, all the while professing loyalty to Jackson. He was able to cloak "the shrewdness with which he not only persuaded Jackson to remove the deposits, but persuaded him also that it was largely his own idea."[14] It was Taney who, as a newcomer to the cabinet, voiced the first criticism of the administration's conciliatory tone with the U.S. Bank. It was Taney who was instrumental in drafting Jackson's famous veto message when he rejected the bank's charter renewal, including these words that express an expansive understanding of constitutional interpretation:

> Mere precedent is a dangerous source of authority and should not be regarded as deciding questions of constitutional power except where the acquiescence of the people and the States can be regarded as well settled. The Congress, the Executive, and the Court must each for itself be guided by its own opinion of the Constitution. . . . The authority of the Supreme Court must not, therefore, be permitted to control the Congress or the Executive when acting in their legislative capacities, but to have only such influence as the force of their reasoning may deserve.[15]

There is a certain irony to this passage, given Taney's subsequent confrontations with the other branches when he served as Chief Justice. His approach to constitutional interpretation here seems echoed in the arguments of Abraham Lincoln in the wake of Taney's *Dred Scott* decision.

Taney had had a distinguished private legal career, serving successfully at the Maryland bar with such eminent attorneys as Luther Martin,

William Pinkney and William Wirt.[16] He has been called "a great technical lawyer with a better legal training than any of his predecessors" in
the attorney general's office.[17] Yet, despite his professional skills, he was
more a politician than a lawyer. He ran for every office then open to direct election: the Maryland House of Delegates, the U.S. Congress, and
presidential elector. In fact, "politics ran hot in Taney's blood."[18] This
feature helps to distinguish him as an Advocate attorney general.

Also contributing to his classification as an Advocate was his view
of the law as a means of achieving policy ends. One biographer noted
that Taney made his legal decisions "with a view to economic and social
conditions, and not entirely from a coldly legalistic point of view."[19] For
example, while couching his condemnation of the bank in constitutional
terms, he viscerally understood the issue as a battle between privilege
and the people, a monied oligarchy versus popular sovereignty. He saw
the bank as a dangerous internal enemy of the United States that had
the power to enslave the nation economically.[20] Taney's Southern and
states' rights sympathies also are evident in his work as attorney general. Twenty-five years before *Dred Scott*, he wrote a four-thousand-
word opinion rejecting the notion that free black Americans could be
citizens or have any constitutional rights. The opinion upheld the constitutionality of a North Carolina Negro seaman law that required the
detention of black sailors when their ships were in port. An earlier attorney general had also upheld such laws, but on much more narrow
and legalistic grounds.[21]

With these characteristics, Taney served as an Advocate under Andrew Jackson in every respect except in his role as all-round adviser.
This does not seriously affect his placement, however, because the bank
issue dominated his two-year tenure as attorney general.

Caleb Cushing and "The Amiable Mediocrity"

The attorney general chosen by Franklin Pierce, the vibrant and politically savvy Caleb Cushing, personifies the Advocate model in the
nineteenth century. Pierce, who won office in a dark horse campaign in
1852, selected him partly as payment of a political debt owed Cushing
for his efforts at the party convention. It was also an act of friendship
between the two men, who had known each other twenty years. Cush-

ing came to dominate the Pierce cabinet, assuming more and more responsibilities and expanding the scope of the attorney generalship.

Cushing was a highly political man who wrote editorials and gave speeches on such current events as the Oregon boundary dispute with Great Britain. In 1840, he authored a biographical campaign booklet extolling the virtues of presidential candidate William Henry Harrison.[22] Cushing thrived on political and partisan activity. An ardent Whig until 1844, he served in the Massachusetts legislature and the U.S. Congress. He then became an equally ardent Democrat.[23] As a delegate to the 1848 Democratic State Convention, he and his fellow "Hunkers" successfully advocated a policy of nonintervention in the affairs of other states, which blocked the possibility of a Democratic coalition with the fervently abolitionist Free Soilers, whom Cushing feared would destroy the Union. He ran for governor of Massachusetts and lost. A few years later, he served as the first mayor of Newburyport, Massachusetts.[24] Then with the Civil War, he changed parties again, becoming a Republican.

His political nature is most evident in his behind-the-scenes lobbying for Pierce while he was a delegate to the 1852 Democratic National Convention. The previous summer, he and four other veterans of the Mexican War had decided to work together at the convention, although they had not settled on a candidate. Pierce, a former senator who also had served in the war, joined the group and became their favorite. At the convention, a fierce battle ensued for the party's nomination among four well-known Democrats. Cushing distrusted qualities in each, so he and his friends quietly began to promote Pierce as a compromise candidate, spreading the impression among wavering delegates that he was safe, a man without enemies. By the forty-eighth ballot, Pierce was still in third place, but on the forty-ninth, the exhausted delegates switched almost unanimously for the dark horse. Historians credit the nomination triumph to Cushing. The general election itself was no contest; the tide was in favor of the Democrats and Pierce swept the electoral college. Cushing, a state justice at the time, did not actively participate, nor was he needed. He had done his part already. "Seldom has a party been more completely triumphant than was the Democracy in 1852. To this result, Caleb Cushing had contributed very materially, and sagacious observers expected that he would be one of the new President's chief advisers."[25]

Sagacious observers were right; Cushing was named attorney general and helped to select the rest of the cabinet. He became its leading spirit. Aside from Cushing, Secretary of War Jefferson Davis, leader of the Southern movement, was perhaps the most powerful cabinet member, and he and Cushing often agreed on foreign and domestic affairs. The secretary of State, William Marcy, preferred the show of power to real authority, and he turned to the attorney general for relief when he found his duties too burdensome. Cushing obliged by assuming three State Department functions: pardons, legal appointments, and official correspondence for other departments. Extradition cases also were transferred to him. This arrangement doubled his responsibilities and made his office more important than it had ever been before. Because of it, he played a part in most of the important issues of the day. The New York *Evening Mirror* in 1853 noted that he had earned the sobriquet "Richelieu" for aggrandizing his authority while in office.[26] Cushing differed from his predecessors in his willingness to assume more responsibility. The most active of the earlier law officers, William Wirt, had scrupulously avoided expanding his duties. But Cushing welcomed them and successfully pushed Congress to increase the permanent clerkships in his office from two to four.[27] Further enhancing the prestige and power of his office, Cushing abandoned his private practice, becoming the first full-time attorney general.

In his role as "the mouth piece of the administration," he wrote daily editorials for the administration newspaper, prepared several important state papers, and consulted with Pierce on virtually every vital issue. "He took a lofty conception of his department, which he made, for the time being, 'the great, controlling, supervising office' of the administration. No problem was too great, no question too small, for the attention of the indefatigable Attorney General."[28]

Like many presidents with Advocate law officers, Pierce came to rely on the strong-minded and energetic Cushing. The two men had known each other since the Twenty-fourth Congress, when Cushing was a Whig and Pierce a Democrat. Although of different parties, they agreed on the annexation of Texas and the war with Mexico; Cushing liked the bold foreign policy of the Democrats.[29] As attorney general, Cushing sometimes dominated his unassuming superior, "since he far surpassed Pierce intellectually, and was a master in all the arts of dialectics and persuasion."[30] Pierce has been described as an "amiable mediocrity," principled but too willing to let others make his decisions for him. He reportedly lacked "robustness of character,"[31] which left him easily manipulated.

Consistent with the Advocate model, Cushing played a major advisory role on a broad range of issues, in particular, foreign policy. One anecdote illustrates his dominance in this area: ten days after the inauguration, Cushing invited the London *Times* correspondent to his office to explain the administration's foreign policy, and he proceeded to talk for two hours about Santa Anna in Mexico, Spain's power in Cuba, and the possible collision between U.S. and British interests in Central America.[32] His interest in foreign affairs extended over his entire professional life. In 1844, he was the first American commissioner to China, where he negotiated the opening of Chinese ports to U.S. trade. He served in several diplomatic posts in the post–Civil War period as well, including as a special minister to Colombia to negotiate a treaty for a ship canal across the isthmus, as counsel for Mexico before an international commission, and then as counsel for the United States in claims against Spain.[33] Perhaps his most notable work was that of counsel for the United States at the arbitration of the *Alabama* claims with Great Britain.[34] Later Grant named him minister to the Republic of Spain.[35]

An Advocate attorney general, Cushing used the law as a tool to accomplish specific policy ends. Some of his advice to Pierce, in fact, seems more concerned with policy than legality. For example, he encouraged Pierce's support of the proslavery legislature of Kansas, despite the evidence of massive election fraud. Pierce wanted to accept the proslavery faction as legitimate regardless of the fraud because he felt he had made a "gentleman's agreement" that Kansas would be a slave state.[36] Cushing's opinion accommodated that wish.

More concerned with ends than means—specifically the goal of maintaining the Union against the abolitionist threat—Cushing produced a number of other legal opinions in support of slavery interests. Several expanded the authority of U.S. marshals in enforcing the Fugitive Slave Law, including one opinion that a marshal could call on U.S. marines and soldiers for assistance in securing a runaway slave. He also wrote that state courts did not have the authority to issue a writ of habeas corpus to discharge someone arrested on a warrant of the United States. "In these notable cases, Cushing assumed almost the authority of the Supreme Court, and cooperated with the administration by pro-

ducing a canon of constructive opinion in favor of the drastic enforcement of the Fugitive Slave Law."[37] His opinion of October 24, 1855, argued that the Missouri Compromise of 1820 was an unconstitutional
usurpation of the municipal sovereignty of new states. Two years later,
Chief Justice Taney relied in part on Cushing's reasoning for the *Dred
Scott* ruling.[38]

Cushing's continued support of Southern interests, which left him
ostracized in his own state of Massachusetts, illustrates the importance
that he attached to certain policy outcomes. His defense of *Dred Scott*,
for example, ignored the moral issues raised by the institution of slavery
and instead concentrated on slavery as a matter of practical politics. He
did not argue that it was right, but that it was a necessary evil if the Union was to be maintained. His speech in 1857 defending this view was
"a brilliant example of special pleading, such as a clever lawyer might
produce for a client."[39] In fact, his proslavery position represented a reversal of his earlier views. Years before he had opposed the admission of
Arkansas into the Union because it allowed slavery, and he also had argued for the abolition of slavery in the District of Columbia.[40]

But this ability to manipulate the law for policy ends does not mean
that Cushing consciously distorted his legal interpretations. He was an
excellent attorney, with a remarkable skill in "marshaling evidence, in
bringing up an imposing array of precedents and authorities, and arguing from them to an unavoidable conclusion."[41] He could make persuasive legal arguments when he was convinced that his position was the
correct one. His knowledge of the law and his argumentative powers
are especially well displayed in one official opinion rebuking British efforts to recruit Americans for the Crimean War. That opinion—which accused Britain of violating U.S. neutrality—was an important step in the
development of neutrality law; it subsequently "has been accepted as of
high authority in international law."[42]

In addition, there are instances in which Cushing acted with a precise regard for the law, especially international law. When the American
adventurer William Walker declared himself president of Nicaragua in
1855 and reinstituted slavery there, Pierce's cabinet differed on the issue
of U.S. support. Although generally imperialistic in foreign policy,
Cushing argued against support, convincing Pierce to label the takeover
a disreputable and criminal undertaking. Cushing also refused to recog-

nize Walker's envoy as an accredited minister, and he detained a Nicaragua-bound vessel loaded with munitions.[43]

Advocate law officers are often accused of being mere instrumentalities. Such is the view held by many toward Roger Taney in his efforts to dismantle the U.S. Bank. He and Cushing certainly felt loyalty toward their presidents, but the assumption that they were henchmen for legally questionable policies is inaccurate. Cushing is especially vulnerable to charges that he was fickle and unreliable. Asserting that he was a dangerous influence on the malleable Pierce, one historian writes that Cushing's "capacity to invert his thoughts might have made him an invaluable attorney to a client with a doubtful or delicate case; but, in an attorney general of the United States, who had to tell the president simply what the law was, and not what it might be or should be, it was incontestably more desirable, that things should not change form before his intellectual eyes with every change of position."[44] The historian draws his harsh conclusion from the opinions of Cushing's contemporaries, including one who called him "unscrupulous, double-sexed, double-gendered, and hermaphroditic in politics—with a hinge in his knee which he often crooks. . . . He governs by subserviency."[45]

Cushing had the misfortune of being a highly partisan man at a time when parties were dramatically realigning. Strongly and consistently pro-Union, he switched from the Whigs to the Democrats and eventually to the Republicans, which caused his political enemies to doubt his sincerity. Pierce, who thought well of Cushing, later attributed his inconsistency to his comprehensive intellect. In a conversation recorded by Nathaniel Hawthorne, Pierce explained that Cushing's unreliability was intellectual, not moral. "He has such comprehensiveness, such mental variety and activity, that, if left to himself, he cannot keep fast hold of one view of things, and so cannot, without external help, be a consistent man."[46] Cushing's biographer also challenges the charge of opportunism:

> Once having made up his mind, he was both loyal and unyielding. . . . The side which he espoused became at once the *right* side, and the other was just as surely the *wrong* one. Cushing was . . . entirely honest in his opinions, but vigorously partisan. He changed his views more than once, but it can never be said that he wavered weakly between two alternatives. Nor is there any evidence that he

ever altered a political conviction in order to gain any emolument or advantage for himself.[47]

In fact, in following his convictions, Cushing damaged his public career, in particular his ambitions for the presidency.[48] He continued to hope for the Chief Justiceship. When Salmon Chase died in 1873, Cushing finally received the nomination from President Grant, but Senate opposition was so formidable that he had to ask Grant to withdraw his name. He had made too many enemies during his long political life, which outweighed his reputation in international law and diplomacy.[49]

The Law Officers of Franklin D. Roosevelt

Franklin Roosevelt's first three attorneys general were all active partisans and may be located toward the Advocate end of the continuum. Homer Cummings, the first of the New Deal law officers, had been active in party affairs since 1900 and even received substantial votes for the Democratic nomination in 1920 and 1924. He met FDR during Wilson's 1912 campaign, and twenty years later he worked for Roosevelt before and during the 1932 convention.[50] As attorney general, Cummings also seemed to be an Advocate, focusing on the ends to be won. He argued, for example, that the essence of law is natural justice, not legal or institutional justice. "The letter of the law, even the text of any written Constitution, is dead unless it conforms to the needs of living men."[51] In one radio address, he said that part of his duty was to "give practical effect to the ends sought by the recent legislation and the policies of the administration. In this effort, I shall hope to be governed by a sense of economic realism rather than by any narrow legalism."[52] It was Cummings who suggested the Court packing plan to Roosevelt; he considered it his "brain child."[53] Cummings served almost six years, longer than any other twentieth-century officer.

Frank Murphy, Roosevelt's second attorney general, also shows Advocate features. He, too, had a political background. His biographer notes that politics, not the law, was his true mistress. As mayor of Detroit, he organized the National Conference of Mayors and became a champion of the New Deal. In 1932, he campaigned in Michigan on Roosevelt's behalf and was rewarded with the governor generalship of the Philippines. Returning in 1936, he ran for governor at Roosevelt's request and won. When he was defeated in 1938, Murphy was named attorney general, a move that surprised even Roosevelt's political intimates who had expected the post to go to Solicitor General Robert Jackson. He was not long at Justice, but "temporary or not, Murphy gave Washington an object lesson in how quickly traditional government operations could be transferred onto the center of the political stage."[54] He crusaded for civil liberties and for government ethics, and was a master at public relations, which irritated other men in the administration, such as Jackson and Francis Biddle. Substantively, Murphy formed two new units in the criminal division and proposed legislation for an administrative office of the federal courts. Roosevelt eventually named Murphy to the Supreme Court, a move that he resisted but could not reject without embarrassing the president. His elevation opened the attorney generalship for Jackson, who had been waiting in the wings.[55]

Robert Jackson's eighteen months in office require more than a cursory overview because he served during the uncertain period leading up to U.S. involvement in the Second World War. Out of this time came several opinions that have since been criticized as examples of legal reasoning distorted to suit policy ends.

Jackson clearly fits the model of the Advocate attorney general. Committed to his party and the New Deal political vision, he was an early supporter of Franklin Roosevelt. As Democratic National Committee secretary in 1932, he served as liaison between Roosevelt headquarters and friendly U.S. congressmen, and he was active in the 1932 convention.[56] It was on FDR's insistence two years later that the largely self-taught Jackson was induced to come to Washington as the general counsel to the Bureau of Internal Revenue. In rapid succession the talented Jackson was named assistant attorney general in the Tax Division, head of the Antitrust Division, and solicitor general. By 1940, his name was appearing as a possible presidential candidate, before Roosevelt decided to seek a third term.[57] He had close personal relations with the president as well, more so than Cummings or Murphy. Roosevelt and Jackson spent many leisure hours together, including regular poker games. On occasion, Jackson joined the president for a fishing trip. He also maintained his role as political adviser after he became attorney general; at least once he and other political insiders like Ickes and Harry

Hopkins dined with the president to discuss the Democratic platform and the chairmanship of the 1940 convention.[58] He continued to call on the White House "off-the-record" after he joined the Supreme Court, as did Murphy.[59]

In a few respects, Jackson seems more of a Neutral than an Advocate. He was, for example, widely regarded for his legal skills.[60] Interior Secretary Ickes paid him one of his rare compliments: "Jackson is one of the ablest lawyers in the Government service," adding later that he was "one of the real men of character and ability on the Washington stage."[61] Personally, Jackson was known for his independence. During the hysteria of World War I, he went against community sentiment by representing striking traction line workers; the cause was so unpopular that no other attorney would defend them.[62] The trait of independence was evident again during the red scare of the early 1950s, when he displayed the four flags of the Nuremberg courtroom in his office, including the Soviet hammer and sickle. He had served as the U.S. prosecutor during the Nuremberg war crimes trial while on a leave from the Supreme Court. Sir Elwyn Jones, later the British attorney general, considered Jackson an independent and brave idealist for continuing to display the highly unpopular Soviet flag.[63]

In another apparent break from the model, Jackson stressed his commitment to strict adherence to civil liberties, regardless of public pressure or wartime need. On his appointment, he told the president that he would run the department "in a lawyerly way, . . . with prosecutions based on criminal acts, not merely reprehensible attitudes or opinions, and without yielding to cultivating hysteria among our people."[64] Jackson's statement is a veiled reference to the fact that Murphy's support of civil liberties had started to yield under the pressure to rout out suspected subversives. In office, Jackson proceeded with restraint. For example, he rejected his predecessor's suggestion that Justice fingerprint all workers at munitions factories. He would accept fingerprinting only if the War Department required it in their defense contracts and it covered managers as well as workers. He also suggested dropping indictments against Americans who had enlisted on the Loyalist side in the Spanish war, unless indictments also went out to pro-Francoists.[65]

But these qualities do not negate his classification as an Advocate. Cushing and Taney also were known as able lawyers and strong-minded thinkers. As a member of the executive branch, Jackson had a broad view of the law as a means of accomplishing desirable policy ends; in this he was very much an Advocate law officer. On at least two occasions, even his avowed commitment to civil liberties was bent. Concerned about subversive activities, Roosevelt in May 1940 instructed his reluctant attorney general to authorize FBI agents to use wiretaps on suspected Nazi spies. He also asked Jackson if there was a legal way to open outgoing or incoming mail to or from certain countries. The FBI soon began a mail opening operation, although there was no clear legal sanction.[66]

A few of Jackson's opinions continue to be used to illustrate how legal interpretation may be made to fit policy, in particular his opinion supporting the bases-for-destroyers exchange. The case involved the transfer of fifty overage but reconditioned destroyers to Great Britain, in exchange for leases on several naval and air bases in the Atlantic. The transfer took place in September 1940, before the United States had entered the war. Still in effect was the Act of June 15, 1917, which read in part: "During a war in which the United States is a neutral nation, it shall be unlawful to send out of the jurisdiction of the United States any vessel built, armed, or equipped as a vessel of war."[67] In addition, Congress had passed neutrality resolutions in 1935, 1936, 1937, and 1939 placing further prohibitions on the sale of war materiel to any belligerent except on a cash-and-carry basis; American ships were forbidden to carry supplies to belligerents. Roosevelt had protested that the resolutions helped Hitler at the expense of Britain and France, but the law was not repealed until three weeks before Pearl Harbor.[68]

In the spring of 1940, Britain's First Lord of the Admiralty Winston Churchill (soon to be prime minister) and France's Premier Paul Reynaud requested a loan of dozens of old destroyers, to counter Nazi efforts to cut shipping or cross the channel. Roosevelt cabled back that he first needed Congress's authorization. Meanwhile, France and the Low Countries fell to a devastating German war machine. With the European crisis mounting, Roosevelt recalled, he and his cabinet spent one August day "devising ways and means to sell directly or indirectly fifty or sixty old destroyers to Great Britain." Congressional approval seemed unlikely given its isolationist mood. To strengthen his case before Congress, Roosevelt tried to extract a promise from Churchill that the ships would not fall into German hands. Churchill could not make that promise but offered a different *quid pro quo*, the transfer of seven British bases in Bermuda, Newfoundland, and around the Caribbean.[69]

Harold Ickes and Frank Knox of the Navy Department continued to press for the transfer, although Ickes believed that the Neutrality Act had to be amended first. Other cabinet members, notably Jackson and Secretary of War Henry Stimson, persuaded the president that he did not need to submit this new plan to Congress.[70] Jackson was in a delicate situation. He had previously issued an official opinion that the president did not have the legal authority to send the reconditioned ships to England. But by August, Ickes writes in his diary, "Bob Jackson has apparently found a legal method by which this transfer can be consummated without legislation."[71]

Jackson advised that the president, as commander in chief, had the power to transfer title and possession of the destroyers in exchange for bases that would enhance national security. The arrangement could be made by executive agreement. His opinion does seem a little strained in parts, particularly his distinction between selling armed ships to belligerents and building armed ships to order for a belligerent. Under this distinction, the transfer of the destroyers would not violate neutrality law but the sale of "mosquito boats" then under construction would.[72]

Scholars are ambivalent about whether this opinion constitutes a manipulation of the law. Some have held that the exchange and the lend-lease program of four months later were "essentially belligerent acts that might well have precipitated a German declaration of war."[73] Others have criticized the transfer on legal rather than policy grounds. Herbert Briggs argued in 1940 that it violated national and international law and the neutrality of the United States. He wrote, "The destroyers have by now been transferred, but let no one say that it was accomplished 'legally.'"[74] This view was shared by Edward Corwin, who was alarmed at the growth in executive power. He argued that the transaction violated at least two statutes and "represented an exercise by the President of a power that by the Constitution is specifically assigned to Congress." Jackson's opinion, he added, rested on the president's power to "dispose" the armed forces, "which was ingeniously, if not quite ingenuously, construed as the power to *dispose of* them."[75] There may be no way to reconcile the destroyer deal with neutrality status, U.S. law, or international law. But, as some writers of the time noted, the United States was not a genuine neutral; it had become a supporting state. The exchange was simply a recognition of the fact that the nation already was engaged in a limited war.[76] By pretending otherwise in his opinion, Jackson may have hoped to avert the real thing, while at the same time assist the side with which the United States identified its national interests. He may have felt he had little choice, given the potentially catastrophic outcome of any alternative.

The categorization of Cummings, Murphy, and Jackson as Advocate models is tempered somewhat by the personality of the president under whom they served. It is questionable how much of an advisory role any cabinet member could play under someone like Franklin Roosevelt. The strong-willed Ickes, for all his seniority, complained: "The cold fact is that on important matters we are seldom called upon for advice. We never discuss exhaustively any policy of Government or question on political strategy. The President makes all of his own decisions and, so far at least as the Cabinet is concerned, without taking counsel with a group of advisers."[77] Roosevelt wanted to run the show himself and was unwilling to delegate broad powers, even during the war. The competitive managerial system he developed kept him at the center of aggressive and diverse advisers. No one voice monopolized his ear.[78] This necessarily restricted the influence that his attorneys general could exercise in the administration.

The Advocacy Role of Robert F. Kennedy

Robert Francis Kennedy may be the century's embodiment of the Advocate attorney general. To him, politics was a positive force to be utilized to right wrongs. Instead of serving narrow self interests, politics could promote the interests of justice. He expressed this view in 1964: "The challenge of politics and public service is to discover what is interfering with justice and dignity for the individual here and now, and then to decide swiftly upon the appropriate remedies."[79] He saw law and policy as inextricably linked, and throughout his tenure as attorney general, he had no qualms about using the political tools at his disposal to rectify societal ills. Decrying the evils of poverty, discrimination and corruption, Kennedy wrote, "We have got to make our legal system work. We have got to *make* it responsive to legitimate grievances."[80] This activist view of the law was a theme that he repeated several more times over the next three years.[81] In one Law Day address, he asserted that "government has positive responsibility to make individual freedom more than a legal fiction. . . . It may be said that in a democratic society law is the form which free men give to justice."[82] Nowhere is this goal-oriented view of the law more evident than in his aggressive stance in the field of civil rights, although he also took an activist approach to the problems of juvenile delinquency, poverty, and organized crime.[83]

His own political training began early. "As far back as I can remember, politics was taken with special fervor and relish in our house."[84] In his mid-twenties, he successfully managed his brother's 1952 campaign for the Senate. Although he stayed out of electoral politics for the next seven years, he was his brother's only choice for campaign manager in 1960. "He could be trusted more implicitly, say 'no' more emphatically and speak for the candidate more authoritatively than any professional politician," Theodore Sorensen writes.[85]

John Kennedy's selection of his younger brother to be attorney general was not without political risks. JFK himself recognized that when he "privately predicted that the nomination of his brother as Attorney General . . . would prove to be his most controversial choice then and one of his wisest choices later."[86] Journalist Robert Novak, calling Robert a "free-swinging, relentless political warrior," wrote in late 1960, "The result could be a mammoth record of accomplishment by the Justice Department. Or it could be an unqualified disaster." Novak recounted Robert Kennedy's lack of legal experience or interpersonal skills, but noted his abilities as an administrator. To liberal criticism that Robert might be too conservative, Novak responded, "His brief career has been marked by intense concentration on the task at hand—usually the furtherance of his brother's political career—with little interest in issues as such."[87] The criticism of liberals seems strange now, given Kennedy's record. But even more curious is Novak's comment that he was not interested in policy per se. Robert Kennedy was only thirty-five when he became attorney general. Clearly, he grew while in office, becoming aware of the demands of racial minorities, the poor, and the young, and sensitized to the importance of due process guarantees.[88] Even so, his passion for causes was evident early on. Washington journalist Clark Mollenhoff, who had known both brothers since the early 1950s, described their differences in terms of this passion: "Bob was one who had to believe. Jack was all things to all men. He didn't really give that much of a damn. But Bob really had to believe. It was one of the things that made him controversial because if he believed against you, he'd tell you. If he believed for you, he was one hundred percent for you. Jack could kind of glaze the whole thing over; he wasn't too much for you or too much against you. He wanted your political support next year."[89]

Robert Kennedy initially resisted the appointment to head Justice. He worried about charges of nepotism, and he was tired of chasing "bad men" after his years as chief counsel of the McClellan Labor-Rackets Committee in the Senate.[90] Later, he explained that he knew civil rights would become an explosive issue and his brother would be hurt politically in 1964 if the attorney general had the same last name, "plus the fact that I thought I'd like to get away from [John Kennedy] for a while."[91] If he was to serve in government, he preferred to be assistant or undersecretary of Defense or State. But their father, Joseph Kennedy, convinced him that, as the president's brother, he would place a cabinet secretary in an untenable position. Instead, Joe Kennedy urged Robert to accept the Justice post, because "John needed someone in the cabinet whom he knew intimately and trusted utterly."[92]

At first, some of his critics were pleased that Robert was placed at Justice rather than in the White House where they thought he might exercise more influence.[93] But the planned push for civil rights legislation and stricter enforcement meant the office was going to be at the center of a political vortex no matter who was attorney general. In addition, Justice covered a broad range of domestic and foreign policy on which the attorney general would have input. Victor Navasky writes, "No other agency of government with the possible exception of the Bureau of the Budget would have offered a President's brother such a panoramic view of what was happening or so many levers to do something about it."[94]

But while RFK is clearly an Advocate law officer, he was not insensitive to the need to ensure nonpartisanship in the department. For the top positions at Justice, he hired some of the most talented attorneys of the day. Byron White, later associate justice of the Supreme Court, was the deputy attorney general; he recruited other excellent Yale Law School graduates, including Nicholas Katzenbach, who would serve as Johnson's attorney general. "Robert Kennedy's personal appointment was in the political tradition, but he staffed the Department in the legal tradition."[95] One of the lawyers described the atmosphere: "We felt that we were . . . in a way, a kind of an elite corps. You know, everybody—your colleagues were first rate—obviously had not been picked on any kind of a crony basis. And it was just a great compliment, a great lift to the ego to be included in that bunch."[96]

In addition, Robert Kennedy attempted to maintain a separation between the legal and political spheres under his jurisdiction. He told his staff at their first meeting that politics was forbidden, from attending political functions to speaking on political topics.[97] He tried to insulate the department from the demands of politics. When a member of the South Carolina Progressive Democratic party wrote for his aid, his administrative assistant, John Seigenthaler, responded, "As you know, Mr. Kennedy since coming into the office of Attorney General has of necessity divorced himself from political activities. He cannot inject himself into partisan politics in any state."[98] This policy was followed in investigations and prosecutions as well. For example, the attorney general did not interfere with the case of Vincent Keogh, even though he was the brother of New York Congressman Eugene Keogh, a man Robert Kennedy described as among the "five people most helpful to the President in the election." In fact, Robert called this case one of the most unpleasant ones he ever faced.[99] Vincent Keogh, a New York Supreme Court justice, had been bribed to ask a federal judge to give a more lenient sentence to a man convicted of bankruptcy fraud. Although "the decision to investigate was an extremely sensitive one for the Attorney General," he placed it under the man who headed Eisenhower's Organized Crime Section so there would be no question of favoritism.[100]

He also pursued other cases that had negative political and personal impact on the Kennedys. The Justice Department's investigation of organized crime adversely affected several friendly Democratic politicians, including Mayor George Chacharis of Gary, Indiana.[101] But perhaps the case of James Landis, a longtime friend of their father, serves as the best illustration of how the Kennedy code of loyalty could conflict with Robert Kennedy's responsibilities as a prosecutor. Landis and Joe Kennedy had been friends since the early 1930s; Landis even did financial and legal work for the family without charge. In 1937, he became dean of Harvard Law School and later was named special assistant to President John Kennedy. He "was a virtual member of the immediate family. His relationship to the Kennedys could not have been closer." Then the Internal Revenue Service discovered that he had not filed his tax returns in five years, apparently because of psychological problems and not criminal intent; Landis paid the taxes, interest, and penalties. Nevertheless, after the attorney general disqualified himself, the deputy attorney general, Nicholas Katzenbach, decided to prosecute. It was 1963, and the upcoming presidential race may have influenced the decision; if Landis had not been a family friend, the prosecution might have been dropped. In any event, Landis pleaded guilty in order to spare the administration further embarrassment, although a plea of not guilty might have been sustained.[102] Robert Kennedy said that these types of cases were one reason he did not want to become attorney general. "That's why I think it's . . . got some dangers to it for a person involved in politics to be Attorney General. . . . It is a position that should really be removed from politics or as completely as it can be."[103]

He did not sever all of his political ties, however. Not only did he help his brother Ted in his 1962 Senate race, he continued to monitor the activities of the Democratic National Committee.[104] For example, in the summer of 1961 Robert Kennedy advised the DNC Chair to begin voter registration efforts, and he named a few people who could help with the upcoming congressional races.[105] He received political reports from various sources, including Roy Reuther of the AFL-CIO, who analyzed upcoming campaigns and state voter registration drives,[106] and Interior Secretary Stewart Udall on congressional elections in the western states.[107] He kept up with key gubernatorial races, apportionment, campaign contributions to Democratic senators, the national party's payroll, and electoral strategy.[108] The attorney general also helped to place state party leaders in government positions.[109] New York politics held a special interest for him. Kenneth O'Donnell in the White House informed Robert that he was meeting the head of the DNC "to work out a procedure for dispensing patronage in New York City and State," and he promised to keep the attorney general advised.[110] He also tried to use patronage to advance desegregation in government, pushing minority hirings in the Post Office and Justice departments in particular.[111] His continuing interest in the party's voter registration drive in 1963 also may reflect a concern with civil rights.[112] His partisan and political efforts were largely indirect, consisting of keeping informed of activities handled by others.

If Robert Kennedy illustrates the fact that Advocate law officers can combine their legal and political lives, he also demonstrates that Advocates are not necessarily dependent and subservient. Because Robert was perceived as the dedicated younger brother, many in the press and public assumed that he would do whatever the president wanted. But Robert was an independent force in the administration. For one thing, he "did not define himself in terms of his status as President's brother, [instead] Robert and John alike drew their sense of identity from membership in the Kennedy family," according to Navasky. Loyalty was a powerful norm in the family, but so was excellence, courage, and integrity.[113] Second, John Kennedy did not want blind devotion from his brother. He relied on Robert precisely because "he could be counted on to disagree—to 'talk back' when others might withhold their views in the President's presence."[114] One insider explained that the president put Robert on the cabinet in the first place because he needed to be told the truth when problems arose, "and Bobby will do that."[115] This combination of loyalty and candor was invaluable to John Kennedy; in fact, the candor would not have been possible without the loyalty.

With their shared vision of political good, Robert and John Kennedy seldom disagreed on issues of substance; on many occasions, Robert was able to persuade the president to change course, although John Kennedy did not hesitate to reject his advice either.[116] On one fairly significant policy decision—involving the Volta Dam project in Ghana— the two men did differ sharply. Robert Kennedy opposed the dam on the grounds that it was contrary to the interests of true African nationalism; he had strong misgivings about Ghana's leader, Kwame Nkrumah.[117] He argued vehemently with his brother, who was under pressure by the State Department to approve the project. When the National Security Council met to decide, the attorney general attended but deferentially remained silent. Deciding to support the dam, the president remarked, "The Attorney General has not yet spoken but I can feel the cold wind of his disapproval on the back of my neck."[118] In the end, part of the loan was made, but "the whole State Department was having one hell of a time overcoming Bobby Kennedy."[119]

Perhaps more than any Advocate law officer except Cushing, Robert Kennedy became a pivotal actor in foreign policy. "In foreign affairs, his brother was navigating tricky waters with a crew of strangers. When storms blew up, there was all the more reason to summon a shipmate of longer standing."[120] One of the worst storms occurred in April 1961 when reports of the failed Cuban offensive at the Bay of Pigs reached the White House. Informed of the covert activity just a few days before the landing, Robert, along with John Kennedy's other advisers, had acceded to the plan formulated during Eisenhower's tenure. After the fiasco, the president wanted better control over the Central Intelligence Agency, so he "quietly gave Robert Kennedy an informal watching brief over the intelligence community."[121] He began by naming his brother to a board of inquiry headed by Gen. Maxwell Taylor.[122]

After that time, he remained an important foreign policy adviser, a role that might have been resented by State Department people in another administration. "But in the Kennedy Administration, they didn't complain very loudly about the President asking his brother's advice about foreign affairs questions because obviously he was going to do that and he didn't care whether they liked it or not."[123] Among his nondomestic activities, Robert Kennedy was the instigating force in securing the return of the 1,113 members of the Cuban Brigade who had been captured during the Bay of Pigs.[124] In addition, he was a member of a special counterinsurgency group, formed to coordinate federal efforts to counter guerrilla insurrection outside of the United States.[125] He participated in White House discussions that led to Undersecretary of State Averell Harriman's mission to Moscow to negotiate the Test Ban Treaty, signed in August 1963.[126] Others in the administration began to solicit his advice on foreign policy.[127] In addition, he served as an informal channel to the president for U.S. ambassadors who needed immediate access.[128] Visiting foreign officials also found his office a useful contact, including a member of the Indian Parliament, the Indonesian National Police chief, and a minister of Korea.[129] On occasion, foreign heads of state would write to him with requests for aid, which he then referred to the State Department.[130] He also helped to arrange CIA subsidies for the leaders of the liberation movements in Mozambique and Angola.[131]

This means of informal access to the president worked well in the often strained U.S.-Soviet relationship. Early in 1961, Robert Kennedy became friends with a Soviet embassy press attaché named Georgi Bolshakov, considered by the CIA to be a top KGB agent. Through them, John Kennedy and Nikita Khrushchev could relay messages unofficially. This channel proved invaluable during the Berlin crisis of 1961 when American and Soviet tanks confronted each other. RFK told Bolshakov that the president wanted the tanks removed within twenty-four hours, and they were.[132] Unofficial contacts played a critical part in resolving the Cuban missile crisis as well. Robert Kennedy's association with Soviet Ambassador Anatoly Dobrynin provided the American and Soviet leaders with a method of communication outside of the inflexible foreign and military establishments of both countries.[133]

In diplomacy, Robert Kennedy assumed a more visible foreign policy role. His most important venture was a four-week global goodwill mission in February 1962, when he and his wife visited Tokyo, Hong Kong, Singapore, Taipei, Djakarta, Saigon, Bangkok, Karachi, Beirut, Rome, Berlin, Bonn, and The Hague.[134] The extensive journey brought two notable successes. First, he skillfully handled a crowd of three thousand Japanese students at Waseda University, turning around their anti-American sentiments. Eisenhower had been forced to cancel a visit to Japan in 1960 because of anti-American violence. Second, Kennedy was able to persuade Indonesian President Sukarno to negotiate with the Dutch in their heated territorial dispute, thus averting a possible war.[135] When he returned to the capital, he briefed the administration on labor and student groups in Japan and Indonesia, trade policy, and his perceptions of world opinion on the Berlin Wall.[136]

In other travels, he attended ceremonies marking the first anniversary of the Republic of the Ivory Coast in August 1961. He visited Brazil and the Canal Zone in December 1962. At President Johnson's request, Kennedy returned to Indonesia in early 1964 as American emissary in a territorial dispute with Malaysia; he was able to achieve a six-month cease-fire. A few months later, he traveled to Germany to commemorate his brother's trip to Berlin and then continued on to Poland.[137]

While clearly an activist attorney general in domestic affairs, particularly in civil rights, Robert Kennedy is criticized more for being an activist in foreign affairs. His legal opinions here have been criticized as attempts to justify President Kennedy's policy preferences, especially his opinion supporting a limited blockade of Cuba in October 1962. Some have compared it to Jackson's bases-for-destroyers opinion that provided the legal defense Roosevelt needed.[138] Scholar Arthur Miller points out that Robert Kennedy was in an analogous situation in the missile crisis. Without time to thoroughly research the question, he and attorneys from the Justice and State departments were compelled to produce an opinion that the quarantine was not an act of war under international law, when in fact it was. "Here again, grave questions of constitutional and international law were involved; here again, the attorney general was able, under the most adverse circumstances, to help produce a viable legal document to legalize what the President wanted to do."[139] Griffin Bell, attorney general under Jimmy Carter, also sees a similarity between the two opinions. "Pressure forced the Attorney General's opinion to be hammered out in oral discussions between lawyers for the Justice and State Departments. Not surprisingly, it was favorable to the President's wishes."[140] The claim that legal opinions simply support presidential wishes is often leveled at Advocate law officers, and a review of this particular case might illuminate the legitimacy of the general charge.

The criticism of the missile opinion is threefold: that it was drafted hurriedly, without sufficient analysis; that the attorney general and others involved were less concerned with legal issues than policy outcomes; and that the opinion was crafted specifically to support the president's policy choice. A review of the events leading to the opinion suggests that these criticisms are based on inaccuracies. First, the legal reasoning on a possible blockade had been developed two months before the Cuban missile crisis, not in the heat of the moment. A CIA memo of August 22, 1962, noted a progressive and alarming Soviet military buildup in Cuba during the preceding month.[141] Although there was no hard evidence of offensive weaponry yet, Robert Kennedy requested that the Office of Legal Counsel draft an opinion on U.S. intentions should the Soviets establish missile bases there. Norbert Schlei, assistant attorney general at the OLC, sent him a memorandum on August 30, 1962, that expressly mentioned a "total blockade or . . . 'visit and search' procedures as appropriate reactions by the American states or by the United States to meet a threat to install missile bases in Cuba."[142] A "visit and search" blockade would not cut off all traffic but would filter out traffic in offensive weapons. It was John Kennedy who characterized it as a "quarantine," which Schlei considered a "startlingly important contribution because that word conveyed to the whole world . . . what was happening." When the actual crisis came, then, "the legal spade work that was done far in advance was very helpful."[143] The legal experts in the Justice, State, and Defense departments drew heavily on this earlier opinion, which in turn influenced the president's proclamation of October 23 that announced the interdiction plan.[144]

Secondly, the August opinion, the October opinion, and the debates in the Executive Committee of the National Security Council (called the ExComm) reflect a sensitivity toward international law. While policy outcomes played the major role in the discussions (given that nuclear war was one possible outcome), the participants recognized that their measures had to be on solid legal ground if world opinion was to be won and the Soviets were to be persuaded. Kennedy, acting in accordance with the UN Charter's prohibition on the unilateral imposition of a pacific blockade, sought the sanction of both the Organization of American States and the UN Security Council. The Security Council was asked to consider the issue October 22 but took no action; some argue that this could be construed as tacit authorization. The OAS met on October 23 and gave the blockade unanimous approval.[145] Some members of ExComm did not consider the quarantine viable without at least a two-thirds vote of the OAS, because without its sanction, "allies and neutrals as well as adversaries might well regard it as an illegal blockade. . . . If so, they might feel free to defy it."[146] Robert Kennedy wrote that it was "the vote of the Organization of American States that gave a legal basis for the quarantine." The vote made the blockade difficult for the Soviets to ignore.[147]

The third charge, that the opinion merely justified John Kennedy's preferences, seems particularly difficult to sustain. He had no vested interest in the blockade plan as such; his primary object was to resolve the dispute without further endangering the nation. Far from promoting a specific plan of action, he did not attend many of the ExComm meetings those first four days, to permit the various options to be debated aggressively. When the president met with advisers on Saturday, October 20, to review the options and make a decision, he still had reservations about a blockade because it would not remove the missiles. That last doubt ended when one military chief informed him that even a major surprise air attack might leave intact some missiles.[148] The blockade had disadvantages, but the other alternatives had even more. If he ordered an air strike or invasion, he would risk nuclear war with the Soviet Union. Yet doing nothing left the United States vulnerable to potential blackmail. The quarantine not only seemed less risky, it permitted him greater freedom of movement should it fail.[149] It was pragmatic and flexible, attributes that appealed to John Kennedy. He had no hidden policy agenda, which Roosevelt had had in the bases-for-destroyers exchange.[150] In sum, it was not the president who ordered the attorney general to support a blockade; it was the attorney general who finally convinced the president.

There is some justification for Gerhard von Glahn's comment that "the legal position of the United States in instituting the Cuban blockade was somewhat dubious by traditional standards of international law." Pacific (as opposed to hostile) blockades are acceptable as coercive measures short of war, but they apply only to the ships of the blockaded nation, not of third parties. Hostile blockades apply to all ships, but they are considered legal only during war. Kennedy's quarantine used features of both. It applied to all ships carrying offensive weapons to Cuba, which is usually understood to be an act of war. Yet there was no belligerent intent on the part of the United States. Even so, it remained a pacific blockade only as long as the countries involved, including Cuba, chose to treat it that way.[151]

Throughout the crisis, Robert Kennedy acted in a manner consistent with the Advocate attorney general. He was a central figure in the ExComm meetings. Secretary Robert McNamara, in assessing the government's performance during the crisis, credited Robert Kennedy with organizing the effort and framing and promoting the quarantine strategy.[152] Sorensen also considered the attorney general "the best performer" . . . "not because of any particular idea he advanced, not because he presided (no one did), but because of his constant prodding, questioning, eliciting arguments and alternatives and keeping the discussions concrete and moving ahead."[153] When Khrushchev sent two letters—the first one rambling but conciliatory and the second one more belligerent—Robert had the idea of ignoring the second and responding only to the first. The State Department had drafted a severe response to the second letter. John Kennedy suggested that RFK and Sorensen draft their response to the first letter, and he would decide which one to send. The president's choice of the Kennedy/Sorensen reply proved to be tactically astute.[154]

Robert Kennedy was not a deputy president, however. Throughout the missile crisis, John Kennedy remained the controlling actor. "He supervised everything, from the contents of leaflets to be dropped over Cuba to the assembling of ships for the invasion."[155] During the regular course of the administration, Robert Kennedy did not participate in certain policy areas at all. Except for poverty issues, he was not consulted in economic affairs. His involvement with foreign policy began to taper off as he became increasingly enmeshed in civil rights.[156] John Kennedy, using a collegial management style, relied on many advisers other than his brother, including Arthur Schlesinger, Jr., Sorensen, Kenneth O'Donnell, McGeorge Bundy, Lawrence O'Brien, Pierre Salinger, Clark Clifford, and such outside advisers as Henry Kissinger and Joseph Alsop.[157] Robert McNamara, secretary of Defense, was "clearly the star and the strong man among the newcomers to the Kennedy team."[158] Even so, Robert Kennedy was a mainstay of the decision process. Schlesinger explained: "John Kennedy used Robert in part as Franklin Roosevelt used Eleanor—as a lightning rod, as a scout on far frontiers, as a more militant and somewhat discountable alter ego. . . . At the same time the Attorney General was John Kennedy's Harry Hopkins, Lord Root of the Matter, the man on whom the President relied for penetrating questions, for followup, for the protection of the presidential interest and objectives."[159] Navasky adds that Robert, as the president's brother, "had the opportunity to be the maximum Attorney General. When he spoke, he was assumed to hold the President's proxy."[160] Yet other presidents had had brothers who served them in public office without being such central figures. The fraternal relationship can only be a part of the explanation for Robert Kennedy's effectiveness in office. The rest of the explanation lies in those traits that he shared with the Advocate law model. He was personally close to John Kennedy, trusted and loved. But he also had an active conception of the law. The president gave him an opportunity to employ that conception in attaining their shared vision of the political good.

The Advocate law officer, as reviewed in this chapter, exhibits certain characteristics that enhance his ability to work well in an administration. He sees himself as part of a team whose chief has been elected by the people to enact a particular policy agenda. Given this conception of an electoral mandate, he feels an obligation to pursue the administration's policy goals. His unabashed commitment to those goals and his long association with the man who is president may create a high level of trust between the two. This, in turn, could lead to his inclusion in a vast array of policy fields and give him a broader influence within the administration.

These same characteristics, however, may serve to undermine his public credibility. If he is perceived as being the president's man, to the exclusion of being the nation's lawyer, the public—influenced in part by the national media and Congress—may not completely trust him to give honest legal advice or to handle fairly the government's litigation. Furthermore, his commitment to policy ends may appear to be pure politics, if those ends are controversial and highly partisan. These factors could leave him vulnerable to the charge of politicizing the office. The Advocate law officer must be especially scrupulous, therefore, to mitigate any appearance of partiality. An awareness of this may be found in the Kennedy Justice Department's handling of the James Landis prosecution, despite Landis's close ties with the family. Robert Kennedy sought to maintain the appearance (as well as the reality) of unbiased and nonpolitical justice.

But not every Advocate has been as sensitive to the importance of appearances. This has left individual incumbents and Advocates as a type open to the charge of bringing politics into the administration of justice. Such charges were levied at J. Howard McGrath of the Truman administration, for example. McGrath was an Advocate attorney general. He had been chair of the Democratic National Party for two terms before his appointment and was an important campaigner in the 1948 presidential race. As a U.S. senator, McGrath had a 99 percent proadministration voting record and was considered a Truman man. Although he saw himself as an organizer more than a policy maker, he was committed to some substantive goals, in particular a more progressive civil rights policy. While head of the DNC, he ended racial segregation of the staff and supported Truman's 1948 civil rights program despite a threatened revolt of Dixiecrats. Later he eliminated Dixiecrats from high party positions. He was named attorney general when Truman elevated Tom Clark to the Supreme Court in 1949. As Harold Gosnell points out, however, "His political credentials were impeccable after the successful election of 1948, but his legal qualifications were questioned by some. While serving in various public offices at modest salaries, he had acquired great wealth through his connections with race tracks."[161] McGrath's partisan past also haunted him as attorney general. He was accused of politicizing Justice, particularly for his department's lax investigation of the Kansas City Democratic political machine. He also became tainted in the worst scandal of the administration, involving tax collection fraud in the Internal Revenue Service, although most of the blame fell on the head of the Justice Department's tax division, T. Lamar Caudle. McGrath mishandled both Caudle's dismissal and a special assistant's investigation of government corruption. The exasperated Truman, under pressure, eventually asked him to resign.[162]

A more recent example of an Advocate charged with politicizing his department may be found in the tenure of Edwin Meese III. His experience illustrates what may happen to an Advocate attorney general who fails to recognize the office's unique position in the executive branch.

Edwin Meese III and the Reagan Presidency

Ronald Reagan's controversial appointee, Edwin Meese III, displayed numerous Advocate characteristics during his three-year tenure. His long and close association with the president, his view of the law as a means of accomplishing policy ends, and his influence within the administration on diverse policy issues are defining traits of the Advocate type.

He and the president had known each other almost eighteen years when he was named attorney general. In the late 1960s, when Meese was a deputy district attorney in Alameda County, California, he came to Governor Reagan's attention because of his "record for prosecuting pot smokers and student protestors around Berkeley."[163] He joined the governor's staff in 1967 as extradition and clemency secretary but soon expanded the job to legal affairs secretary. From 1969 to 1975, he served as Reagan's executive assistant and chief of staff.[164] He played an active part in the 1980 race as Reagan's deputy campaign manager.

Yet Meese had not been active in political or party affairs before meeting Ronald Reagan. He explained in 1984, "I am not a political fire horse to start with. I have never been involved much in political activity. The campaign of 1980 was the first one in which I had any kind of a major role." Actually, his characterization of himself as no "political fire horse" may be a little disingenuous. Various reports at the time suggested that he was the real power in the 1980 campaign, although he publicly deferred to William Casey. It does seem that he played only a minor role in Reagan's 1976 campaign for president, with his other campaign experience limited to a 1966 nonpartisan district attorney race.[165] In this electoral aspect, he may fit the Advocate only partially.

Meese was a member of Reagan's first term White House triumvirate, with Michael Deaver and James Baker. While in the White House, according to one cabinet member, Meese was the "keeper of the radical right dogma," and by 1982 was "fast becoming the most powerful man in the government next to the president."[166] Larry Speakes considered him something of a "prime minister" in Reagan's first term, more conservative and less pragmatic than his rivals Baker and Deaver. Meese, he writes, "was old-line Reagan, tuned in, knew all the players. He also knew how to work Reagan by playing to the President's conservative leanings."[167] Meese has been described as the man whom "Reagan's conservative backers believe to be the most ideologically 'pure.'"[168]

This ideological role continued after Meese joined Justice in 1985, although he had already lost some influence in the Oval Office. For one thing, he was notoriously disorganized. In addition, during his second term Reagan was less preoccupied with promoting the conservative agenda. Finally, as attorney general, Meese was no longer close to the seat of power. As Speakes notes, "A member of the Cabinet may have rank, but it's proximity that counts."[169] Even so, Meese continued to have some effect on the policies of the Reagan administration. One former associate said, "My guess is that Meese has more roles than any previous attorney general."[170] Some of these roles kept him linked to the White House; for example, he was a member of the NSC and head of the Domestic Policy Council of the cabinet.[171] Conservative writer Patrick Buchanan, then White House communications director, said in 1985 that "Ed is well on his way to becoming one of the best political Attorneys General we've had in this country."[172] By 1986, he was one of the few of the California coterie—those most intimate with the Reagans—to remain in government. A strong Reagan supporter with solid conservative backing, Meese "has taken center stage in an ideological debate that previously lacked a credible point man within the Government. Now it has one: pornography or drug smuggling, abortion or school prayer, the Attorney General's legal agenda is the President's political agenda. . . . In the process he has become the most forceful leader [of the Justice Department] since Robert F. Kennedy."[173] Other writers also have found a parallel with the Kennedy years. "In a way, Meese is Reagan's Bobby Kennedy. No Attorney General since Kennedy has been so close to his President. None has wielded such influence on so many matters."[174] Like the Kennedys, Reagan and Meese shared a vision of the United States that Meese tried to implement during his tenure at Justice; the attorney general became the president's ideological alter ego. In some respects, Meese became more of a leader of the conservative movement than Reagan, who moved away from the social agenda toward other issues.

Meese denied that there were political dimensions to his policy decisions,[175] and thus he could insist that he had not introduced politics into the department. Yet his broad, activist approach to the law is evident in his actions and speeches. For example, while at Justice, he referred to a two-page outline called "Policy Goals," drawn from the conservative political agenda of Ronald Reagan. These goals included an end to affirmative action programs, a return of abortion decisions to the states, and support for school prayer.[176] He often challenged the constitutionality of the special prosecutor law and vocally advocated the reversal of several court rulings, such as *Roe v. Wade*,[177] which had overturned state laws banning abortion, *Miranda v. Arizona*, which required that a suspect be informed of his constitutional rights, and *Mapp v. Ohio*, which extended the exclusionary rule to all criminal cases. One of his more famous public pronouncements was this: "Neither Mapp nor Miranda helps any innocent person. They only help guilty people."[178]

His activism extended beyond specific policy areas and into his whole approach to law and the Constitution. He argued, for example, that the executive is as authoritative as the Supreme Court or Congress in interpreting the law, a view that is reminiscent of Taney's famous veto message. This attitude represents an expansive understanding of executive authority. As one writer explained his position, "If the Supreme Court handed down decisions with which the Executive Branch disagreed, then officials in that branch of government should treat their own views as authority for the true meaning of the law."[179] Furthermore, Meese challenged the doctrine of incorporation, by which the Supreme Court since 1925 has gradually applied most of the Bill of Rights to the states. His criticism of the doctrine as being "intellectually shaky"[180] even brought a repudiation from Justice John Paul Stevens, "the first time in scholars' memory that a Supreme Court justice had publicly rebuked an Attorney General by name."[181]

Also consistent with the Advocate model, Meese stressed majoritarian principle over rule of law. The people had given Ronald Reagan a mandate, he noted, and Reagan's policies therefore had to be pursued. Judicial restraint, which he repeatedly called for, "stands for a presumption in favor of the power of political majorities and against the claims of individual rights."[182] His and Reagan's notion of restraint was goal-oriented; a restrained court would be active in overturning the precedents of prior "unrestrained" courts. Although couched in terms of judicial restraint and the "jurisprudence of original intent," his agenda clearly was oriented toward substantive goals. His approach to the law had definite policy outcomes, reversing a long liberalizing trend in criminal procedural rights and civil liberties. Recognized by the press and the conservative movement as the standard bearer, Meese moved quickly from issue to issue, fomenting old disputes on constitutional interpretation that many legal scholars had thought long since resolved. *Business Week* noted in late 1985, "Meese has made it clear that he'll use his new post to propose controversial policy changes on a host of subjects. With his unique access to the President and the broad powers of the Justice Department at his disposal, Meese's agenda could become the nation's."[183]

The qualifications that Meese sought in judicial appointees reflect a political view of the law as well. He considered a nominee's position on *Roe* to be a litmus test, because it revealed a particular judicial philosophy. "I think that a potential judge's views on *Roe v. Wade*, which I view as a usurpation of the legislative authority, might be indicative of the way in which that judge would generally approach the whole subject of judicial activism," he explained.[184]

Meese also rejected a long-standing ethic that the president should not take a position on a pending case. At his confirmation hearings, he defended the White House role in reversing established policy of both Justice and the IRS in the Bob Jones University case. Previous attorneys general of both parties consistently had held presidential interference in specific cases to be inappropriate.[185] This 1982 incident is worth further consideration, both because of Meese's involvement while still in the White House and because the case captured the attention of the movement conservatives. At the time, William French Smith was attorney general, a man described by Larry Speakes as "lowkey" and "adequate." Most of the controversial cases handled by Justice came not from Smith himself but "from Meese over at the White House."[186] Smith, the longtime lawyer of the Reagans, was close but not as intimate with the president as Meese, and he may not have been as activist.

The Bob Jones case[187] involved a fundamentalist Christian university that had its tax exempt status revoked in 1970 because of its discriminatory admissions policy, which worked to exclude blacks. The acting solicitor general considered the case to be a routine tax question, long settled by IRS and Justice policies. But he agreed to ask the Court to review the case in order to clarify the law. The White House (particularly Edwin Meese) and a group in the Justice Department, however, wanted him to reverse the government's position and side with the university. Such a switch is highly unorthodox. The acting solicitor general resisted the pressure, but finally signed a new government brief, with his own caveat attached. A year later, the Supreme Court, in an eight to one vote, supported the IRS position.[188]

According to Reagan's Education Secretary Terrel Bell, the conservative political agenda affected the administration's handling of *Grove City College v. T. Bell* as well. During the Carter administration, the Department of Education moved to declare that Grove City College was ineligible to receive federal funds because the school violated Title IX rules when it refused to complete certain mandatory forms showing that it was not discriminating on the basis of sex. Since 1972, the executive branch had interpreted the law to mean that if any part of a university was in violation, the university as a whole would lose federal funds. The college and some of its students challenged the action.[189] After Reagan's election, the Department of Education still was "reasonably happy with the interpretations that had been established in prior years" and prepared to continue with the case. But the White House and Department of Justice instead wanted to ask the court to limit federal aid cutbacks to those specific programs on a campus that had violated Title IX rules. Bell and Attorney General Smith planned to discuss their disagreement with the president, but when Bell arrived, he found they were meeting with Ed Meese instead. "I spelled out to Meese the consequences . . . of such a radical change in interpretation of the law. But given the fact that I wasn't going to be able to talk to the president directly, and knowing Meese's affiliation with the people of the movement, I knew that mine was a lost cause."[190] Bell considered the position of Justice mean-spirited. But Smith told him that "he had come to Washington to make a difference and that I was obstructing his good intentions." This comment, Bell adds, "was just a harbinger for more Justice Department actions," particularly under Meese.[191] In the end, the Supreme Court agreed with the administration, a ruling that surprised Bell. Congress also was surprised and in 1988 passed, over the president's veto, a statute to overturn the effects of the court decision.

These examples illustrate that, as White House counsel and later as attorney general, Meese operated with a sense of mission, in the words of Benjamin Civiletti, attorney general under Carter.[192] And the mission required him to attack "conventional notions about constitutional law."[193] Those who did not share his mission were concerned. In part, his detractors were critical not because he was activist and goal-oriented, but because his goals conflicted with their own. But others had more fundamental concerns with the way that the Department of Justice was operating. One writer perceived a threat to rule of law in the administration's conception of the law:

> The President's confusion of the law with his own moral and social agenda was often repeated by the Justice Department under Meese. Again and again, in situations where the Administration's desired social policy required it to make a choice between conflicting values . . . the Reagan Administration chose not to follow established legal practices while presenting its position. It read cases, construed statutes, and represented both trial records and legislative history in radically unorthodox ways.[194]

In some respects, Meese seemed to accomplish less of his legal agenda as attorney general than he had as White House counsel. Except possibly in the area of judicial appointments, his agenda did not become the nation's, primarily because of Ed Meese himself. He was prone to disastrous lapses of judgment that bordered the line of legality; after 1985, he was under almost continual investigation. To illustrate the press scrutiny he faced, the *Washington Post* carried 103 articles and cartoons on him from January to December 1987 and 218 from January to July 1988, when he left office. In the month of February 1988 he garnered an astonishing forty-three news articles, editorials and cartoons in that one publication. In addition to his media woes, he was investigated three times by an independent prosecutor and frequently called to testify before Congress. This left him little time to devote to his agenda, much less to administering his department.[195] One 1988 editorial commented, "Edwin Meese seems to be spending more time under the magnifying glass of justice than wielding it."[196]

His tenure as attorney general did not begin auspiciously; an investigation by independent counsel Jacob Stein interrupted his confirmation hearings by almost a year. Meese and Democratic Senator Joseph Biden had jointly requested the investigation to clear up repeated questions about Meese's financial dealings while he was White House counsel. One set of allegations concerned a real estate developer who had helped Meese sell his San Diego home, including loaning money to the buyer. That developer subsequently was named an assistant secretary of Commerce. Another man who had loaned Meese $60,000 received an appointment to the Board of Governors of the U.S. Postal Service. Meese sat on the committees that had approved both appointments. Four officers of the bank where Meese received his house loans also received government jobs while Meese was in the White House. There also were suggestions of improprieties in his 1981 promotion to colonel in the army reserves, when he had been ineligible. Another allegation was that he had improperly accepted a check from a private trust for moving expenses to Washington, in violation of federal law. When he learned of the illegality, he had the record altered to show the check was for consulting fees.[197]

The independent counsel investigated these allegations for five months and concluded that, although some were indictable offenses, he would not pursue them. No indictments were issued, so Meese and his lawyers said that the report exonerated him. Many of the senators were unconvinced. Meese attempted to assuage their fears when he told them that "I have a much higher level of sensitivity to these matters now than I did when I arrived in Washington. And I can assure you that I would take great pain to avoid any kind of a situation . . . that might give rise to a misunderstanding . . . of my acts."[198]

The lesson remained unlearned, however. Confirmed as attorney general, Meese found himself called before another Senate committee investigating ethics to answer questions regarding his relationship with the Wedtech Corporation, a Bronx military contractor. Wedtech officials were under investigation for bribery and racketeering, and seventeen people had already been indicted when Meese appeared before the committee.[199] Meese had first been contacted about Wedtech in 1981, by his old friend E. Robert Wallach. Wallach had asked Meese to help Wedtech in its efforts to obtain an Army engine contract. Eventually, the company received the lucrative army contract and another one from the Navy. Wallach also introduced Meese to W. Franklyn Chinn in 1985 to manage his investment portfolio; both Wallach and Chinn were then under contract to Wedtech. Meese and Chinn then entered into a limited partnership that garnered the attorney general a profit of 80 percent on an investment in an eighteen-month period. Later, Meese omitted the partnership from a list of holdings that he had to compile on potential conflicts of interest. At the Senate ethics hearings, Meese maintained that he had never had an interest in Wedtech, that the omission had been inadvertent, and that the partnership had been legitimate.[200]

In another case of poor judgment, Wallach contacted Meese on behalf of a billion dollar Iraqi pipeline project that needed U.S. support. After a phone call from Meese, National Security Council Adviser Robert McFarlane agreed to meet with the project's sponsors. Meese also exchanged letters with Israeli Prime Minister Shimon Peres on the issue. The State Department was unaware of these communications. Wallach, who had a financial interest in the pipeline, sent a memo to Meese that mentioned that bribes had been offered to leaders of the Israeli Labor party in exchange for their assurances that the pipeline would not be attacked. Meese denied having read the memo and insisted he did not know of any bribery scheme. If he had known, he was under a legal obligation to report Wallach's activity, in accordance with the Foreign Corrupt Practices Act.[201]

Because of these and other allegations, Meese came under the scrutiny of a second independent prosecutor, James McKay. McKay examined Meese's association with Wedtech, his participation in telecommunications cases at Justice while holding AT&T stock, his failure to include a $55,000 sale of securities on his 1985 federal income tax return, his finances, his involvement in the Iraqi oil pipeline project, and Mrs. Meese's job at the Multiple Sclerosis Society, where her $40,000 salary was paid by a foundation headed by a wealthy Washington businessman. McKay released his report on July 5, 1988, after a fourteen-month investigation. He had decided there was insufficient evidence that Meese had been bribed, or that he had violated the Foreign Corrupt Practices Act in connection with the pipeline. However, he found that Meese probably did violate federal laws in the telecommunications matter, and two provisions of the Internal Revenue Code. In both of these cases, prosecution was not warranted, McKay concluded.[202]

Meanwhile, Meese was implicated in the Iran-contra affair. Independent counsel Lawrence Walsh included the attorney general in his investigation, and in July 1987 Meese was called to testify before the joint congressional hearings. Oliver North, who had testified earlier, told senators that the attorney general had known of the Israeli sale of eighteen HAWK anti-aircraft missiles to Iran at the time it occurred in November 1985 and even had helped draft the intelligence finding authorizing it. North also asserted that Meese knew that North's chronology of events, drafted in November 1986, contained false information. Meese denied knowing either.[203]

The congressional committees also questioned a Justice Department opinion of December 1986 that supported the legality of the Israeli arms transfer to Iran. In their final report, the congressmen concluded that the arms transfer appeared to be a clear violation of the Arms Export Control Act, and the Justice Department opinion was incorrect, based on false assumptions about the role of the Israelis in the operation. The committees' primary concern regarding legal advice, however, was that there was too little of it. Many of the national security findings were not reviewed by the attorney general, nor was his legal opinion solicited on such questions as raising money from third countries, diverting proceeds from the sale of U.S. property, or establishing a source of funds autonomous of Congress.[204]

Meese's amateurish investigation early in the Iran arms sale scandal, undertaken at Reagan's request, raised the most serious questions about his commitment to uncovering the truth. Although he disclosed the evidence of the diversion of profits to the contras, his investigative methods were criticized because they violated the most rudimentary techniques. Among the lapses, he had met alone with CIA Director William Casey, National Security Adviser John Poindexter, and Vice-President George Bush, and had not taken notes. He had not asked critical and obvious questions: Casey on his knowledge of the diversion, Poindexter on his receipt of North's memos or his notification of the president, Reagan on his awareness of the affair. He did not involve the criminal division of his department until after key documents had been altered or destroyed by North and his secretary.[205] When North told the committee that he had continued shredding documents while the Justice Department investigators were just ten feet away, some were incredulous. The revelation "raised further doubts about the competence of the Justice Department's preliminary inquiry and led some law makers to speculate that the department might have been part of an effort to hide the facts."[206] Most congressmen tended to believe it was a case of incompetence more than corruption.[207]

Meese's casual investigation stemmed in part from his Advocate traits. He acted as an adviser to the president and not as attorney general. North and Poindexter testified that they understood Meese was acting as "a friend of the President" when he interviewed them.[208] Senators William Cohen and George Mitchell write that Meese simply wore too many hats, "and it was never clear which hat he was wearing during the course of his investigation."[209]

Journalist Haynes Johnson remarked that the attorney general's Senate testimony "was a curious study in incuriosity. It was also a study in contradictions between Meese's role as the president's longtime personal adviser, friend and political confidant and his position as the nation's chief legal officer."[210] Meese's view of the law, including his unfriendly attitude toward judicial review, may have contributed to the Iran-contra scandal and many other misjudgments in the administration. Members of the executive branch did not feel obligated to follow what they considered faulty legal determinations of Congress or the courts. Such a philosophy may invite abuse of public office. In fact, even before Iran-contra and Wedtech, more than one hundred senior Reagan administration officials had been accused or found guilty of illegal or unethical conduct.[211]

Throughout these ordeals, Reagan remained steadfast to his attorney general. White House aides commented on the intense loyalty that the president seemed to feel toward his old friend.[212] The loyalty remained strong despite repeated judgment errors on Meese's part (including his lobbying in 1987 in favor of Douglas Ginsburg's nomination to the Supreme Court) and despite the special prosecutor investigations, which Reagan believed were politically motivated.[213] "Ed Meese has been loyal to the President. Ronald Reagan has more than reciprocated that loyalty. His loyalty to Meese is enduring, perhaps even endearing, but ultimately it blinds him to all other considerations."[214] In the end, however, loyalty was insufficient to protect Meese from the sheer volume of allegations against him. Tension in the Department grew as morale dropped, pending the release of McKay's report on Wedtech and the pipeline. In late March 1988, in an unexpected blow, two top Justice officials resigned. The men, Arnold Burns, deputy attorney general, and William Weld, head of the criminal division, told the White House that "the department's reputation was being severely tarnished by Mr. Meese's continued presence." Both were conservative political appointees, who were deeply troubled by the attorney general's continual legal difficulties. Weld even said that if he had been the prosecutor in the case involving Meese, he would have seriously considered an indictment.[215] In and out of government, criticism of the attorney general continued to build.[216] Despite the increasing pressure to resign, Meese insisted that to do so would be an admission of guilt.[217] Finally, the day McKay filed his 830-page report without any indictments, the attorney general announced his plans to leave office. He labeled the report a vindication. He could resign without the appearance of being forced out. Five months later, Meese again was in the headlines when an internal Justice Department ethics report was released. The report concluded that he "engaged in conduct which should not be tolerated of any government employee, especially not the attorney general." It recommended disciplinary action by the president had Meese remained in office.[218]

While his abuse of the office does not seem to extend to criminal culpability (he was never indicted), Meese repeatedly exercised poor judgment in many of the decisions he made. Speakes described him as someone who seems to be "totally above board, totally honest," and yet, "he was always on the hotseat for questionable activity . . . and it did make you wonder."[219] For whatever motive, Meese permitted unscrupulous associates to use his office for their personal gain. This not only damaged his own reputation, but it also undermined the morale and credibility of the department he headed.

Meese did not leave the office as he had found it. His repeated difficulties had exacted a price: his successor would be scrutinized by the GOP, the White House, Congress, and the press. White House aides urged the president to appoint someone who could be confirmed quickly, who had strong legal credentials and no hint of ethics problems.[220] In other words, an officer more toward the Neutral end of the continuum than Meese, someone who could restore morale and confidence in the department. Meese's successor, Richard Thornburgh, has some Neutral characteristics, although it is premature to classify him. Active in public life,[221] the two-term governor of Pennsylvania was known for his integrity. The news media reported that "because of his reputation as a 'Mr. Clean,' several Republicans and Democrats agreed that Mr. Thornburgh was an ideal replacement for Mr. Meese."[222] The Neutral law officer, and the tendency of presidents to appoint them in the aftermath of scandal, will be examined in chapter five.

Beyond the problem of appearances of impropriety, not every Advocate has been scrupulous of the need to avoid illegal or unseemly actions while in office. The Advocate traits of partisanship, loyalty to the president, and pursuit of ends over means may take such a law officer into questionable legal and ethical terrain. The next chapter is devoted to a study of those Advocate attorneys general who have clearly abused the office and the public trust.

Chapter Four

The Danger of the Advocate: Abusing the Office

Because of the emphasis on ends over means, the Advocate type risks overstepping the law whenever he considers ends of paramount importance. This has happened in the case of at least three attorneys general, whose scandal-plagued administrations will be reviewed in this chapter. All three are of the Advocate type. While many Advocates do not abuse the powers of the office, the traits by which they are categorized contribute to an environment that permits abuse, in particular their ends-oriented approach to the law and their position close to the seat of power.

The worst government scandals—Teapot Dome and Watergate—occurred during the tenures of Advocate law officers, and other Advocates have been linked with lesser wrongs. This has created a tendency by some in Congress, the public, and the executive branch to view the Advocate as illegitimate or at best inappropriate. Critics often associate abuse with a law officer's political past; they make a normative argument that the attorney general must be removed from politics. Other writers seem to recognize that politics as such are not the problem. Instead of rejecting all politically active attorneys general, they try to delineate good and bad camps within the Advocate tradition. Victor Navasky, describing Robert Kennedy as an example of a good attorney general, attempted to draw this distinction in a question he posed about Carter's nominee, Griffin Bell: "Will he be an activist in the tradition of Robert F. Kennedy, or a fixer in the Mitchell-Kleindienst image?"[1] In other words, does the attorney general engage in legitimate policy judgments or in illegitimate political/partisan ones? The distinction between the two is often made. Elliot Richardson notes that there is a "difference between the proper role of the political process in the shaping of legal *policies* and the perversion of the legal *process* by political pressure."[2] One deputy attorney general in the Eisenhower years also distinguishes between politics and policy. General policies, even if we disagree with them, are legitimate concerns for an administration, but not "permitting partisan factors to dictate key decisions in the Department."[3] These issues will be examined in greater depth in the concluding chapter, but three case studies will illustrate the way in which the powers of the office have been abused, either out of political ambition, corruption, or blind partisanship.

A. Mitchell Palmer and the Red Raids

One risk of having an Advocate law officer is that he may place his own view of good policy above the law, and the danger is magnified if he is politically ambitious. These traits came together in the person of A. Mitchell Palmer of the Wilson administration. In office just two years, Palmer instituted a program of mass arrests of alien radicals, which he hoped would catapult him into the Oval Office. Known as the Palmer Raids, the arrests involved the wholesale violation of criminal procedural rights, including due process, search and seizure, and self-incrimination. It is for his disregard of civil liberties that he is remembered.

Palmer has many characteristics of the Advocate attorney general. His partisan life began early. While still in his twenties, he was elected president of the Democratic club in Stroudsburg, Pennsylvania, and a member of the county executive committee. After a bitter struggle with the old guard, the reformist wing of the party succeeded in having Palmer chosen the national committeeman for Pennsylvania in 1910; he ran the state party with an iron hand until 1921. In the meantime, he also won a seat in the U.S. House of Representatives, where he served from 1909 to 1913. Palmer's intelligence and persuasive powers brought him to the attention of the House leadership, and he soon was elevated to a spot on the powerful Ways and Means Committee.[4]

Also like the Advocate model, Palmer played an important role in Wilson's election and reelection. Wilson had not been his first choice in 1912, although Palmer admired him. He felt obligated to back Wilson's rival, Speaker of the House Champ Clark, until internal Pennsylvania politics forced him to switch his allegiance. But once he decided on Wilson, Palmer was a committed champion, soon "inducted into the inner circle of Wilson's preconvention advisers."[5] He worked hard in his state primary, where fifty-two delegates were won in an important victory. At the national convention, Palmer served as Wilson's floor leader in the grueling battle for the nomination, at some cost to his own career.[6] Wilson finally was nominated. In the general election, Palmer campaigned hard in Pennsylvania. Although the state went to the third party candidacy of Theodore Roosevelt, Wilson did beat his Republican opponent there, which boosted Palmer's political prospects.[7]

Palmer hoped for a reward, a place on the cabinet where he could build a national following. He specifically wanted to be attorney general because, with the issue of antitrust dominating the 1912 race, that office promised to attract public attention. He was seriously considered for Justice until Col. Edward House pushed for the appointment of his friend James McReynolds. Wilson characteristically acceded to the Colonel and named McReynolds, even though Wilson did not know him. Palmer was left in Congress.[8] Wilson's inability to place him in the cabinet "was not the result of any qualms about Palmer's loyalty. Wilson wanted Palmer in his cabinet . . . but he relied most heavily on the advice of Colonel Edward House, who did not like Palmer."[9]

Palmer remained a faithful lieutenant, however, pushing the administration's progressive legislation through the House, even tariff reduction, which was politically unpopular in his home state. His support helped Wilson win large majorities on all his measures during his first year and a half in office. Palmer "probably was closer to the President than any other representative. In part, this was because of Palmer's high place in the party organization, which obliged Wilson to deal with him on a variety of small matters." He also had a political savvy that Wilson needed, steering the president away from some bad political decisions and advising Wilson on how to handle the party demands that he serve only one term.[10] In 1914, Wilson convinced Palmer to run for the Senate seat of arch conservative incumbent, Boies Penrose. It was a hopeless race, yet when Palmer lost, he still received no offers from Wilson. Now out of office, he returned to his private practice, except for a period in 1916 when he actively campaigned in Pennsylvania for Wilson's reelection.[11]

He did not join the administration until 1917 when, with the declaration of war, he offered his services in any capacity. He was named Custodian of the Office of Alien Property, which seized, administered, and later sold enemy-owned property in the United States. By the end of 1918, the agency was handling thirty thousand trusts worth $500 million. Although he named eminent attorneys and bankers to the top positions, Palmer also filled the organization with political supporters for a planned 1920 run for president. For example, of the fifty-one state counsels he retained to advise on state laws, seventeen attended the national conventions of 1916 or 1920 as delegates or national committeemen, and others were high in the national party. As his biographer notes, "With such appointments as these Palmer went a long way toward making himself the Democratic politicians' choice for the Presidential nomination in 1920."[12] Palmer, for his own political future, was determined to keep the operation scandal free, despite the tempting sums of money involved. He was not successful; his subordinates were implicated in several illegal activities. Although he himself was never charged with wrongdoing, he was subject to harsh criticism for his failed oversight and legal laxity, problems that were to resurface later in his public life.

Finally, in March 1919 he received the appointment that he wanted. Palmer became Wilson's third attorney general. Edward House again had preferred someone else, but in his absence Wilson was influenced by Palmer's supporters. Wilson also may have wanted to replace the rather repressive Thomas Watt Gregory with a recognized progressive like Palmer. Attorney General Gregory had treated pacifists and other opponents of the war ruthlessly, and progressives wanted Palmer in his place. The progressives would come to rue their support.[13]

In the Advocate manner, Palmer had a very broad conception of the scope of his office. He met little resistance from the president because Wilson was preoccupied with the peace treaty from July 1919, when he returned to the United States from the Paris Peace Conference, to September of the same year. Then in October, Wilson was incapacitated by a stroke from which he never completely recovered. For months, Edith Wilson kept her husband insulated from political affairs because she did not want him disturbed. By then, Colonel House was no longer a factor in the administration; he and Wilson had split over the conduct of the peace negotiations in 1919. Palmer quickly filled the resulting power vacuum in the executive branch, becoming the most powerful member of the cabinet. The new attorney general assumed responsibility for several pressing domestic problems, including the enormous rise in prices and the threat of labor unrest.[14]

One trait shared by many Advocate law officers is an activist approach to legal interpretation; Palmer was no exception. In handling spiraling inflation and disruptive labor strikes, he moved aggressively, using (and even bending) the law to achieve domestic tranquility and order. When several bombing incidents attributed to communists and anarchists occurred in May and June of 1919—creating public hysteria—Palmer again employed an expanded vision of his legal authority. Under tremendous pressure to eliminate strikers and radicals, whom he considered related, Palmer decided on mass deportations of alien radicals, particularly Russian immigrants.[15]

At first he moved cautiously, but demands for action poured into his office from citizens and members of Congress alike. "As Palmer became aware of the widespread popular hostility toward radicals, his interest in civil liberties abated," noted his biographer.[16] He may have felt an obligation to satisfy the demands of the electorate. As a man with presidential aspirations, he certainly could not afford to ignore them. A Red scare also could be useful politically; he could ride its waves all the way to the White House. Soon Palmer was feeding the public fear with exaggerated reports of violent conspiracies; he warned of bloody outbreaks on July 4, 1919, and on May 1, 1920, neither of which occurred.[17]

Not only was there a compelling political reason for Palmer to act against the aliens, but he came to believe that the threat they posed was genuine. A plot to assassinate the nation's leaders on May 1, 1919, was uncovered; riots and bombings followed. Then, on the night of June 2, his own house was bombed and partially destroyed. His advisers in the Justice Department and his colleagues in the cabinet convinced him that the threat of a serious national uprising was real. His own xenophobia caused him to place the blame on recent immigrants. By December, he accepted the idea that the national situation was grave.[18] Once he reached that point, he could justify massive infringements of civil liberties as emergency measures.

The Justice Department, with the cooperation of the Labor Department, made its first mass raid on November 7, 1919, when agents broke in on Russian homes and meeting places in twelve cities. People were taken into custody without arrest warrants; homes were torn apart without search warrants; many of those arrested were beaten with blackjacks. The wide dragnet captured many innocent people. Some were citizens; some passers-by; most of the others were innocent aliens who had joined Russian clubs for fellowship. The process was so indiscriminate that the great percentage was released; of the 650 arrested in New York, for example, only forty-three were actually deported, less than 7 percent. Despite these reports of abuse, public approval soared, with newspapers almost unanimously in favor.[19]

Two months later, an even more comprehensive net was cast in forty cities, to capture and deport all aliens who were communists. About three thousand arrest warrants were issued, but thousands of people were placed under custody without them. Once again, searches were conducted and property seized without warrants. Suspects were not allowed to see their attorneys before questioning. Many were coerced into signing confessions. Some were kept in prison or deportation centers for months, held incommunicado and then released without ever having been formally arrested. The beatings continued, and there were reports of torture. Deportation centers were crowded and unsanitary, and food was inadequate and sometimes spoiled.[20]

By now, there were a few indications that Palmer had taken his crusade too far. The U.S. attorney in Philadelphia resigned publicly in protest. The assistant Labor secretary, suddenly made acting secretary, rejected most of Palmer's deportation cases and then effectively defended his actions in front of a congressional committee. One federal judge, ruling on the release of eighteen aliens on writs of habeas corpus, angrily chastised the government for wanton lawlessness. Furthermore, Palmer's predictions of a 1920 May Day reign of terror did not materialize, which made the attorney general look like an alarmist. Newspapers began to suggest that Palmer hoped to capitalize on the Red Scare for his political advantage.[21]

In April, representatives of several civil liberties groups decided to investigate the raids and publish their findings. Their report, issued by the National Popular Government League, was endorsed by such outstanding legal figures as Felix Frankfurter, Roscoe Pound, and Zechariah Chafee of the Harvard Law School, and Ernst Freund of the University of Chicago Law School. Citing numerous violations of the Constitution, the sixty-seven-page document noted that "there is no danger of revolution so great as that created by suppression, by ruthlessness, and by deliberate violation of the simple rules of American law and American decency."[22] The report led to hearings before the Senate Judiciary Committee in early 1921.[23] Harlan Fiske Stone and Charles Evans Hughes, both later on the Supreme Court, added their voices to the growing chorus denouncing Palmer's tactics, as did several leading industrialists who feared that cheap foreign labor would be restricted.[24]

Still the attorney general did not concede. Insisting that the danger continued, he called on Congress for strict sedition legislation. "Palmer was running for President as his country's protector; only if the peril seemed great would his past efforts be fully appreciated and his future services appear needed."[25] He remained convinced of his rightness and hinted that his accusers were not true patriots. The raids had been legal, he argued. Arrest warrants were not necessary because the suspects were simply detained and not imprisoned. He blamed the Labor Department for the long detentions and unpleasant conditions.[26] His self-defense was aggressive but unconvincing.

One should note that Palmer did not exercise direct control over the raids or over the detention centers. He was ill much of the time and busy with the other problems plaguing the administration. Nevertheless, he had been warned beforehand of constitutional problems and then informed of reported abuse after both raids. On December 27, 1919, for example, the U.S. attorney in Philadelphia, disturbed over the November raids, wrote to Palmer that injustices were inevitable in mass arrests. Palmer replied that he had received the letter too late for consideration. The U.S. attorney later resigned, repeating his objections to Palmer and to the president.[27] In spite of such reports, the attorney general continued to give his subordinates in the department, especially J. Edgar Hoover, who headed the project, a virtually free rein. He admitted as much before a Senate hearing on the operation when one senator asked him about the use of search warrants. Palmer confessed that he could not answer the question and referred the senator to Hoover, who was sitting beside him.[28] Lack of oversight might also have accounted for the brutality. Justice Department agents themselves were instructed to avoid beatings, but local police and private patriotic organizations who assisted in the roundups were not so constrained. Because he was "unable to supervise closely the assistants he chose, Palmer's reckless policies had the worst possible effect."[29]

In the midst of the controversy, Mitchell Palmer announced his candidacy for the 1920 presidential race, the first Democrat to do so. He had the backing of many state politicians, and his campaign was reasonably successful, considering an ongoing investigation by the House Rules Committee.[30] But his actions as attorney general had alienated labor and the progressive wing of the party. At the convention, he was never able to garner more than 267.5 delegates. His support steadily dwindled until he finally withdrew after the thirty-eighth ballot. He returned to the Justice Department, but his last seven months in office were inactive; Congress and the public were tired of the Red Scare and anxious to start a new decade.[31]

Palmer did make speeches for later Democratic hopefuls, including Al Smith, for whom he campaigned in the South in 1928. On Franklin Roosevelt's request, he and Cordell Hull drafted a unifying party platform in 1932 that was subsequently adopted. But his long absence from politics, his continuing ill health, and his growing disillusionment with Roosevelt's New Deal kept him out of active politics.[32]

The fact that the policy goals he pursued so relentlessly were his own, not the president's, does not alter his basic classification as an Advocate attorney general. He believed that the law served as a means to an end rather than an end in itself. He did not feel bound by any legal restraints when they hampered his ability to achieve a greater good, even though that conception of good was defined in part by his xenophobia and paranoia. Even during his service as Alien Property Custodian, Palmer tended "to take important public matters into his own hands and to act as though any means were justified if the end was desirable. . . . Palmer apparently believed that any action which protected the nation in any way was justified in time of emergency, and the Custodian had a very loose definition of emergency."[33] An identical statement may be made about his tenure as attorney general, in particular his actions against the Red menace that he saw threatening the United States.

In one major respect, however, Palmer does not suit the type: he never became a close and trusted adviser to the president. That role was filled by Edward House. One can speculate that, had Wilson remained healthy and actively engaged in his administration, such a relationship might have developed; after all, Colonel House—who had disliked Palmer—was gone by 1919 and there were few other personalities in the administration as dominant as Palmer. Yet the same reason that Wilson and House ended their friendship would have mitigated against any intimacy between Wilson and Palmer: both House and Palmer were politicians. Palmer was even something of an opportunist. For example, in 1920, he initially backed the League of Nations and the peace treaty, but he dropped his support when he discovered the strong sentiment against them when he went on the campaign trail.[34] In contrast, Wilson viewed politics and compromise with disdain. Conceivably, if Wilson had not become ill and embittered, he might have imposed limits on Palmer, making the attorney general less of an Advocate than he was.

Palmer's actions in office should remind us of the potential for danger inherent in an Advocate law officer's tendency to stress majoritarian demands over rule of law. As his biographer writes, "Certainly a public official is obligated to heed the will of a vocal majority . . . [but] the crucial question raised by Palmer's action . . . is whether a leading government official has a higher duty than giving the public—or his party— what it wants." He concludes: "If Palmer was one of the most dangerous men in our history, it was not because he attempted to impose his rule or his policies upon the people, but because he tried to win power by carefully attuning himself to what he felt were the strong desires of most Americans."[35] While Palmer's story is one of majoritarian principle run wild in the advancement of a political career, it is also a reminder of how easily minority rights and other legal restraints may be sacrificed in the name of emergency.

The "Morally Ambiguous" Harry Daugherty

Harry Daugherty, Warren G. Harding's attorney general, is another example of an Advocate law officer who failed to delineate between proper and improper conduct in office. If Palmer is known for his excessive Red Raids, Daugherty is remembered for his moral blindness, which allowed corrupt associates to make fortunes from the administration of justice.

First and foremost, Daugherty was a political animal. Elected to the Ohio state legislature in 1889, he served as the "extremely partisan" house floor leader for Gov. William McKinley. He soon became one of McKinley's most important political managers, helping him secure delegates at the Republican National Convention in 1896 and traveling more than nine thousand miles on his behalf during the campaign. He was rewarded with the chair of the Republican state central committee, the most important party office in Ohio. Later, he became a leading champion of William Howard Taft in his 1908 and 1912 races,[36] and he was a pivotal figure in the nomination and election of Harding in 1920. His political successes came about because he was "combative and clever, pragmatic and amoral, ambitious and courageous."[37] Another historian notes that Daugherty was "morally ambiguous" from the beginning.[38]

Even in his private legal work, he was essentially a politician, more adept at lobbying for his corporate clients than at working out technical problems. He used his political connections to help his clients and occasionally—by covertly introducing hostile legislation—to hurt them and so force them to solicit his aid. Twice he used his connections with President Taft and Attorney General Wickersham to appeal for special treatment on behalf of convicted clients. He was successful in one case when he persuaded Taft that the client was dying, and Taft commuted the fifteen-year jail term.[39] Daugherty made no distinction between his two interests of politics and law, "and indeed the two became for him a single Janus-faced image."[40] This inability to distinguish between the law and politics contributes to his classification as an Advocate model, although unlike most Advocates he was more concerned with politics per se than policy outcomes.

His relationship with Harding, another Ohio Republican, also fits the model. Harding and Daugherty first met in 1899 at a Republican rally, when Harding was a candidate for state senator.[41] A dozen years later, they became close associates after a bitter state party fight.[42] Daugherty was the self-appointed publicist for Harding's 1920 presidential bid. By that time, he had twenty-five years of experience in state and national politics: in organization, publicity, and political backing. He could provide inside advice on Ohio politics, and he had friendly contacts elsewhere. Harding was initially hesitant to run, but Daugherty promoted his candidacy anyway. Daugherty's open and untiring support brought Harding closer to him and eventually won him the post of preconvention campaign manager, where he put in eighteen-hour days. Although the party chair replaced him as campaign manager in the general election, Daugherty continued to work for the ticket. Harding trusted Daugherty's political instincts, in spite of criticism by other Republicans concerned about his reported ethical lapses, including allegations that Daugherty and several friends misused depositors' funds of a bank that then declared bankruptcy.[43] Once elected president, Harding continued to trust Daugherty, naming him attorney general, the position Daugherty wanted. The appointment received almost universal press opposition, yet Harding remained steadfast. He did not want the country to think he was ungrateful to Daugherty. In the end, the Senate confirmed the entire cabinet in less than ten minutes.[44]

Not only were Harding and Daugherty close political associates, but they were, without question, longtime friends. Their wives had even grown up together. Throughout the Harding years, the two men usually met weekly to play poker; Harding found it easier to relax with the convivial attorney general than with Herbert Hoover at Commerce or Charles Evans Hughes at State. They spoke several times daily on the telephone, on a special direct line between their two offices.[45]

In some respects, however, the Advocate type does not seem to apply. Daugherty was not a trusted presidential adviser, nor did he contribute to policy-making on the diverse range of issues that confronted the Harding administration. For decades, historical convention portrayed Daugherty as a kingmaker and important adviser, who exercised a powerful influence over a passive and dependent president.[46] This myth was constructed by Daugherty himself, ten years after his service, with the publication of his autobiography, *The Inside Story of the Harding Tragedy*.[47] Contemporary accounts and historical documents refute this version of the relationship, showing instead a president who did not wholeheartedly trust his attorney general's judgment even on issues involving the Justice Department. For example, Harding's release of Eugene Debs in 1921 was contrary to Daugherty's advice. Harding also ran background checks on several of Daugherty's patronage suggestions and criticized Daugherty for making railway officials U.S. marshals when a rail strike seemed imminent. When Daugherty advised him that an executive proclamation was not necessary to terminate the state of war with the Central Powers, Harding decided to seek and follow the legal advice of the State Department, which recommended formal executive action.[48] Feeling increasingly bypassed, Daugherty complained to a friend that Harding "never took any advice from me about anything; he never listens to me, never pays any attention to me, doubts my loyalty to him, he doesn't see how I am serving him or the government and on the whole considers me of very little good. I guess he is right."[49] Perhaps contributing to the myth of Harding's reliance on Daugherty is the fact that Harding never publicly repudiated him. If anything, the president's sympathy and public expressions of support seemed to grow even as he relied on the beleaguered Daugherty less and less. Although he might have begun to suspect the attorney general of malfeasance by 1923, he did not admit it, instead attributing the accusations to partisanship. "Ultimately, [Harding] probably shifted the blame upon himself for appointing a political intimate who lacked the character and training to be attorney general."[50]

A review of Daugherty's actions in office illustrates the dangers inherent in such an appointment. Daugherty evidently wanted the post initially "to vindicate a past which was constantly under suspicion," and not to seek financial gain. And in fact, some of his early moves strengthened Justice, which had been neglected by Mitchell Palmer. He recommended legislation to expand the federal judiciary, pushed for stricter enforcement of antitrust laws, called for an investigation of war frauds and high retail prices, and made a few solid appointments.[51] He also was instrumental in having Taft appointed to the Supreme Court. Because Daugherty often relied on Taft for federal court recommendations, Harding's judicial selections were generally good ones.[52]

But too often the attorney general exercised poor judgment in filling top positions, rewarding old Ohio cronies who were less interested in the law than their bank accounts. His director of the bureau of investigation, for example, was implicated in jury packing, spying on political opponents, breaking and entering, and fomenting labor unrest, partly to build up his private detective business. Daugherty may not have known of these activities, but he was guilty of using the bureau to retaliate against congressmen investigating him. Even more troubling, two of his closest friends, Jess Smith and Howard Mannington, operated a criminal ring from the Justice Department. They were involved in influence peddling, withdrawing confiscated liquor from government warehouses, securing immunity from prosecution for clients, selling liquor permits, working shady stock deals, and selling government jobs. Historians speculate that Daugherty must have been aware of some of their actions because Smith was his housemate and Mannington was a frequent visitor.[53] After a year in office, Daugherty began to generate growing public and congressional criticism. His heavy-handed response to a railroad union strike in 1922 fueled the opposition, and the House

Committee on the Judiciary began hearings to consider fourteen grounds for his impeachment. The evidence was so flimsy, however, that the effort died.[54] Some criticism, including the impeachment effort, was politically motivated, and Daugherty did not help his cause when he reacted with belligerency. But a foundation of truth underlay many of the accusations.

The scandals associated with Daugherty's department were just starting to surface when Harding died suddenly in August 1923.[55] Coolidge, who felt no special obligation to Daugherty, became president. For the sake of continuity, he tried to keep Harding's cabinet intact for many months. As the Teapot Dome oil lease scandal grew, however, the attorney general became a political liability and an embarrassment, especially as the election of 1924 neared. In fairness to him, Daugherty probably did not know of Teapot Dome. He was not friends with Albert Fall, the Interior secretary who took bribes to lease naval oil reserves without competitive bidding; nor did Fall seek his advice on the legality of the venture. But because he and Harding had approved the leases, Daugherty was pulled into the Senate investigation. After Fall and Navy Secretary Edwin Denby resigned, the brunt of the investigation fell on him. The scandal provided an excuse for his congressional enemies to reopen his case; they passed a resolution to investigate him for his failure to prosecute Fall and the others. The hearings degenerated into a sensationalistic and partisan attack, with unsavory witnesses called to testify. Daugherty was also hurt by his own department, especially the attempts by his bureau of investigation to harass witnesses and steal evidence. In March 1924, when the committee demanded access to Justice files, Daugherty refused. Coolidge promptly sent word that he expected his resignation.[56] "The culmination of charges that he was ethically unfit to serve as attorney general led to his forced resignation."[57]

After Daugherty left office, a Senate select committee investigated his handling of the Department of Justice, including charges of obstruction of justice in war fraud and land fraud cases, of failing to prosecute illegal monopolies, and of selling jobs, including judgeships. The hearings also sought to uncover the illegal activities of Smith and Mannington.[58] The committee failed to implicate him in the Teapot Dome or Veterans' Bureau scandals, but it did uncover Jess Smith's criminal activities, the abuse of the bureau of investigation, and the existence of large unexplained sums of money in Daugherty's bank account.[59]

His past continued to be scrutinized. One investigation, involving the American Metal Company, led to his indictment and trial in 1926. The company was German owned, so its assets had been seized during World War I and held by the Alien Property Custodian. In 1921, however, $7 million was returned to the company when the German owner claimed the seizure had been illegal. Questions were raised about the release of the money, and Harding asked the attorney general to investigate; Daugherty did so and approved. Later, a special attorney appointed by Coolidge discovered that the German had given a prominent Republican $391,000 in Liberty Bonds, with $50,000 traced to the Alien Property Custodian. The remaining $341,000 was untraced. After the special prosecutor resigned, a U.S. attorney found some of the bonds in an Ohio bank owned by Daugherty's brother. In addition, documents placed Daugherty in the area the day before the bonds were cashed. The evidence was circumstantial but damaging. Daugherty was indicted and tried twice for conspiracy to defraud the government. If convicted, he would have been the first cabinet member imprisoned for maladministration. But both trials resulted in hung juries, and the government finally dropped the charges.[60]

Daugherty's political days were over. He was elected a delegate-at-large for Coolidge to the Republican National Convention in 1924 but was powerless and inconspicuous.[61] By then he was aware that he had become a political pariah. In one rather touching incident in 1932, when news photographers caught him chatting with Democrat James Farley of FDR's campaign, Daugherty asked the photographers to destroy the plates. He was afraid that the public might misunderstand and discredit Farley. In recounting the incident later, Farley considered Daugherty's gesture generous.[62]

John Mitchell and the 1972 Campaign

John Mitchell, the first of several attorneys general to serve under Richard Nixon, was a Wall Street lawyer who specialized in the arcane area of municipal bond law. He had been Nixon's law partner in New York before becoming manager of his successful 1968 presidential bid. Mitchell was very much an Advocate in some respects: in his closeness to the president, in his prior campaign service, in his role as an all-round adviser, and in his ends-oriented approach to the law. Yet he breaks with the type in respect to his previous partisanship. A political neophyte in 1968, he later told a reporter that he did not enjoy political work. "I did it because I believed in the cause and the individual," he said. Even so, Mitchell received most of the credit for the smoothness of the campaign.[63]

Mitchell had known Nixon for years. After the personally devastating loss in the California gubernatorial race in 1962, Nixon went to New York to practice law. He was shattered, Mitchell noted, but the law firm helped him rebuild his self-esteem. Even more of an influence was the presence of Mitchell himself, who was "a magnitude of his own in the Nixon circle." He was one of just five people who had a "critical influence on [Nixon's] thinking."[64]

As attorney general, he remained on intimate terms with Nixon. "Unlike any other Cabinet member, he gets through to the President almost whenever he likes. They usually see each other two or three times a week, and often talk on the phone in the evening."[65] The attorney general's preeminence in the administration was a direct result of his friendship with Nixon. Journalists Dan Rather and Gary Paul Gates commented, "Like Robert Kennedy in his brother's administration, Mitchell's power had almost nothing to do with his Cabinet status as Attorney General, and everything to do with the special relationship he had with the President." They described Mitchell as "a kind of senior partner—a patient, pipe-smoking front man who absorbed much of the public heat for unpopular policies."[66]

During the first term, Mitchell felt so comfortable with Nixon that some White House guests remarked on Mitchell's ease in speaking his mind, even when it was evident that the president wanted to speak. He often attended NSC meetings, although he generally said little; people assumed he was waiting to discuss the issues when he was alone with the president.[67] He was similarly inscrutable during cabinet meetings, but those who observed closely could see Nixon glancing toward Mitchell for reaffirmation when the president was making a point. "If the Attorney General grunted and nodded his balding head, the President would usually press on, and with increased enthusiasm. But if Mitchell grunted and looked away, or stopped puffing, then Nixon would backtrack a bit, or sometimes change the subject altogether."[68] Considered a major power in foreign affairs in those first two years, the attorney general reportedly formed an alliance with Henry Kissinger, NSC adviser, to exclude Secretary of State William Rogers from policy-making.[69] He was, one *Wall Street Journal* writer argued, no mere political operative: "Rather than serving as a 'political operative' in the usual sense, Mr. Mitchell is fitting the grander role of personal adviser to the President on political matters, as on other subjects. And thus one of his associates concludes, 'He is possibly the second most powerful man in the country—second only to the President.'"[70] This preeminence began to wane during the third year, when H. R. Haldeman and John Ehrlichman in the White House became increasingly influential. By the end of 1970, a tension between Mitchell and Haldeman was evident. The attorney general's descent from power was rapid after February 1972, but especially so after the Watergate break-in the next June.[71]

Characteristic of the Advocate model, Mitchell had a broad conception of the law that is evident in his handling of several policies and programs. He authorized a much broader use of wiretapping than had his predecessor, permitting its use against domestic radicals as well as in cases of national security and organized crime. The attorney general also approved the federal prosecution of the Chicago Seven for inciting riots at the 1968 Democratic National Convention, against the advice of some Justice attorneys, and approved the indictments for conspiracy against Daniel Ellsberg for leaking the "Pentagon Papers." His efforts to put an injunction on the *New York Times* and the *Washington Post* to block publication of the papers was later overturned by the Supreme Court. He praised local police for arresting thirteen thousand demonstrators in the May 1971 march on Washington, a mass arrest that was later ruled unconstitutional. His legislative proposals also reflect a goal-oriented approach to the law. In one anticrime bill, for example, he advocated preventive detention, whereby a defendant could be jailed for up to sixty days before trial without bail, and "no-knock" provisions to permit police officers with search warrants to enter premises without knocking.[72]

Mitchell's role in the Watergate break-in and cover-up seems ironic given his policy emphasis on law and order. But his almost blind commitment to Nixon's reelection created a situation where any means were justified by that end. Proud of his pragmatism, he had no respect for rule of law per se that would have alerted him to the inappropriateness of the illegal steps he authorized. Mitchell resigned as attorney general on March 1, 1972, to head the Committee to Reelect the President, but the questionable activities began well before then. Jeb Magruder's Senate testimony alleged that the break-in had first been mentioned to Mitchell in his Justice office on January 27, 1971, as part of a grandiose and expensive scheme of political sabotage that included abductions and blackmail. Mitchell dismissed the plan as unrealistic; he did not expressly reject the notion of illegal activities, nor did he expel from his office the plan's author, G. Gordon Liddy, counsel to CREP. A week later, Liddy presented a scaled-down version that still was not approved or rejected. Finally on March 30, 1972, Liddy presented a less ambitious project involving electronic surveillance, specifically of the Democratic National Committee headquarters. This plan Mitchell approved. Magruder, former chief of staff of CREP, also testified that Mitchell had developed the burglars' cover story and helped Magruder prepare false testimony for the grand jury. He also knew that evidence was destroyed and hush money paid to the defendants.[73]

Mitchell denied the charges that he had authorized the break-in or participated in the cover-up. He also denied having informed Nixon of Watergate or of the other White House "horror stories," such as the break-in of Daniel Ellsberg's psychiatrist's office. He was concerned with Nixon being reelected. Sen. Herman Talmadge (D.-Ga.), noting Mitchell's closeness to Nixon, asked, "Am I to understand . . . that you placed the expediency of the next election above your responsibilities as an intimate to advise the president of the peril that surrounded him?" Mitchell answered in the affirmative: "In my mind, the reelection of Richard Nixon, compared with what was available on the other side, was so much more important that I put it in just that context." Later, in response to questioning by Sen. Howard Baker (R.-Tenn.), Mitchell said that he still believed Nixon's reelection was more important than Watergate or the other so-called horrors.[74] This attitude reflects Mitchell's underlying belief that, in battling political enemies, anything was justified. One of his successors, Elliot Richardson, writes: "When the will to win is coupled with an uncritical belief in the rightness of one's own patriotic motives, it is hardly surprising that a byproduct should be the gut feeling that anyone who questions or obstructs the chosen path . . . is 'the enemy.' . . . And to beat an 'enemy,' convention allows you to do anything you have to do."[75] Even if there had been no wrongdoing, Mitchell's campaign activities while still attorney general were very irregular. He told the committee that he simply succumbed "to the President's request to keep an eye on what was going on over there and I had frequent meetings with individuals dealing with matters of policy." He also said he had participated in hiring personnel. But Mitchell insisted that he had consulted more than supervised. Then Talmadge produced several documents where Mitchell clearly was operating as director, dated June 22, 1971, and January 14, 1972, well before he resigned the attorney generalship.[76] The senator also asked about Mitchell's earlier and unqualified denial that he had engaged in any political activity while attorney general, given at the confirmation hearings of his successor, Richard Kleindienst, on March 14, 1972. Denying that he was Nixon's campaign director yet, Mitchell had testified that he had no party responsibilities.[77]

A federal grand jury, meanwhile, continued its investigation of the break-in and cover-up. It indicted Mitchell on March 1, 1974, on six counts involving obstruction of justice and perjury. One of the counts was dropped, but John Mitchell was found guilty of the remaining five on January 1, 1975, the first attorney general to be convicted. He, Haldeman, and Ehrlichman were sentenced to serve from two and a half to eight years.[78] Mitchell was in prison for nineteen months, from June 1977, until January 1979. Of the two dozen Watergate conspirators who were jailed, he was the last to be released. He also was disbarred in New York in July 1975.[79] One of the U.S. attorneys to serve under him concluded, "The verdict confirmed that John N. Mitchell had acted in a fashion totally inconsistent with the standards of integrity and impartiality required of the chief legal officer of a great nation."[80]

In addition to Watergate-related charges, Mitchell was indicted on charges of conspiracy to defraud the United States and obstruct justice, centering on a secret campaign contribution of $200,000 by Robert Vesco, who was then the subject of an investigation by the Securities and Exchange Commission. After the donation came in, Mitchell allegedly had arranged a requested meeting between Vesco's lawyer and SEC chair William Casey. But the SEC staff blocked the meeting. Mitchell and Maurice Stans, chair of the campaign's finance committee, were tried in New York and eventually acquitted.[81]

Jack Landau explains, "His first and only loyalty in his public life was to Nixon. And that was ultimately his problem. He viewed himself primarily as Nixon's lawyer, not the nation's lawyer."[82] As a result, he adds, Mitchell did not strike a deal to disclose Nixon's role in the scandal and thus escape serious prosecution and prison. While Mitchell does seem to have seen his role as the president's lawyer, he may not have been as committed to Nixon as Landau remembers. Nixon himself, according to the White House transcripts, did not believe that Mitchell was as concerned with saving the presidency as he was with saving himself. Ehrlichman, on Nixon's suggestion, met with Mitchell on April 14, 1973, to urge him to accept legal and moral responsibility for the Watergate events in order to spare the White House. Reporting back later in the day, Ehrlichman told Nixon that Mitchell refused. He was "an innocent man in his heart and in his mind and he does not intend to move off that position." Mitchell had insisted that the break-in plans were made without his knowledge, which Haldeman disputed. Mitchell had also implicated Haldeman in the plans, an allegation that angered Nixon.[83] Clearly, Nixon, Haldeman, and Ehrlichman intended Mitchell to take all of the blame, but Mitchell himself was not cooperating in the role of scapegoat. In fact, Nixon seemed to feel little reciprocal loyalty to his once close friend. At one point on April 14, he asked Ehrlichman, "What do Colson, et al. . . . think we ought to do under these circumstances? Get busy and nail Mitchell in a hurry?" Later that day he said, "Whatever his theory is, let me say one footnote—is that throwing off on the White House won't help him one damn bit."[84]

Haldeman, in his 1978 account of the Watergate affair, argued, "I will never believe that the politically astute Mitchell would specifically approve a break-in at the Democratic National Committee Headquarters." Mitchell was too cautious, and, besides, he would have targeted George McGovern's headquarters if he had decided to wiretap any offices.[85] But perhaps that is the point—that Mitchell was not as politically astute as he was thought to be at the time. Sen. Sam Ervin, who chaired the congressional investigation, held this view: "If President Nixon had entrusted his campaign for reelection to the Republican National Committee, there would have been no Watergate. Its members would have known that the activities . . . were outside the political pale."[86] Instead, Nixon placed in charge close associates like Mitchell who were political amateurs. It is ironic that this one missing characteristic of the Advocate model—a politically astute background—might have given Mitchell the judgment he needed to avoid the events that led to Watergate.

Chapter Five

The Neutral Attorney General

Professional eminence, nonpartisanship, and widely recognized integrity distinguish attorneys general of the Neutral type. Before appointment, they have not been close to their presidents, either politically or personally. Defining their goal of neutral exposition of the law, they may be less active than the Advocate in two possibly related ways: Their advisory role generally does not extend to foreign affairs or domestic politics, and they often have a more restricted view of their own and the president's authority. These characteristics imply independence and give such law officers a high public credibility, which may explain why presidents who assume office in the difficult aftermath of major scandal turn to the Neutral type. Such an appointment has the advantage of soothing congressional and press criticism and helping to restore public confidence. While the Neutral seems well suited to such times of crisis, the type may surface in other periods as well; the presence of scandal is not a defining feature. In fact, the first attorney general to exhibit Neutral characteristics—William Wirt—was brought into office during a noticeably nonscandalous and noncontroversial time.

William Wirt: The Eminent Attorney

When William Wirt was appointed James Monroe's attorney general in 1817, he was a well-respected lawyer noted for his integrity, intellectual acumen, and oratorical skills. His legal prowess is confirmed in the quality of cases that he argued, including *McCulloch v. Maryland*, *Dartmouth College v. Woodward*, and *Gibbons v. Ogden*. He first gained fame among his contemporaries for his four-hour argument in the 1807 prosecution of Aaron Burr.[1]

126

The comments of his peers reinforce this image of him as a man of honor and eminence, "a great lawyer, an acute statesman, a consummate advocate and last, though not least, an honest man."[2] On Wirt's death, Daniel Webster called him "one of the ablest, one of the most distinguished members of this Bar." Adjourning the Supreme Court for the day, Chief Justice John Marshall said that the Court had "long been aided by [his] diligent research and lucid reasoning." Former President John Quincy Adams, then a member of the House of Representatives, presented a House tribute in his honor, an unusual step because Wirt had never been a member. Noting the importance of the attorney general's tasks, Adams said they had never been "more ably or more faithfully discharged than by Mr. Wirt."[3]

Attorney General Wirt was hesitant to assert powers for himself or for the president. One historian writes that he was "philosophically opposed to strong executive action, and inclined to shift the responsibility to Congress."[4] Repeatedly in cabinet meetings, Wirt differed with Secretary of State John Quincy Adams over the need to involve Congress in such areas as diplomatic recognition of the government of Buenos Aires. He and Monroe also were more concerned than the pragmatic Adams with the legality of the actions of Gen. Andrew Jackson in Florida in 1819 and of belligerents' taking enemy property on neutral vessels under international law. Adams, who had respect for Wirt's positions, described one meeting where "Mr. Wirt argued the point, as he naturally and properly does all questions in the Cabinet, as a lawyer." Wirt's argument, Adams added, "appeared to me to be very sound reasoning, taking departure from the Constitution and laws of the United States, with all our principles restrictive of power."[5] Monroe, who suffered from indecision, often acceded to his attorney general's cautionary advice.[6] The president had sought a cabinet that would be both a genuine advisory body and a congenial and representative group. But the body was so representative that it was seldom congenial. Monroe nevertheless relied on cabinet discussions to formulate major administration policy, in foreign affairs and in such controversial domestic affairs as the Missouri Compromise.[7]

Wirt suits the legalistic type in other ways as well. He was not animated by party loyalty; neither were many men during Monroe's era of good feelings. Yet Wirt was nonpartisan even for those nonpartisan times.[8] On one occasion in 1823, he urged a Supreme Court appointment for a well-qualified Federalist, because he had "the loftiest range of talents and learning and a soul of Roman purity and firmness." Denigrating partisan feelings, Wirt explained to Monroe:

> In making the appointment, I think that instead of consulting the feelings of local factions . . . and instead of consulting the little and narrow views of exasperated parties, a President of the United States should look to the good of *the whole country, to their great and permanent interests.* . . . The strongest features in your administration have been the boldness, the independence and magnanimity of your course. . . . Will it be in keeping with the other measures of your administration, to fill such an office as this with an inferior character, from deference to local and party feelings?[9]

His apolitical stance continued in the 1824 presidential race, when Wirt refused to endorse any of the candidates for the nomination, including three cabinet colleagues. He even refused to tell his closest friend whom he preferred. "As I have cautiously forborne to make the Attorney General a partisan in this election, . . . so I am determined that nobody else shall entrap me into a partisan feast," he wrote.[10] In this, he was following the example of the president, who believed he ought to remain above the fray in the matter of his successor.

Wirt never became adept at politics. After the election of Adams, he agreed to stay on as attorney general, but he was not happy with his life in the capital. He wrote a friend that political life had been forced on him, adding, "As for what are called political honours, I would as soon put on the poisoned shirt of Hercules."[11] On an earlier occasion, he wrote, "I am sick of public life. My skin is too thin for the business."[12]

He complained in his last month in office, "The more I see of public life the more sick I become of it, and the more deeply I am convinced that all is vanity and vexation of spirit."[13] These repeated complaints evidently were sincere, yet Wirt's assertions seem puzzling, given his tenacious twelve-year hold on the office, a record yet to be matched. There is even evidence that he attempted to retain the attorney generalship in the administration of Andrew Jackson, a man with whom he was not comfortable. He asked Monroe if cabinet officers had to resign with a new administration. The former president's response provides an interesting insight into Monroe's conception of the office and its relationship to the chief executive, especially as compared with other cabinet posts: "As the heads of departments are counsellors, and wield important branches of the Government, I do not see how they can remain in office without the President's sanction. . . . This view is much less applicable . . . to your case than to the others. Your duties are different. The President has less connection with, and less responsibility for the performance of them. Your standing is, likewise, such, . . . that I should think he [Jackson] would wish to retain you."[14] However, Jackson did not, and Wirt resigned when the new president was inaugurated in 1829.

In several minor ways, Wirt violates the ideal type. For example, he had known Monroe for twenty years at the time of his appointment and considered the elder statesman something of a patron. He also had dabbled in public office, but this amounts to a superficial break only, because in politics he was more of a dilettante than a politician. Before 1817, his public life was limited to a single term in the Virginia House of Delegates, one year as a U.S. attorney under James Madison, and a few months as chancellor of the eastern Virginia Court of Chancery. He could have continued in public life and in fact was urged to do so by such friends as Thomas Jefferson, but—in keeping with the Neutral type's emphasis on being a professional—he refused to abandon his private practice.[15] Even his acceptance of the attorney generalship rested on professional, not political, considerations; he was attracted by the opportunities for career advancement, particularly the chance to practice before the Supreme Court.[16] As one scholar has written, "Wirt was that rarest of early American phenomena, a lawyer who was actually satisfied with the practice of law."[17] His post-1829 activities, after he had retired from the attorney generalship, also constitute only a minor variation from the type. He did become increasingly involved in national politics after he left office, but it was more out of fear of Jackson than any newfound affection for politics. By 1832, he so loathed the incumbent Jackson that he allowed himself to be drafted as the nominee of the Antimasonic party, but he was a reluctant candidate. He never took his electoral chances seriously and even tried to withdraw from the race once Henry Clay was nominated by the Whigs. In the end, the voters returned Jackson to the White House. Wirt died two years later.[18]

Nonpartisanship and perceived independence from the White House, two pivotal characteristics of the Neutral law officer, suggest that this type of attorney general is useful in restoring shaken public confidence. If this is true, we could expect to find the Neutral type in administrations needing credibility after episodes of corruption or scandal. Although not the norm, attorneys general with these features can and do serve in ordinary times, but the three officers closest to the ideal type—other than Wirt himself—were appointed by presidents who had to cope with the worst administration scandals, as the case studies to follow will illustrate.

The "Star Route" Scandal and Benjamin Brewster

The first time that a Neutral law officer was chosen in response to scandal occurred in the 1880s, after the public exposure of one of the most corrupt schemes of the Grant administration. It was the Star Route scandal, involving enormous fraud in the awarding of postal route contracts on the frontier. In the post–Civil War era, the U.S. Post Office had difficulty extending service to the growing population in the West, so it began to award private contracts for mail delivery along thousands of miles of so-called star routes.[19] Little government oversight was possible, so bid fixing and route manipulation flourished. Before Garfield's inauguration in 1881, press reports of the corruption began to appear. Once in office, the new president was stunned by an internal post office report that implicated a powerful Republican senator named Kellogg and the secretary of the Republican national party, Stephen Dorsey, both of whom had been pivotal in Garfield's election victory. Attorney General Wayne MacVeagh warned the president that once the investigation began there could be no retreat, because any wavering on Garfield's part would suggest a cover-up. Garfield agreed, and MacVeagh opened his investigation. Later, in answer to a cabinet suggestion that civil and not criminal suits be instituted against the schemers, Garfield reportedly said, "No, gentlemen. I have sworn to execute the laws. I shall do my full duty. Go ahead, regardless of whom or where you hit."[20] MacVeagh assumed charge of the criminal prosecution, sending inspectors to the frontier, canceling fraudulent contracts, and collecting evidence. Kellogg and Dorsey used their influence to attempt to obstruct the investigation, even trying to pressure Garfield to remove Mac-Veagh and the postmaster from the cabinet.[21]

In the midst of this controversy and in his first year in office, Garfield was shot. He lay dying for ten weeks, leaving Vice-President Chester Arthur—whom some accused of complicity in the assassination—hesitant to take charge.[22] The star route prosecution languished. MacVeagh tried to insulate the trials from political turmoil by naming Benjamin Harris Brewster senior counsel for the government. MacVeagh knew that his own tenure as attorney general was temporary, pending Garfield's death, and he prepared the way for Brewster to be his successor. Brewster seemed a suitable choice: he was an outstanding private attorney, known and respected by the bar. He was from the same wing of the party as Vice-President Arthur.[23] As George Howe notes, Brewster was chosen in part because of his "cordial personal and political relations with Mr. Arthur." When Garfield died, Arthur—as MacVeagh had anticipated—named Brewster attorney general, "largely because of his previous work in preparing prosecutions."[24]

Unlike most Neutral law officers, Brewster had been fairly active in electoral politics. Originally a Democrat, he had worked for Buchanan's and then Polk's election in 1844. Because of his strong pro-Union sentiment, he switched to the Republican party and actively supported Lincoln's reelection and Grant's election in 1868.[25] His own political life, however, was minimal. His repeated attempts to be appointed to public office met with failure for most of forty years. At various times, he was considered for the posts of state attorney general, district attorney, U.S. senator, and U.S. attorney general under Grant,[26] but had been passed over because he was considered too frank and independent. These liabilities became assets in the crisis of confidence facing the Arthur administration. He was "a noted non-conformist . . . famed for fighting in a losing cause" if that cause involved honor or principle.[27] His biographer, writing just ten years later, noted that the attorney generalship came to Brewster "absolutely aside from political considerations, because the entire national press and sentiment demanded his integrity and legal power in a high post at a critical time."[28] For these reasons, Brewster is placed at the Neutral end of the continuum.

His actions in office are consistent with the Neutral. The new attorney general, realizing the need to free the star route cases of any political taint, named a prominent Democrat to join government counsel.[29]

Throughout the ordeal, Brewster attempted to insulate the proceedings from partisan demands. In answer to cabinet criticism, he wrote: "I made up my mind that I would not permit any body to talk with me upon the political relations of this case or of any other case. I thought it would be a scandalous thing for me to do. I did not come into the office of Attorney General to dispense the justice of the United States upon political considerations. I would rather never have taken it; I would rather leave it than do that."[30] Along similar lines, he wrote that he had done his public duty in an honorable and upright manner, rejecting all efforts to persuade him to drop the case because "there was too much to be remembered, the honor of the Department of Justice, but besides that, the honor of Mr. Brewster."[31]

Brewster's task, though difficult, was not as formidable as that which later faced Harlan Fiske Stone and Edward Levi. The Department of Justice was not involved in the fraud in any way, although the press criticized it for being desultory and ineffective in its efforts to prosecute the politically powerful malefactors. The cases were fraught with political peril. For one thing, Senator Kellogg controlled fifteen delegates to the 1884 party convention, delegates whom Arthur needed to secure the nomination. Furthermore, the badly divided party enjoyed only a one-vote majority in the Senate, which it would lose if Kellogg was convicted. A majority of the Republican party, therefore, was opposed to the prosecution, and eminent Republicans even tried to shield guilty friends.[32] Brewster also had to contend with jury fixing, delaying tactics, biased newspaper coverage, infiltration of the prosecution team by spies paid by the defendants, and difficulty in reaching frontier witnesses. The trial itself was a carnival, according to contemporary reports, with the judge contributing to the general levity. Then, despite the overwhelming evidence amassed by the government, convictions were lost, blocked by four jurors who had been bribed. Jurors in a second trial also were bought.[33]

In the end, only a few minor convictions were won. This lack of success was politically damaging to Arthur because "contemporary opinion ascribed failure to the half-hearted nature of the Administration's efforts."[34] The defendants reportedly believed that, while Brewster was serious, Arthur was less than committed to the prosecutions. Brewster's own testimony before the Springer Committee in the House, which investigated the Department of Justice in 1884, repudiates these allegations. He reported that Arthur's words to him were: "I want this work to be done as you are doing it; . . . I want it to be done earnestly and thoroughly. I desire that these people shall be prosecuted with the utmost vigor of the law."[35] The prosecutions were a politically thankless task, bringing little credit to the administration even if successful. But the effort was not without value; the prosecution cleaned out an entrenched and corrupt conspiracy, resulting in an estimated annual post office savings of between $500,000 and $2 million. In addition, "public opinion was roused against corruption in office, and impetus given to the movement for civil service reform."[36]

Brewster also handled the politically sensitive case against Garfield's assassin, Charles Jules Guiteau. Guiteau's insanity defense was unsuccessful, and he was sentenced to hang. Arthur and his attorney general were pressured by some fellow Republicans to reprieve the pitifully insane Guiteau and send him to an asylum, but others argued that a reprieve would be suspicious in light of vicious rumors that Arthur had been involved in the assassination. Either action would damage the administration's reputation. The question of reprieve rested with Brewster and, despite his own committee's recommendation of leniency, he decided against it.[37] There is no evidence that Brewster took this course because it was politically expedient for the president. In fact, he based it on a very narrow interpretation of presidential power, writing that it would be a dangerous precedent if Arthur substituted his own judgment for that of the court. The trial had been thorough, he argued, and the regular appeals process had upheld the conviction. Furthermore, Brewster questioned the president's power to appoint a commission to reverse the sentence.[38]

Another scandal erupted during Arthur's tenure, this one involving the Department of Justice itself. For years, U.S. marshals and commissioners had defrauded the government by rendering false accounts and arresting people on frivolous charges for the sake of fees. Such officials often were locally powerful and controlled many Republican convention votes. Brewster attempted to end these abuses with criminal proceedings, but his efforts encountered a storm of protest that he was once again harming the party and Arthur. The president was asked to remove his attorney general as a political necessity. Eugene Savidge writes, "The discontinuance of these reforms would . . . insure [Arthur] the nomination and a second term."[39] Arthur must have been tempted but he did not relent; the prosecutions continued. Capitalizing on the public disclosures of the scandal, the Democratic Congress started an investigation of Justice and the attorney general. Congress eventually exonerated Brewster, but the whole affair further polarized the party and undermined Arthur's chances for the 1884 nomination. In the end, Brewster's activities contributed to Arthur losing the nomination to James G. Blaine, who then lost the election to Grover Cleveland.[40] To his credit, Arthur steadfastly supported his maverick attorney general, which repudiates his early image as a political spoilsman and hack in a New York City machine.[41]

Neutral law officers generally are unknown to their presidents at the time of appointment. This aspect of the type is difficult to gauge, because it is unclear how close Arthur and Brewster were in 1881. Both men had been delegates to the Republican national convention the year before, when Arthur had been chosen Garfield's running mate. Both were supporters of Grant in the internecine party warfare.[42] The fact that MacVeagh brought in Brewster as senior counsel on the star route cases suggests that he and Arthur were personally acquainted before Garfield's death. Their friendship deepened in the two and a half months after the shooting, because of Brewster's sympathetic support of the harassed vice-president.[43] As president and attorney general, they developed an intimate friendship. Brewster's tenure of three and a half years, comparatively long in an administration troubled with high cabinet turnover,[44] may have contributed to this closeness.

In time, Brewster became one of Arthur's trusted advisers in political as well as legal affairs.[45] This broad advisory role seems to conflict with the Neutral type, except that Arthur himself acted in such a surprisingly nonpartisan way while in office. Brewster's dual loyalty—to the law and to the president—appears never to have been tested, because Arthur did not waver in his support despite the heavy political costs incurred. It is conceivable that, given his reputation for candor and independence, Brewster would have sided with the law over the president if Arthur had forced him to choose. He once explained that lawyers owe their clients fidelity, but he concluded his comments on a moralistic note: "In law we should know not only how to control ourselves and our own knowledge and act with honesty and fairness, but we must command others and their knowledge and force them to be honest and just."[46]

Restoring Confidence: Harlan Fiske Stone

The second administration to turn to a Neutral attorney general was that of Calvin Coolidge, who like Arthur came into office on the death of a president facing scandal. Coolidge inherited from Warren G. Harding a controversial and colorful attorney general named Harry Daugherty, whose three-year tenure had been rife with corruption. Even before Daugherty, the Department of Justice had not been in good repair. The preceding attorney general, A. Mitchell Palmer, had neglected all business but an imagined Bolshevik threat.[47] The scandals of the Harding administration were starting to surface just as the president died. Initially, Coolidge sought stability by keeping the cabinet intact. But as the Teapot Dome scandal unraveled so did the cabinet. Evidence of corruption in the Justice Department brought increased pressure in Congress and the party for Daugherty's dismissal. Coolidge finally asked for his resignation; later Daugherty was charged with conspiracy to defraud the government.[48]

Coolidge was in need of an exemplary attorney general. After Palmer and Daugherty, the morale of the department was extremely low and public trust even lower. He turned to a Columbia University law professor and dean, Harlan Fiske Stone. Stone speculated in 1944 on the reason for his appointment: "I think he had confidence in me, and that about tells the whole story."[49]

More than Brewster, Stone fits the Neutral type, perhaps because the attorney generalship was itself the object of scandal, which it had not been in the Arthur administration. Consistent with the type, Stone and Coolidge were not close associates. The two men had known each other since their college days at Amherst, but Stone had been a year ahead and they had not been friends. Responding to criticism that they had been college "chums," Stone wrote in 1924, "We were not of the same class and therefore were not intimates, although I doubt if many were intimate with [Coolidge]. His extreme reticence made that difficult." Stone was hardly aware of the younger Coolidge until the year after his graduation, when he returned to Amherst and heard Coolidge speak. "I was impressed by the humor, quiet dignity and penetrating philosophy of his oration," he said.[50] Stone never became close to the reclusive president. In 1929, for example, he wrote to his sons that

Coolidge had accepted his dinner invitation; only once before had the Coolidges accepted a private invitation while in office.[51]

In addition, Stone was new to the political world. His background was almost exclusively academic. He taught many years at Columbia Law School and then served as dean from 1910 until 1923, when he left to join a Wall Street law firm. A few months later, Coolidge asked him to come to Washington. His full-time private practice encompassed little more than five years out of twenty. As an eminent legal scholar, Stone had published extensively in law journals, and his legal analyses were cited by the U.S. Supreme Court, several lower federal courts, and the appeals courts of at least eight states.[52] A colleague at Columbia, Charles A. Beard, called him "judicial in temper, and eminently fair in judgment. . . . In politics and jurisprudence he was reckoned a conservative" except where the liberty of opinion was at stake.[53] Stone's biographer explained his conception of the lawyer's function, which also fits the Neutral type: "The chief value of legal counsel to the client, and to the economy, was, he believed, in guiding and aiding the client to conduct his affairs in such a way as to avoid possible pitfalls. Lawyers should not be merely a salvage crew to rescue as much as possible after a crash. The lawyer's job was rather to prevent litigation by helping the client to do his job properly."[54]

While not politically involved, Stone had not avoided public life before 1924. During World War I, he had served on a special board of inquiry looking into the conscientious objector status; he was disturbed at the widespread attitude that such people "should be put to death," as the *New York Times* suggested in 1919. The postwar period brought further episodes of repression against pacifists, as well as socialists and anarchists. Although Stone disagreed with their views, he demanded their right to due process of law. He was especially critical of Attorney General Palmer's tactics in his "Red Raids" against alien radicals.[55]

Coolidge evidently began to consider Stone for the post some weeks before Daugherty left, at the suggestion of New York Congressman Bertrand Snell, another Amherst classmate. Meeting with Coolidge to press for Daugherty's removal, Snell had mentioned Stone as an outstanding lawyer of unblemished character. Coolidge made no comment at the time, but a few weeks later had Snell contact Stone. Initially Stone demurred because of the difference between his private practice salary ($100,000 a year) and a cabinet salary ($12,000). But when

Coolidge met him face to face and said, "Well, I think you will do," Stone accepted the post because he felt it was his duty.[56]

The nomination did not immediately satisfy the Senate nor the media, because Stone was largely unknown outside of legal and academic circles. Because of his brief association with the Wall Street firm, he was called an eastern business attorney by some. Others remembered his work for due process.[57] In time, the press hailed the appointment. The *New York Times*, for example, wrote that he was "about as far as possible from the type of the preceding attorney general. In character, in legal attainments, in the approval of his brethren of the bar . . . Mr. Stone is unusually well qualified."[58]

He was confirmed April 7, 1924, and his subsequent actions in office reinforce his classification as a Neutral. Concerned with rebuilding the battered department, he dismissed the Daugherty holdovers and reorganized Justice, including forming a new bureau of investigation, headed by a young lawyer named J. Edgar Hoover and modeled on Scotland Yard. He also cleaned out the Atlanta federal penitentiary by sending in undercover FBI agents.[59] Because of his prestige, he was able to recruit top professionals, some of them former students, for salaries much lower than in the private sector.[60] Beard wrote that, while Stone "did not go as far as I then hoped he would. . . , [he] did go far in throwing out witchburners and restoring the supremacy of law and judicial procedure, perhaps as far as circumstances would permit."[61]

Stone was not a party man; he did not allow political considerations to deter him from removing a Republican from office or prosecuting a Republican politician. However, he was not politically naive. While he sometimes appointed high caliber Democrats to office, as he did with Hugo Black of Alabama, Stone was cognizant of partisan obligations and would choose the Republican if two men were equally able.[62] He also recognized the need to consult senators before making personnel changes in their states. Writing one U.S. district attorney, he explained: "The best interests of the United States . . . must be our guide. Where those interests are concerned, I do not intend to give ground. However, tact, consideration of the sense of dignity of others and recognition of the fact that we have to live under a system of party government, are considerations which we must not leave out of account."[63] His classification as a Neutral is confirmed by the descriptions of colleagues. Solicitor General Philip Perlman, at a 1948 memorial service, said he was "a judicial craftsman of the highest order." His successor on the Court, Chief Justice Frederick Vinson, noted his reputation as an outstanding legal scholar.[64] One biographer called him "a judge's judge."[65] Beard wrote that "Stone . . . had the independence of the free-hold farmer . . . tempered by a keen awareness of social obligations, small and great."[66]

Stone may have been more independent than Coolidge liked. When he was named to the Supreme Court after just one year, some senators and newspapers thought he had been "kicked upstairs" for cleaning up the Department of Justice too zealously. Editorials appeared charging Coolidge with wanting someone who would play the game his way.[67] Press accounts speculated that Stone had been too committed a trust-buster as attorney general.[68] This seems unlikely, however, given his short tenure and the years needed to prepare an antitrust case. Another possible reason for the move may have been the limitations Stone had placed on the executive branch; Coolidge may have wanted a broader interpretation of his powers. For example, the attorney general had argued before the Supreme Court that the Senate had the power to compel testimony from executive branch officers. He also appeared as *amicus curiae*, arguing against his own department's lawyers, in support of the judiciary's position that the president cannot pardon contempt of court offenses.[69] It is also possible that Coolidge simply saw Stone as an excellent choice for the coveted post. In any case, without Stone, Coolidge was able to form a more compliant cabinet. Donald McCoy writes that, with the exception of Herbert Hoover, cabinet members either "bent themselves to his will, or saw eye-to-eye with him to begin with."[70]

Although Coolidge did appoint two special counsel to prosecute Teapot Dome, an indirect repudiation of Daugherty, he does not seem to have been conscious of the need to appoint a particular type of attorney general to restore public confidence, even though his choice of Stone did so. He seemed reluctant to restructure Harding's cabinet, making changes only when forced to; he retained Daugherty for six months after Republican senators first called for his removal. The cabinet changes Coolidge did make—in the Justice and Navy departments—probably reflected his different governing style as much as any conscious break with the previous administration to satisfy public or congressional demands for greater independence.[71] Regardless of Coolidge's reasons for handling the scandals as he did, the majority of the public seemed to have regained its trust by the time of the 1924 election. His actions in response to the various scandals helped his electoral chances,[72] even if he was unaware of it.

After the election, however, Coolidge learned the importance that the public and Congress attach to an attorney general's background during postscandal administrations. Determined to name a politically sympathetic attorney general to replace Stone, Coolidge nominated Charles Beecher Warren, his 1924 convention floor leader and a prominent figure in the Sugar Trust then under indictment. This Advocate-type background, coupled with Coolidge's failure to consult party leaders about the appointment, led to a disastrous confrontation with the Senate in March 1925 when Warren's confirmation was rejected by one vote. For the first time since 1868, a cabinet nominee was refused by the Senate.[73] Coolidge angrily renominated Warren, but he was rejected again, this time by a decisive vote of forty-six to thirty-nine. With this defeat, the president conceded to congressional expectations. His next nominee, John Sargent, was a former Vermont attorney general. Sargent was confirmed unanimously, and his tenure was considered honest and conservative.[74]

Although many of Stone's traits are consistent with the Neutral type, his judicial philosophy, which fully matured after he was on the bench, suggests a vision of the law as a tool for accomplishing social ends, a trait more compatible with the Advocate type. At Columbia, he had preached judicial restraint and considered public demands for social justice to be lawless. But these views gradually changed; he came to see the Constitution as a broad charter to be adapted to the times. He said at a 1936 conference, "Law is not an end, but a means to an end. . . . [The] end is to be attained through the reasonable accommodation of law to changing economic and social needs."[75] Accommodation would occur through an enlightened application of the common law. Stone did not want the social sciences to permeate legal studies, but he did believe that judges needed a well-grounded knowledge of social and economic forces. By the time he became attorney general in 1923, he believed that the sources of all true legal doctrine were logic, history, and the method of sociology. He argued that sociological jurisprudence had a contribution to make.[76] This approach to the law more often characterizes politically active law officers, but it is not necessarily incompatible with the Neutral type.

Edward Levi and President Ford

Gerald Ford, as with Arthur and Coolidge, assumed office in the difficult aftermath of major scandal. He recognized the immediate and overriding need to restore confidence in the attorney generalship. Revelations about Watergate and related campaign abnormalities significantly damaged the Justice Department because of the involvement of Attorney General John Mitchell, who was President Nixon's campaign manager in 1972. Mitchell was convicted of obstruction of justice, perjury, and making false statements to a grand jury; he spent nineteen months in prison.[77] Public faith was further eroded when Richard Kleindienst, the next attorney general, pleaded guilty to a contempt-of-Congress misdemeanor charge for failing to report a phone call from Nixon pressuring Justice to drop an antitrust suit against ITT.[78] Reports that one assistant attorney general had passed grand jury testimony to the president also lowered public trust. Perhaps the darkest days for the department occurred in October 1973, when Nixon ordered the firing of the first special prosecutor, Archibald Cox, and the sealing of his office's files. During the so-called Saturday Night Massacre, Attorney General Elliot Richardson, the one who was supposed to bring confidence back to Nixon's Justice Department, resigned. His deputy was then fired.[79] The assistant attorney general in the antitrust division, Thomas Kauper, describes the demoralization that followed: "The Department was a very depressing place for awhile. I met with all of my people on Sunday. The only question was that if I was going to resign, the rest of the division would also. That went on for some days, and even much longer." Kauper added that Watergate had seriously damaged the prestige of the Justice Department even in the federal courts. When government attorneys attempted to argue cases, "they encountered disbelief in what they were saying. For a long period, the major task was to reestablish the credibility of the Department."[80]

Arguably, Ford's task to rebuild confidence was more difficult than that faced by either Arthur or Coolidge. Unlike them, he did not have the mantle of legitimacy conferred by winning an election as vice-president. He had been appointed to the post after the forced resignation of Spiro Agnew. Also, he replaced a president who had resigned to avoid an impeachment trial for his alleged complicity in the cover-up. Neither Garfield nor Harding had been directly implicated in their administration's scandals. Ford's need to restore faith in the presidency as well as in the Department of Justice led him to select as attorney general a man who embodies more of the Neutral characteristics than any of his predecessors, Edward Hirsch Levi of Illinois.

Contradictory needs for continuity and for change pressured Ford when he entered office. Continuity was critical in a Justice Department that had been damaged by the rapid turnover of attorneys general; Levi would be the fifth in just over three years. Jokes about the short tenures abounded. Secretaries reportedly had signs on their desks reading: "If the attorney general calls, for God's sake get his name!"[81] Yet Ford also was pledged to restore the executive office to a position of respect and trust by instituting certain changes from the previous administration. In addition, the Republican party's chances in the upcoming congressional elections were shaken by the Watergate scandal, and he had to distance the party from it.[82] For this reason, a new attorney general had to be named.

The current officer, William Saxbe, was not involved in Watergate in any way, but he was too closely associated with the previous administration and with the political world. Formerly a senator, Saxbe had joined Nixon's Justice Department in the wake of the Saturday Night Massacre and Richardson's resignation. He had made gains in improving affairs. Not only had he kept Justice together for the critical last eight months of the Nixon presidency, he had introduced procedural regularity and a system of clear authorization for warrantless wiretaps.[83] But he was not the right man to move forward. In addition to his political past, he "repeatedly got himself into trouble with poorly timed, ill conceived remarks about pending cases."[84] Ford made no immediate changes, however. Like Coolidge, he stressed stability and continuity in the cabinet,[85] keeping Saxbe four more months. Then, on December 12, 1974, he named Saxbe ambassador to India. The way was open for Ford to name his own man to the important post. A month later, the press announced the nomination of Levi.

Ford emulated Coolidge in another sense. His attorney general, a former president of the University of Chicago, was an academic well versed in legal scholarship and university administration, as was Harlan Fiske Stone. The similarity between Stone and Levi was noted by the *Economist* when it called Levi "the first genuine legal scholar to be named as attorney general in half a century. The last one was Mr.

Harlan Stone, appointed . . . also at a time when the Justice Department was plagued by scandal."[86] But Ford differed with Coolidge in the matter of intent. Ford consciously sought certain characteristics in his nominee that would reassure the public and Congress. His choice was not accidental. Writing later of his decision to appoint Levi, Ford noted, "In my judgment, a new attorney general . . . had to be someone of unquestioned integrity and impeccable legal abilities and background and ought to come from outside the traditional political arena."[87] Not only did he look beyond the political world, he also looked beyond his circle of friends, including his longtime friend and eminent attorney Philip Buchen. If it had not been for the pressures brought by Watergate, Buchen might have been named attorney general, had he wanted the post. But his association with Ford was too close for him to have been a serious candidate in that highly sensitive atmosphere. Instead, he was named White House counsel.

Levi fits the Neutral type even more thoroughly than Stone, his scholarly predecessor. Levi and Ford were not personally acquainted; in fact, they had never met when, on December 5, Ford interviewed him as a possible nominee. Ford was impressed, calling Levi "soft spoken, reserved, clear-eyed about the problems in the Department, forthright."[88] Noting the widespread doubt about the Justice Department, the new president explained that he wanted a different kind of law officer, one who could restore confidence in the "integrity and trust of our legal system," and who "understands the meaning of rule of law and its limits."[89]

The Senate agreed with Ford's assessment. Levi's name was submitted for confirmation on January 16. After three days of hearings, he was confirmed by voice vote on February 5 and sworn into office on February 7. While Levi himself may have regarded the hearings as long and grueling, they were noticeably shorter than those of other attorneys general in the post-Watergate period. For example, the hearings for Richard Kleindienst lasted twenty-four days; for Elliot Richardson, six days; for Griffin Bell, seven days; for Edwin Meese, seven days over a fifteen-month period (to allow time to investigate charges of ethical lapses when he served in the White House). William Saxbe's two-day confirmation hearings may have been due to the fact that he was a fellow senator at the time of his appointment. Before Watergate, hearings often were perfunctory, with Congress seldom challenging a president's cabinet preferences. Nicholas Katzenbach in the Johnson administration, for instance, was queried for just half an hour. After an administration scandal, Congress assumes a much more aggressive and partisan role in the confirmation process, which may partially account for a president seeking such qualities as eminence and nonpartisanship in his nominee.

Consistent with the Neutral type, Levi was nonpartisan. During the hearings, he informed senators that he had not registered with any political party for several years, lest he imply that the University of Chicago was endorsing one party over another.[90] Illinois Senator Charles Percy, in introducing Levi, reiterated his nonpartisanship: "He is not a partisan. He is beholden to no one. . . . For too long politics has been permitted to intrude into the Justice Department." His nonpartisanship was not without critics. Sen. Roman Hruska suggested that it might take a politician to avoid partisan entanglements within the department. "Virtually every decision that is made of policy within that department, as within other departments, has political connotations or implications one way or the other. One inexperienced in politics might make the mistake of misjudging or not being able to appreciate that type of impact," Hruska said.[91]

But Levi's perceived independence was an important factor working in his favor with most senators. Responding to a question by Edward Kennedy on improper contacts from the White House on pending cases, the nominee answered: "I'm going to call them as I see them. I cannot imagine why anyone, including the President of the United States, would think of asking me to take this office . . . except for my independent judgment as to the legality, which includes frequently my independent judgment as to the kinds of policies which are involved in the legality, and I would give my independent judgment."[92] It was the kind of answer that the Senate was seeking. Independence from the White House had been a recurring theme in the confirmation hearings of Kleindienst and Richardson, and even appeared briefly in the hearings on Mitchell's appointment, in relation to his role as Richard Nixon's campaign manager in 1968. In his confirmation hearings, Levi was asked more questions on independence than on any other topic, including his law enforcement priorities and pending legislation revising the criminal code.[93] The issue of independence generally does not figure highly in attorney general confirmation hearings, but in postscandal periods, senators as well as the president are especially concerned with it.

Different strengths in the nominee are stressed, depending on the political environment, a fact that was noted by Lawrence Walsh, then president-elect of the American Bar Association, when he testified for the nominee. He said that Levi's absence of political involvement was good at that time, though not perhaps at other times. "The office of the attorney general encompasses many functions. No one man can know them all to perfection, and the President must choose, subject to confirmation by this body, whether or not the particular group of capabilities selected at a particular time are the best."[94]

Also in keeping with the Neutral type, Levi made it clear to the senators what he would do if the White House made improper demands on his office. "I will try to proceed through explanation and discussion, but ultimately I do not feel any reason to give in to pressure of any kind. . . . If there were really, really serious interference, . . . I would resign."[95] At the same time, Levi recognized the need to work in harmony with the president as a member of his cabinet. He noted that the president has the authority to set policy in general directions, as in the proper interpretation of the Sherman Act and other antitrust legislation. Levi then explained his view of the office: "I have not any doubt that the attorney general is the lawyer for the government, in a sense a lawyer for the president, only the president has other lawyers as well. And that there is a proper loyalty which we all recognize as lawyers to the idea of law itself."[96]

The press generally approved the appointment. An editorial in the *Wall Street Journal* defended Levi against the fears of Senate conservatives that he was a liberal academic. The editors wrote that Ford simply was responding to the concerns of both conservatives and liberals "in defending traditional values against the onslaughts of neo-barbarism." Levi, they added, was a man of courage and integrity.[97] Outside the media, however, Levi's conscious nonpartisanship was viewed with suspicion. Republican activists in Ohio and Kentucky, for example, wrote Ford that Levi was too liberal, or at least not partisan enough. Ford reassured them not to be concerned.[98]

Ford and Levi repeated the need for an independent attorney general during Levi's swearing-in ceremony. Ford called on the new attorney general to make Justice a great department again, a necessity if citizens were to have faith in the law. Levi then said: "We have lived in a time of . . . corrosive skepticism and cynicism concerning the administration of justice. Nothing can more weaken the quality of life or more imperil the realization of the goals we all hold dear, than our failure to make clear, by word and deed, that our law is not an instrument of partisan purpose."[99]

Ford's concern with partisanship in the Justice Department seems to have predated Levi's arrival. For example, in the 1974 congressional races, Saxbe played a minor role at most, unlike some department heads who actively campaigned.[100] Ford also minimized the partisanship of all cabinet positions. Twice he issued guidelines to his cabinet in the 1976 federal elections, prohibiting federal officials and employees from soliciting or receiving political contributions. Cabinet secretary James E. Connor reminded the department heads that speeches before nonpartisan groups were official in nature, adding that official activities should not appear political.[101]

Although Levi generally was removed from partisan activity, he was involved in policy, and in this sense became a political actor in the administration. As with most attorneys general, Levi's policy/political activities stemmed largely from his function as head of a large government department, including such responsibilities as testifying before Congress on legislation affecting Justice.[102] And while Ford wanted Levi to remain nonpartisan, he also sought the assistance of his attorney general and other department heads in communicating with the Republican leadership in Congress, so that Congress could understand the administration's programs.[103] He participated on several administration policy committees, including the Domestic Council, the Energy Resources Council, and the Committee on Urban Development and Neighborhood Revitalization. In addition, Levi undertook a few diplomatic functions, such as representing the United States at the twentieth anniversary commemoration of the Austrian State Treaty.[104]

The Neutral attorney general may find himself isolated in his department, removed from other important policy areas, including ones with legal repercussions. To some extent, this happened to Levi. It was not because he was an ivory tower academic; his long career administering a major university gave him sufficient bureaucratic skills. In addition, his professional reputation enhanced his power. According to Kauper, Levi's words carried weight because he was viewed as a truly brilliant lawyer.[105] But the very traits that commended him as an attorney general in time of scandal—his independence, his nonpartisanship, his newness—operated against his full participation in the broad range of policy issues confronting the president.

For one thing, Ford, in keeping with a growing trend among presidents, relied on his White House counsel, Philip Buchen, for much of his legal advice. Buchen and Ford had been fraternity brothers and had opened a law office together in 1941 (closed the next year when Ford joined the navy).[106] Their long association, which Ford did not share with his attorney general, may have contributed to the trust that the president placed in Buchen; he was one of the very few whom Ford asked for advice on the Nixon pardon. Buchen was involved in virtually all legal issues facing Ford.[107] For example, he advised on the legality of the legislature's response to the pocket veto.[108] He also advised on the seizure of aircraft belonging to the People's Republic of China.[109] He may have played an advisory role in the *Mayaguez* incident as well, to be examined later. On occasion, Buchen turned to the attorney general's office for an opinion, especially on issues of institutional prerogative, such as executive privilege.[110] He also served as a liaison between the president and the attorney general: the Justice Department notified Buchen of politically sensitive cases in order to prepare the president for media questions,[111] and Levi also contacted Buchen for administration guidance in some legal areas that had policy implications.[112] In another instance, Buchen referred to the Justice Department the case of *Drinan et al. v. Ford et al.*, a suit brought by several congressmen to enjoin the administration from further military activities in Cambodia.[113] To some extent, Buchen's office served as a buffer between the political world and the Justice Department. That was the role it played in March 1975, when Rep. James Blanchard of Michigan asked Ford to intervene personally to prevent the Department of Justice from filing a school desegregation suit against a Michigan school district. Buchen responded to the congressman, "Your request must be considered in light of the President's general policy not to interfere in litigation conducted by the Department of Justice except in the most unusual circumstances."[114] Perhaps because of the jurisdictional overlap in the area of legal advice and justice policy, press speculation arose that a tension existed between the White House counsel and the attorney general. Rebutting the rumor that his relationship with Levi was not harmonious or effective, Buchen told one reporter:

From the time the Attorney General was appointed, he and I have worked very closely on many critical issues. There is hardly a day that we do not confer either by telephone or in a conference. On these occasions, we have useful exchanges of ideas which have helped me a great deal in my work, just as I believe they are helpful to the Attorney General. There is no member of the President's Cabinet for whom I have higher respect and admiration.[115]

In addition to Buchen, White House aide James Cannon also served as a conduit to the president for information on lawsuits, legislation, and other Justice issues.[116]

Not only must the attorney general face competition in the giving of legal advice, but his own advisory role is circumscribed by the fact that presidents are not compelled to seek legal advice, or to abide by legal advice once it has been tendered. Because he is outside of the inner circle, the Neutral type is especially vulnerable to exclusion from discussions of important issues. A review of Levi's advisory role during the trying days of *Mayaguez* illustrates the typical Neutral pattern.

Early on Monday, May 12, 1975, Ford received word during his CIA briefing that the Cambodian armed forces had seized in international waters the SS *Mayaguez*, a merchant vessel under U.S. registry with a crew of U.S. citizens. The vessel was forced to Koh Tang Island. The next morning, after the failure of indirect diplomatic efforts to return the crew and ship, and to prevent the *Mayaguez* from being moved to a mainland port, the president ordered U.S. aircraft to fire warning shots across the bow. U.S. armed forces then isolated the island in an effort to prevent the crew from being taken to the mainland, where rescue would be more difficult. In the process, three Cambodian patrol boats were destroyed and four others damaged. One boat, suspected of carrying U.S. captives, succeeded in reaching Kompong Som. Needing to act quickly, Ford ordered a marine landing on Koh Tang to rescue any Americans still there. Naval aircraft attacked mainland military targets to prevent any reinforcements. The marines were able to retake the *Mayaguez* on May 14; two hours later, the crew was safely taken aboard the *Wilson*.[117] American losses were high; fifteen men were killed in action, three were missing, and fifty wounded. Another twenty-three died when their helicopter crashed.[118] The incident raised a number of legal questions, both in international law, where the seizure could be considered an act of war, and in domestic law, specifically, the application of the War Powers Resolution of 1973, the Cooper-Church Amendment of 1971 (banning use of U.S. ground combat troops in Cambodia), and other prohibitions against U.S. combat activities in Indochina found in certain appropriations acts.[119] But, according to a chronology of the president's activities from May 12 through May 15, the attorney general was never consulted. During that three and a half days, Ford conferred most frequently with Gen. Brent Scowcroft, deputy assistant for national security affairs, and Secretary of State and National Security Adviser Henry Kissinger. He also frequently consulted Defense Secretary James Schlesinger. Ford met almost as often with his White House senior staff, especially Assistant to the President Donald Rumsfeld, who later became secretary of Defense, and counselors Jack O. Marsh and Robert Hartmann. Press Secretary Ron Nessen regularly attended meetings that week as well.[120]

The chronology does not include attendance at NSC meetings, but this gap is filled by Richard Head, Frisco Short, and Robert McFarlane in their book on crisis resolution. Their account reinforces the conclusion that Levi was not an adviser. The attorney general did not attend these NSC meetings, nor did he do so normally during the Ford years except as an observer on the Operations Advisory Group, which made recommendations on foreign policy objectives.[121]

A relevant point to consider is that participation of legal counsel in these deliberations may not have been essential. Many questions pertaining to the War Powers Resolution had been addressed the previous month, when Ford sent naval vessels to assist in an international evacuation effort of South Vietnamese refugees from Da Nang.[122] In addition, Levi's absence does not mean that Ford received no legal advice; he may have relied on other sources, including Buchen, who attended two meetings with the president that first afternoon and two more later in the week. He also attended the fourth NSC meeting, which reviewed the diplomatic status and the details of the landing plan.[123]

Yet a comparison of Levi's absence during *Mayaguez* with Robert Kennedy's participation in the Cuban missile crisis illustrates the different roles assumed by Neutral and Advocate attorneys general in the area of foreign affairs and national security. Given his close relationship with the president, Kennedy probably would have been included even if he had had no official function in the administration. Advocate attorneys general, because they are close to their presidents, have often been among the select. This raises the disturbing possibility that presidents appoint Neutral officers in response to external demands and then proceed to circumvent them when their legal assessments are unwelcome. In the case of Ford, however, Levi does not seem to have been consigned to play only a public relations role. He may have been more influential than the average Neutral law officer because of Ford's governing style. According to several former White House staff members, Ford was an open, action-oriented president, who liked to have his staff and department heads exchange ideas. With his background in Congress and collegial politics, he brought a different institutional view to the office than did Nixon.[124] The cabinet, which met relatively frequently, was given a more active policy-shaping role under Ford; cabinet agendas were broad, covering such diverse topics as amnesty for draft evaders, the summit conference on inflation, U.S. involvement in Chile, Kissinger's trip to the Mideast, aid to Cambodia and South Vietnam, and energy policy.[125] After one cabinet meeting, Secretary of Transportation William Coleman praised the president for allowing cabinet members to discuss their differences openly.[126] Ford told his department heads to be more than narrow specialists, explaining at another cabinet meeting, "I want to be able to use all of you in ways that cut across your departmental lines," specifically mentioning Levi in higher education and Carla Hills in legal affairs.[127] Ford's style may have permitted the attorney general to be involved in many more areas than one might expect of a Neutral. Cabinet Secretary Connor explained, "I don't recollect that the senior White House staff usually agreed on a single recommendation. . . . The counsel's office would stress one thing and the people with congressional perspective would stress another. The whole purpose of the exercise, from my position, was to flesh it out, to show that there were different perspectives on decisions and to ensure that the President knew what they were."[128]

This style began to change after the pardon, when Rumsfeld joined the White House staff and Ford's more open "spokes-of-the-wheel" approach shifted to a more orderly pyramid arrangement.[129] Even then, Levi was in regular communication with the president outside of the cabinet, meeting more frequently and for longer periods of time with Ford than many of the other department heads. This conclusion is drawn from a review of the president's meetings with his cabinet officers from August 1975 to March 1976. Meetings were most frequent with Kissinger, who had a double role in foreign affairs and national security. The secretary of Defense also was a regular visitor. But Levi is third in terms of the total number of hours spent with the president individually or in small groups (of up to six), and he is third in terms of the average length of each meeting, both in individual/small groups and in larger groups. Levi is fifth in terms of the actual number of small-group or individual meetings with the president.[130] While care must be taken in using these figures to infer anything about the influence of the attorney general on Ford, at least we can say that Levi was not denied access to the Oval Office.

Any trust and friendship that Gerald Ford came to feel for his attorney general does not alter their essentially Neutral relationship. Such law officers are not necessarily ineffective or impotent because of their recent arrival to government service or to the president's circle of advisers. The phrases Ford used in 1985 to describe Levi reinforce the classification: "Under his thoughtful, nonpolitical, and highly principled leadership, the integrity and effectiveness of the Department of Justice were restored." The president also praised his "sound legal reasoning, adherence to constitutional principles," and the ability to restore "a sense of trust, credibility and reassurance."[131] This language is often employed in describing such law officers. A fellow cabinet officer used similar language to describe the attorney general during an address to the American Law Institute. Secretary Coleman said Levi's style was "perfect to restore the faith in that Department." Noting that he did not always agree with Levi's positions, he said he was most impressed by Levi's "insistence that he and he alone bears final responsibility for determining the government's legal position."[132]

The stress on rule of law seems to characterize the tenures of Neutral law officers. Levi was acclaimed for his adherence to this venerable legal principle. One former department colleague, Ronald Carr, wrote that "he brought to the office of Attorney General a coherent understanding of the meaning of the rule of law and of its implications for public responsibility." Specific actions or changes are not of fundamental importance in judging Levi's tenure, Carr argued. Instead what mattered was "the intellectual and ethical integrity" with which he approached his office and responsibilities.[133] Carr's point is well taken. When recuperating from the searing public wounds of scandal, an administration may find that procedural integrity assumes greater importance than substantive accomplishment. This stress on procedure over substance and on rule of law over majority will continued into the next administration. But the immediacy of the scandal was fading, and the political world gradually began to reassert itself in the Department of Justice under Griffin Bell.

Griffin Bell's Neutral Zone

Disillusionment because of Watergate was so entrenched that Ford's successor, Jimmy Carter, also sought to build confidence in the attorney generalship by appointing a law officer with Neutral type characteristics. Carter had run on a campaign pledge to establish an independent law office. He and his appointee, former federal judge Griffin B. Bell, agreed that the administration's legal positions were to be decided at the Justice Department and not the White House. The recent scandal, Bell noted, had corroded public faith in government because of the involvement of two attorneys general. He wrote, "That the attorney general be free from political influence is essential to public confidence in his office."[134]

The Senate also had not forgotten Watergate. During Bell's confirmation hearings, Judiciary Committee members repeatedly stressed the need for independence. Referring to the bleak pattern of recent history, including the convictions of Mitchell and Kleindienst, Sen. Donald Riegle (D.-Mich.) said, "I think the legitimate concern that a lot of people have is will there be sufficient independence in the Justice Department different and very much separate from what we saw in the previous administration where there was a tremendous abuse of power."[135]

While Bell himself was committed to remaining independent of the White House, the public did not perceive him as such. His harshest critics targeted those experiences in his past that broke with the general Neutral pattern, specifically his long-standing association with Jimmy Carter and his previous political activity. Because of these experiences and the negative perceptions they engendered, he does not fit the type as well as Edward Levi. For example, Bell was not a stranger to Carter. The two men had known each other since their childhood in Plains,

Georgia, although Bell was closer to Carter's cousin, the journalist Don Carter, than to Jimmy, who was six years younger. "It was a rural area and families all knew each other because there were not that many families," Bell said. Many years later as a federal judge, Bell and gubernatorial candidate Carter periodically met to discuss interesting cases or law articles. Bell also was a law partner of Carter's longtime friend and attorney, Charles Kirbo. In fact, he had introduced the two men when Carter needed an attorney to challenge a crooked state senate race.[136]

Nor was Bell new to politics or government. He had been the chief of staff and legal adviser to Gov. Samuel Vandiver of Georgia in the late 1950s. Like Brewster, he had some partisan experience as well, serving as the state campaign manager for John Kennedy in 1960. The next year Kennedy appointed him to the U.S. Court of Appeals for the Fifth Circuit, where he served for almost fifteen years.[137]

Bell's minimal involvement with the 1976 campaign also elicited criticism, although his responsibilities generally were restricted to lawyerly functions, such as writing a legal memorandum on the difference between a pardon and an amnesty. In addition, he prepared the questionnaire used to guide interviews with prospective vice-presidential candidates, and he helped prepare a few speeches and raise money in Georgia during the Pennsylvania primary.[138]

These Advocate traits were criticized in Congress and the media at the time of his appointment and may have accounted for the three negative votes to ten affirmative that Bell received when the Judiciary Committee reported his nomination to the entire Senate.[139] In a 1978 speech, Bell said he had been a victim of undue suspicion—what he called the "Watergate syndrome"—in his confirmation hearings. "Some opposed me because I was a friend of the President. Because Watergate showed that some friends of one President exercised poor judgment in public office, these people suspected that I would."[140] An article in the *New York Times Magazine* by Victor Navasky asked how Carter could fulfill his campaign pledge of an independent attorney general with the appointment of a personal friend. Navasky went on to cite Bell's political past, writing with some exaggeration that "Griffin Bell seems always to have been involved in politics and organizing."[141] The fact that these suspicions remained salient after Levi's two years illustrates the difficult and slow process involved in rebuilding confidence. Bell recognized that his background was a disadvantage: "It probably wasn't a good thing for me to be the attorney general, being from Georgia. But worse than that, the President and I were from the same county."[142]

Although he does not fit the pure Neutral type, Bell represents that type in many important respects. His self-perception is consistent with the type, in particular his stress on his independence and the "rule of impartial law."[143] The descriptions of others who know him also support this classification, because they emphasize his legal ability, his incorruptibility and his "highest character and integrity."[144] His association with the president was not as close as his critics charged. While he and Carter had been acquainted for many years, they were not intimate. During Carter's years as governor, Bell saw him only a few times annually and never visited the Governor's mansion, even though he lived just two blocks away.[145]

Bell's 1977 interview with Navasky reinforces the Neutral classification, when Navasky writes that Bell talked more of the department's reorganization than his substantive policy goals as attorney general. Bell, he wrote, is "more interested in political process than policy." He suggests that this makes Bell more of a politician and less of an activist.[146] This conclusion is dubious. While clearly not an activist attorney general, Bell was not, by default, a political fixer. On the contrary, this emphasis on organization is consistent with Neutral law officers, who stress procedure over substantive issues because the latter more overtly involve political choices. While process is not politically neutral, Neutral law officers, who tend to insist that their office is nonpolitical, may feel that procedural questions are less politically charged than issues of substance.

Also in keeping with the Neutral type was Bell's view of his relationship to the president. During his confirmation hearings, he said that the president would be one client among many, as would government agencies and even Congress. "And the American people would be a client," he added. "I think you are administering and enforcing a body of law. It is necessary for you to think of the Department of Justice as the people's law department." When asked by Sen. Charles Mathias if the people were not his first client, Bell said, "Possibly so. It is according to what you think about representative government. I think of the Congress and the President as representing the people." If the interests of president and people diverge, however, he would be with the people.[147] Later, he emphasized the attorney general's duty to the people even more strongly. "The people are your client," he said. "At the same time, the president is your client. But if there's a conflict, the people prevail."[148] If confronted with an arguably illegal presidential request, Bell said he would respond this way:

> If one of his people called me, I would refuse to do it and report it to him. And tell him I did not appreciate it. If he asked me to do it, and it was something I should not do, then I would refuse to do it. If necessary, I would resign. When I say 'necessary,' it would not take much effort or much cause to get me to resign. I intend to be independent. . . . [President Carter] has made a mistake if he doesn't know I'm independent. I have my own reputation to worry about. . . . I don't think I will have that trouble, but if I do, I would be prepared.[149]

Bell's emphasis on independence and integrity as qualities needed for an attorney general also reflects a legalistic understanding of the office. "You have got to pick out a person with great integrity, because he is also a leader in the sense that he leads the place" by setting the tone, Bell explained. But integrity had to be coupled with strength and a dominant personality, if an attorney general was to stand up to the competing power centers. He had to have backbone as well as ethics. He said in an interview, "It helps the President to have a strong attorney general to be certain that people advising him are not all but frank. He's got to be stronger. They have a big staff [of lawyers] over at the White House; they would run right over a weak attorney general."[150] Interestingly, Bell added that he would not have done what Ford did in selecting an attorney general he did not know. "Levi was good," he said, "but Ford had a different problem [than most presidents]. He was trying to restore the image of the Department of Justice." Instead, Bell would follow the pattern of Carter and most presidents in naming someone he knew, because there was more opportunity for abuse in that office than in the other cabinet posts. Carter initially sought an outside attorney general; he had asked Bell to head the search. But when Bell submitted a list of five outstanding candidates, Carter instead named him. "I don't know why he picked me out. The only thing I did think about was that he didn't know any of the people that I'd found. And I know that, if I was president, I would not select an attorney general I did not know."[151]

His goal as attorney general was to professionalize and depoliticize the department, and in this he and Carter concurred. They developed a policy to make the Department of Justice a neutral zone in government.

We had some understanding. One was that the Justice Department would be operated on a nonpolitical basis. I think I understand how to do that because I was a judge for fourteen and a half years. Certainly, that was operated on a nonpolitical basis. I intend to operate it on that basis. I intend for the Justice Department to be operated within the strictures of its being a law department which would have nothing to do with politics. Of course you touch politics because you are advising people, but it will not be a medium of politics; and it will not be used for political purposes. I would rather not be Attorney General than to have it turn out otherwise.[152]

Sensitive to the appearance of politics in the department, Bell decided to resign before Carter's reelection campaign. "I was sufficiently mindful of the public perception of my ties to President Carter to know that, in taking the job, I could not serve during a presidential election year," he wrote.[153] He resigned August 3, 1979.

Carter also sought to depoliticize the department. He exempted Bell from partisan activities, such as midterm conventions and political meetings. "I was exempt from all that," Bell said, "and it caused [Cyrus] Vance to ask to be exempt, the secretary of State. Then Harold Brown, the secretary of Defense, said he thought he ought to be exempt, so the president exempted those two. Then Schlesinger came in wanting to be exempt, but the president said he wasn't exempting anybody else. Somebody had to politick."[154]

Repeatedly in his campaign Carter had stressed independence. During Bell's swearing-in ceremony, he touched on these themes again: "I want to be sure that everything I do, everything Griffin Bell does, and everything all of you do is conducive to a restoration of trust and harmony." But restoration of trust included pursuit of certain substantive goals, according to his first comments that day: "One of the most crucial appointments that a President can make is that of Attorney General, because here we have not a department of law but a department of justice. To the maximum degree possible the Attorney General should personify what the President of the United States is—attitudes, philoso-

phies, commitments—to provide equality of opportunity and a sense of
trust in the core of our American governmental institutions."[155] In this
view of the attorney generalship, Carter was slightly less concerned
with Neutral qualities than was Ford. The stress on proper procedure,
which was essential in the Levi Justice Department, was tempered with
a recognition that substantive policy commitments could be legitimate
as well. Public confidence and independence were important considerations, but so were "equality of opportunity" and a law officer's ability
to personify the president's goals in the area of justice. This substantive
orientation is evident in a speech given by Governor Carter in 1974,
where he chastised lawyers who used legal technicalities to abuse the
poor and illiterate of his state.[156]

Despite this substantive approach to the law, Carter had a management style that mitigated against Bell becoming a wide-ranging Advocate. According to one study of the administration, Carter tended to
seek advice from the person who had the formal authority in a given
area, so that "there was no single powerful advisor across the whole
range of topics."[157] Those who seemed to have the most influence across
the board were located in the White House. Carter relied on his vice-
president, Walter Mondale, and the head of the Domestic Policy Staff,
Stuart Eizenstat, in many policy areas. Bell, who wrote critically about
these White House power centers in his 1982 book, discovered that
most of his battles were with them, not with the president. He felt that
the White House staff assumed more and more power during the Carter
presidency, to the detriment of cabinet secretaries.[158]

Once in office, Griffin Bell and Jimmy Carter faced several experiences that tested their assertions of independence and neutrality. Four
cases illustrate the tension between law and politics in the Carter administration. Carter came close to firing his attorney general in one
case, and Bell considered resigning in another. In the end, Carter overruled Bell just once, in an incident dealing with the Comprehensive Em-
ployment and Training Act (CETA) regulations and parochial schools.

The CETA case began when the Department of Labor asked the Office of Legal Counsel in the Justice Department if federally funded
CETA positions could be provided to church schools. The OLC responded in January 1979 that the program could only apply to health
aides and kitchen personnel, but not to teachers, counselors, or mainte-
nance and clerical workers. The decision was not popular with Catho-

lics, and the U.S. Catholic Conference confronted Mondale and Eizen-stat. When the vice-president then asked Bell to intervene in reversing the opinion, Bell had John Harmon, assistant attorney general for OLC, issue an explanation. Then, Bell writes, "President Carter, in a two-par-agraph letter to me, flatly overruled our decision." This action brought him close to resignation. He then learned of the "backstage maneuver-ing" at the White House done by Mondale and Eizenstat, who report-edly were upset that Bell had not consulted them before issuing the CETA opinion. In response, Bell sent a letter to Carter challenging their criticism. He wrote, "Implicit in this complaint is the notion that the proper way to proceed was for you to direct, on their recommendation, the conclusion I would reach in my legal opinion. Because I failed to fol-low that course, you have now taken the extraordinary step of overrul-ing the opinion of the attorney general." He then reminded Carter that he had: "directed me to establish an independent Department of Jus-tice, a neutral zone in the government where decisions will be made on the merits free of political interference or influence. I was asked for my opinion on a question of law. I was under the professional obligation as a lawyer and under an official obligation as your attorney general to state my frank and candid legal opinion on this question." He acknowl-edged Carter's authority as president to overrule him and added that this did not conflict with his view of an independent attorney general. "However," he argued, "the notion reflected in your staff's complaint that I should have given you the opportunity to direct what my legal opinion should be flies in the face of all that we have been trying to do since coming to Washington to rebuild the Department of Justice."[159] In the end, Bell chose not to resign because the issue was not that signifi-cant, and he knew that, in any event, the court would overturn the gov-ernment's position. Threat of resignation is a potent resource, but one that must be used carefully, he said. "You can't quit over nothing. It must be a big thing."[160]

In another instance, dealing with the affirmative action suit of Allan Bakke,[161] the attorney general also faced a confrontation with the White House. The Bakke case came to the Supreme Court just one month after Carter's inauguration. The federal government was not a party, so it chose to file an *amicus curiae* brief. Bell instructed his solicitor general and assistant attorney general for civil rights to develop the govern-ment's position. Their brief argued that the government would support affirmative action but oppose rigid quotas. This meant that Bakke, a white man claiming reverse discrimination, would have to be admitted to medical school. Bell took their draft to the president when he went to discuss the position they were developing. This was his greatest mistake, he wrote later, because the brief was then circulated to Eizenstat and Mondale, among others. Tension grew between affirmative action proponents and antiquota people. Bell wrote, "Nowhere is the tug of power between the White House and a Cabinet department more apparent than in a dispute between the Justice Department and the President's staff over what is law and what is policy." Bell felt pressure from Joseph Califano, secretary of Health, Education, and Welfare, and the Black Congressional Caucus, as well as the vice-president. Bell tried to keep the solicitor general insulated, although the solicitor general knew that the attorney general was under pressure from the White House.[162] Bell instructed the attorneys involved to "lock themselves in a room, write the brief, and finish it. . . . The final product was pretty much in line with the President's policy."[163] It argued that the facts were inadequate and the case should be returned to the lower court for further hearing. In the end, the Supreme Court ruled 5–4 along the lines that Justice had initially presented.[164]

A third battle between Justice and the White House dealt with another civil rights case, this one involving a Dallas police officer who had shot to death a 12-year-old boy named Santos Rodriguez in 1973 during questioning. Although the state court convicted the officer of murder with malice, the jury sentenced him to just five years in prison. The Hispanic community was outraged; Justice reviewed the case initially in 1973 but dropped it after the state court's conviction. Carter, traveling through Texas in 1978, saw photographs of the slain youth and was horrified. Through Press Secretary Jody Powell, he asked Bell to review the sensitive case. The attorney general decided against federal prosecution of the officer, because it might constitute double jeopardy. He believed that the state had rigorously pursued the case in the first trial.[165] Bell explained: "We ran the case through the process; it started in the civil rights division. They recommended against prosecuting. It came all the way up the line to me, and I didn't see any reason to change it. President Carter told me that he thought my decision was a disgrace. . . . So I said, well, Mr. President, you have your rights. Your right is to fire me. You can't tell me who to prosecute. You delegated the prosecutorial discretion to me. I have to exercise it. But you can get rid of me."[166] Although the president considered firing Bell, he did not. Instead he announced to the press that the prosecutorial discretion had to be left to the attorney general. He sent a handwritten note to Bell afterward saying, "The Rodriguez case was/is very embarrassing to me. I hope you made the right decision."[167]

The final incident centered on a small fish called the snail darter. As with the Bakke case, the underlying question for Bell was who determines what is law and what is policy. The attorney general phrased the debate this way: "Who speaks for the government in deciding the law—the attorney general and his 'independent' Justice Department or presidential assistants?"[168] The presidential assistants argued that the decision rightly rested in the White House because it was "a judgment of policy and not a judgment of law. The law is not settled or definitive at this time."[169]

The controversy began when the snail darter was declared an endangered species by the Interior Department in 1975, which meant that construction on the nearly completed multimillion-dollar Tellico Dam on the Little Tennessee River, which would destroy the fish's habitat, was stopped. Lower federal courts upheld the Interior Department's position and rejected the claim of the Tennessee Valley Authority, which was constructing the dam. Supporting the TVA's position, Attorney General Levi had appealed the lower court ruling to the Supreme Court. By the time the Court granted certiorari, the new administration had decided to switch the government's position. Carter, acting on advice from Eizenstat and White House Counsel Robert Lipshutz and with the backing of the Office of Management and Budget and the Council on Environmental Quality, instructed Bell to withdraw the government's appeal. Such an action would affirm the position of the Interior Department and reflect the administration's commitment to the Endangered Species Act.[170] Bell answered that he could not do so unless there was a change in the law or the facts. A reversal on any other grounds would damage his professional reputation.[171] In one memo to Carter, Bell outlined the problem: "A reversal of that position, coming at this juncture, would not but undermine the respect traditionally accorded the Department and the Office of the Solicitor General by the justices on the Court. Second, a reversal of position on the case would well be publicly perceived as the administration imposing its policy views on the Justice Department despite the Department's contrary judgment of the law."[172] The Office of Legal Counsel wrote the White House that the Supreme Court, as the final authority on matters of interpretation, should have the opportunity to review the case. "It is said here that TVA should withdraw its claim because there is a chance that the claim may be *upheld*. . . . In our judgment, the President should not accept such an argument. His duty is to see that the law is faithfully executed, whatever the law may be."[173] Carter initially instructed the Justice Department to switch sides against the TVA, an option supported by Lipshutz and several others, but this was two days before Carter read Bell's memo on the subject and well before he and Bell met.[174] When they did meet, Bell told him that he could not ethically change positions. Carter then "changed his mind and told me to stick with the original position."[175] In a modest compromise, Interior was permitted to file an appendix to the Justice Department *amicus* brief, giving its interpretation of previous judicial decisions.[176] The Court then ruled 6-3 in favor of Interior. The next year, Chief Justice Warren Burger told Bell that the TVA would win if the case was reargued. In 1979, Congress exempted the Tellico Dam from the act.[177]

The major foreign affairs crisis in the Carter years—the Iranian hostage crisis—occurred after Bell had left office, when Benjamin Civiletti was attorney general.[178] Even so, it is worth a cursory review because it further illustrates the attitude of the Carter White House toward the attorney general's participation in foreign affairs. Civiletti's participation in the long ordeal was more than that of Levi during *Mayaguez*. He attended daily briefings at the White House to discuss Iran. Early on, he outlined the various actions that could be taken regarding Iranian nationals in the United States,[179] and gave his legal opinion on the agreement for the release of the hostages.[180] Civiletti also sent a long memo to the president on the Iranian claims litigation.[181] The president did not always follow his attorney general's legal advice. When Iranian students wanted to stage a protest demonstration on federal property in the District of Columbia, Civiletti advised Carter that the federal government could not deny their constitutional rights of free speech and assembly.[182] Carter rejected the advice, arguing that such a demonstration could provoke a violent backlash, which could, in turn, provoke violence against the hostages. In his own words, Carter said he "became quite irritated when my legal advisers and some staff leaders came back repeatedly to argue. . . . After listening to the legal arguments two or three times, I finally directed that no one discuss it with me anymore, and that my orders be carried out without exception and without further delay." The federal courts later upheld his decision as a constitutional exercise of his authority.[183]

Carter used his attorney general more than Ford did, but this may be attributed to the differences between the crises. There was not only a major difference in duration, but also in the options open to each president, and this affected each man's choice of advisers. In the case of Iran, for example, the Carter administration employed economic and immigration sanctions that necessitated coordination with the Treasury and Justice departments. In contrast, Ford had few nonmilitary options available once diplomatic efforts failed to resolve the crisis. This lack of options may account for Ford's almost total reliance on national security advisers.

Even so, and consistent with what we have discovered of the Carter White House, the attorney general was not a pivotal adviser in the Advocate mode. He was not included in discussions concerning punitive action against Iran, the public warning of serious consequences, or the question of consulting Congress. Treasury Secretary Bill Miller was charged with researching the law on freezing Iranian assets.[184] Carter's primary legal adviser seems to have been White House Counsel Lloyd Cutler. While it is unclear if any legal advice was solicited in the five months of planning before the rescue attempt,[185] Cutler did advise Carter immediately afterward. He drafted a legal memo advising the president that his failure to consult Congress did not violate the War Powers Resolution.[186] He helped draft Carter's report to Congress describing the rescue effort.[187] And he reviewed testimony to be given by Acting Secretary of State Warren Christopher before the Senate Foreign Relations Committee.[188]

Carter kept his promise that legal questions would remain with the Department of Justice, but conflict arose over which areas were primarily legal and which were primarily policy. Bell grew increasingly critical of the meddling of the "White House power centers," and what he considered to be their special interest orientation, in particular the vice-president's office and the Domestic Policy Staff. These power centers contributed to the administration's difficulty in speaking with one voice, Bell said. After the May 1978 Camp David conference, they assumed even more power vis-à-vis the cabinet secretaries, and Bell feared that they would upset the system's checks and balances because they operated outside of the process of senatorial confirmation.[189]

Some evidence of the active role the White House sought to play in these legal/policy areas is evident in the files of the Civil Rights and Justice Cluster of the Domestic Policy Staff at the Carter presidential library. Wanting an opportunity to comment on Justice Department drafts to Congress, policy staff members tried to increase their lead time in receiving copies of testimony and proposed legislation. One aide complained, "On at least two occasions, . . . we did not receive advance copies of the testimony." Bell evidently took the position that he would give the material directly to the president, who could then decide if he wanted his policy staff to see it. The aide criticized Bell's direct method because it ignored questions of politics and cost.[190] The staff also seems to have felt that Justice "has become its own client and often ignores views of the agencies it represents, [and] that Justice often resolves interagency matters in a manner contrary to views of all the agencies without White House involvement."[191] Tension between the Domestic Policy Staff and Justice eventually led to a series of meetings. At one, the policy staff presented Justice Department assistants with an eight-point plan for improving relations. The following three points caused the greatest concern for Justice:

- There would be instances when the White House would be interested in individual cases because of their policy implications, . . . and we viewed that interest to be entirely legitimate. . . .
- Justice needs to be sensitive to the political ramifications of particular litigative decisions or policies even if it should not be bound by them.
- Justice has an obligation to identify underlying policy questions and to review legal approaches to them in the light of broad administration policy.[192]

According to a memo on that meeting, sent to Eizenstat to prepare him for an upcoming meeting with Bell, the Domestic Policy Staff hoped to present its case to the department assistants so that they could "soften up" the attorney general, who was known to dislike any hint of White House tampering.[193] Soon after, Eizenstat had lunch with Bell. He later wrote to Carter, "Judge Bell was concerned about insuring the integrity and independence of the Justice Department from political control." He added that they had successfully worked out guidelines to distinguish between cases where Justice needed complete freedom and those where the White House had a legitimate interest. Eizenstat and Bell agreed that Justice should be given complete freedom in deciding whether or not to prosecute a particular person. In civil cases in which the United States is a party, the White House should only be involved in the rare instances when major national policy is affected. In *amicus curiae* cases, as was *Bakke*, White House involvement is more appropriate, because such briefs constitute statements of administration policy.[194]

There was tension between the attorney general and the counsel to the president as well. While Bell occasionally had conflicts with Bob Lipshutz, the mild-mannered first counsel, they generally got along. Later he noted that "Bob was very easy to work with. But [even so] my role as attorney general was a good deal different from the role that he played."[195] Bell faced a greater challenge in dealing with Lloyd Cutler, the second counsel. "When Cutler left his Washington law firm to succeed Lipshutz in the job, the power of the counsel was unmistakable," Bell wrote. It became another power center contending with Justice over law and policy issues.[196]

While the White House counsel and department legal staffs can answer routine legal questions, it is the Office of Legal Counsel alone that provides "the real legal opinion, the true word," Bell said. A president or department head who ignores the OLC may make disastrous decisions. He cited the example of John Poindexter and Oliver North, who received a legal opinion in favor of their Iranian arms deal from the general counsel of the CIA, whom Bell described as "Casey's man." The former attorney general speculated in 1987: "I bet President Reagan wishes Poindexter and North had asked for a Department of Justice opinion. The President would be better off today; the country would be too. I was very surprised that not a single person on that [joint congressional] committee asked that question. They never seemed to pick up on the fact that just a simple thing like following procedures to get a legal opinion would have avoided that whole problem."[197]

There was a distinction, however, between administration contact for the purposes of consultation and that for the purposes of control. To guard against the latter, Bell in 1978 instituted guidelines to ensure that

White House communication would not influence the department's legal judgment. The policy insulated assistant attorneys general, U.S. attorneys, and the heads of the investigative agencies by requiring that all inquiries (especially those dealing with specific cases or investigations) from White House staff or Congress be directed to the attorney general, deputy attorney general, or associate attorney general. All requests for formal legal advice or opinions had to be directed to the attorney general or the OLC. When he announced the policy, Bell said he did not mean to imply that improper attempts were being made. "The policy is simply based on the fact that persons in certain positions of power unintentionally can exert pressure by the very nature of their positions."[198] In 1977, the OLC also produced a memo for Bell specifically examining the role of the solicitor general. The memo, written in response to the conflict between Carter's political and legal advisers during the *Bakke* case, reasserted the tradition of independence in the solicitor general's office.[199]

As is evident from his relations with the White House, Bell consciously and conscientiously pursued political neutrality. Yet as he himself noted, politics is not easily divorced from the attorney general's office, because of the great number of roles that the law officer must play, from serving as chief prosecutor of the nation to head of the FBI. In some of these roles he is more clearly the government's advocate, as when Bell brought a prior restraint suit against a Wisconsin newspaper that planned to publish information on the hydrogen bomb. "In this case I was an advocate for the government," he explained.[200] But other roles make different demands. For example, in prosecuting a criminal case involving espionage, he and his staff had to consider not simply national security and the demands of the agency involved, but also "the constitutional rights of the defendants and the ethical constraints imposed on [them] as lawyer[s]." At such times, the prosecutor is more than house counsel for the bureaucracy; he is an officer of the court and agent of the president in his constitutional task of taking care that the laws are faithfully executed.[201] Legal advice also cannot be divorced from policy. Legal opinions are sought to determine if the executive can carry out a particular policy. "Policy drives the legal opinions. You're asking questions of the law: can we do something?" Bell reasoned. Even so, Bell dismissed as cynical the suggestion that presidents only seek opinions that buttress their preexisting preferences. He cited Carter's genuine concern with legality when the OLC examined the issues relating to the Panama Canal Zone during the treaty negotiations.[202]

Bell does not agree that politically active people should be excluded from the Justice Department, although they should forgo political activity while in office. He argued that government would not work if it only accepted people "on the condition that they have led some kind of cloistered life, that they are absolutely broke, and that they can never have any kind of conflict of interest." In a view similar to that expressed by some senators during Levi's confirmation hearings, Bell added, "I think it might not be a bad thing to have an attorney general who knows something about courts and who knows something about politics and something about life and business."[203] It is the political process, after all, that makes government accountable. Without the safeguard provided by an elected head, a bureaucracy could become arrogant and elitist. A totally independent Department of Justice might arbitrarily ignore presidential orders, "confident in its power and independence." The president, Bell concluded, might then lose control.[204] The danger Bell sees in the ascendance of independence over political loyalty, a defining feature of the Neutral type, and the alternative danger in the Advocate's emphasis on politics, will be examined in the final chapter of this study.

Chapter Six

In Conclusion

This study has established a rudimentary typology for understanding the structural tensions in the attorney general's role as adviser to the president. It is appropriate in a concluding chapter to consider the normative aspects of the typology, specifically addressing the advantages and disadvantages of each model. There is a temptation to apply these ideal types in such a way that a president or Senate can identify a "best" type of attorney general. But the reality is much more complex.

Certain normative conclusions are easily drawn. Attorneys general should not engage in illegal, unethical, or partisan activity while in office. Violating the law—or the appearance of doing so—is a gross abuse of the public trust; Palmer, Daugherty, and Mitchell acted well outside the realm of permissible behavior, and Meese seems to have behaved in ways that undermine the credibility of the office. Also inappropriate is blatant partisan activity in office, because of the threat to public confidence in an impartial system of justice. Few would defend Mitchell's involvement in Nixon's reelection campaign while he still administered the Justice Department, even had there been no illegality.[1] But once these areas are identified and disavowed, the normative task becomes more complex. The proper political role an attorney general should assume in the normal course of making decisions is much more difficult to judge.

The prevailing attitude in post-Watergate Washington has been a suspicion of attorneys general with partisan backgrounds or long associations with their chief executives, two primary attributes of the Advocate model. The Neutral, with its emphasis on procedures over substantive ends, has been promoted, while the Advocate, with its

166

goal-oriented view of the law, is suspected of manipulating means in pursuit of ends. The popular belief is that, even if such manipulation does not exceed legal limits, it sets a dangerous tone. Navasky suggests this in his argument that "a number of the worst transgressions of the Nixon Administration find their lineage in the unwisdom of prior Administrations." The plumbers unit could be the heir of Robert Kennedy's Get Hoffa squad; and the break-in at Daniel Ellsberg's psychiatrist's office was justified on the same national security grounds as the wiretapping of Martin Luther King, Jr.[2] Navasky apparently underwent something of a conversion between 1971, when he wrote the panegyric *Kennedy Justice*, and 1974, when he wrote "The Politics of Justice." In the earlier book, he wrote that "ultimately, the test of any Cabinet officer . . . is his ability to win the confidence of and exert influence on the President."[3] This view gives clear preference to the Advocate model. Three years later he seemed to call for Neutral characteristics when he explained:

> The most effective Attorney General in terms of getting things done is certainly one like Robert Kennedy or John Mitchell who has the President's confidence, can speak for him, and commit his prestige to Justice Department programs. But the most effective Attorney General in terms of preserving the processes of justice, the one least likely to get the department in trouble—not because of bureaucratic timidity but because he puts means up there ahead of ends—may well be the one with some distance from the President.[4]

Navasky has joined a chorus of scholars, legislators, attorneys, and former incumbents who characterize the Neutral as more legitimate than the Advocate. The report of the Watergate special prosecution force in 1975 reflects the widely held view that the attorney general should be apolitical and independent of the White House:

> The President should not nominate and the Senate should not confirm as Attorney General, or as any other appointee in high Department of Justice posts, a person who has served as the President's campaign manager or in a similar high level campaign role. A campaign manager seeks support for his candidate and necessarily incurs obligations to political leaders and other individuals. . . . The

Attorney General and other Justice Department appointees should be lawyers with their own reputations in the legal profession, with capacity and willingness to make independent judgments, and with the authority to choose similarly qualified persons for subordinate positions.[5]

One former Justice attorney wrote that, "whatever the value of the once-sought-after attribute of 'political pragmatism' in a nominee for high office, it has no place in the Department of Justice." He questioned the whole notion that Justice "should be run by lawyers who march to a drumbeat emanating from the White House. This leads to political posturing, political decisions, the sapping of strength and vitality from the career attorneys in the department and the eventual erosion of public confidence in the even-handed administration of law."[6] This view enjoyed particular popularity in the mid 1970s, in the aftershock of Watergate. The selection of Levi and Bell in the ensuing years is testament to the entrenched suspicion of politicized appointees. But once a decent interval elapses, the Advocate again becomes the model of choice.

With the nomination of Edwin Meese, who clearly embodied Advocate traits, the suspicion reemerged. Questions concerning his independent judgment and his loyalty to Reagan peppered his confirmation hearings, raised by such senators as Dennis De Concini, Joseph Biden, Charles Mathias, and Charles Grassley. De Concini (D.-Ariz.), for example, commented that the attorney general "though nominated and appointed by the Chief Executive, must act independently of his particular political concerns."[7] Nevertheless, despite the delay brought by a special prosecutor's probe, Meese was confirmed. But his subsequent actions in office rekindled the old issues, making relevant again the debate about politics in the Department of Justice.

Calls to depoliticize the attorney general's office and the Department of Justice have brought a number of proposals through the past twenty years, particularly during the 1974 Senate hearings on "Removing Politics from the Administration of Justice." Former Supreme Court Associate Justice Arthur Goldberg testified that the attributes of eminence, independence, and courage were needed in law officers, the ability "of saying to a President, no, the law does not permit this; I will not permit this; and you must not engage in activities such as have been contemplated." The bar itself is independent, he added, "it is not a servant of a client, but services a client; . . . men and women of the bar are independent and give counsel and advise independently. The principle law enforcement officers of the Government should be lawyers in that sense, and not organization men, even if the organization is the President." He suggested that attorneys general be prohibited from providing advice on private affairs, campaign efforts, or other political matters.[8] Joining in the call for reform was Archibald Cox, the special prosecutor who had been fired in the 1973 Saturday Night Massacre. Cox told senators that partisan politics had no place in the Justice Department. Not only should attorneys general not be chosen because of their work in political campaigns, but they should not have any party or political role once in office or assume such a role immediately after leaving office. "The country would be very well served if we could establish a solid tradition that attorneys general would not be appointed from such a background."[9]

Congress responded to these sentiments. In 1977, Sen. Lloyd Bentsen (D.-Tex.) attached an amendment to the Ethics in Government Act that would have excluded anyone "who had served as a high-level campaign adviser to the President" from being appointed attorney general or deputy attorney general. It passed the Senate but was deleted from the bill in the conference committee.[10]

Many reformers see the problem in terms of institutional arrangement and not the background or activities of individual law officers. As early as 1924, during the Senate investigation of Harry Daugherty, institutional changes were suggested to depoliticize the department. Sen. Burton Wheeler asked if the Department of Justice should be taken out of politics, "because of the fact that the Department of Justice is the one department in the Government of the United States that ought to enforce the law impartially, regardless of any political affiliation?" John Crim, special assistant to the attorney general, responded affirmatively and suggested the creation of an assistant attorney general to handle all criminal work, and another to handle civil, thus removing the attorney general from immediate control of federal prosecution.[11] These offices were soon created. Since then, many other proposals have followed, seeking to redress what Whitney North Seymour calls "a fundamental flaw in the original conception of the Department of Justice." He argues that the competing demands of law and politics on an attorney general will remain a problem "unless and until that flaw is corrected."[12] One proposal he offers is to divide the functions between two offices: an attorney general cum presidential adviser, and a chief prosecutor. The system would resemble those in Britain and Sweden.[13] Another writer proposes that the Hatch Act be amended to include the attorney general and his top assistants, and that civil service status be extended to all U.S. attorneys and marshals. In addition, Justice should be removed from any role in selecting the federal judiciary, since the attorney general, as chief prosecutor, should not be in a position to name the judges before whom his department will appear.[14] These are some of the recommendations that have been made to address the institutional aspects of the problem.

A third effort to depoliticize Justice, to insulate it from overt political pressures, was instituted during Griffin Bell's term in office through internal departmental policy. Consciously seeking to protect his department from what he considered to be inappropriate meddling from White House power centers, he worked out guidelines to help delineate those areas where Justice alone should make the litigation decisions. He also set up a system to monitor White House contacts with Justice attorneys.[15] And, through an Office of Legal Counsel memorandum, he reiterated the importance of independence for the solicitor general.[16]

But these approaches to reform, particularly the internal and institutional proposals, have limits to resolving the tension in the attorney general's office. Bell's internal guidelines, for example, did not last long in the Reagan Justice Department. An attorney general who chooses to can serve as a buffer between political actors on the one hand and his departmental attorneys on the other. But if the attorney general shares the policy agenda of the administration, as did William French Smith and Edwin Meese, for example, he may become an amplifier of the White House rather than a buffer.

Regarding institutional change, many who have studied the problem of abuse argue that it will not make the office incorruptible. The malfeasance of a few individuals would exist despite proposed changes. Charles Cooper, former head of the OLC, believes that constitutional and legislative arrangements cannot protect the American people from an individual who wants to abuse power.[17] Further, altering the existing structure could pose hazards of its own, especially in terms of accountability if the law officer is removed from the political world. A chief prosecutor who is autonomous of the president and thus of the people could amass vast prosecutorial powers. Former Attorney General William Saxbe warned that removing politics and political party responsibility would leave an unchecked bureaucratic system of justice.[18] Sen. Roman Hruska speculated that such a system of justice could operate in a tyrannical way, because the bureaucrat is not "dependent upon the good will of the people," as is a political appointee whose administration must face voters every four years.[19] The president also must be held accountable for his constitutional duty to "take care that the laws are faithfully executed." The attorney general only serves as his agent in fulfilling this obligation; for the president to be accountable, he must have the authority. The responsibility of an appointed attorney general to an elected chief executive is fundamental to our concept of democratic government. "To make the Department totally 'independent' would be to put it under the total control of the Attorney General and thus render it unresponsive to the public will as that will is reflected by the President," noted Elliot Richardson.[20]

If internal restraints are insufficient and institutional reforms entail too many costs, then the only genuine safeguard may be in selecting people of integrity and ability to the office of attorney general. Political scientist Thomas Cronin, stressing the importance of the individual, assigns 90 percent of the blame for abuse to the incumbent and 10 percent to the office.[21] Theodore Sorensen also has argued that the underlying causes of misconduct are personal, not institutional: "An attorney general of the caliber of Francis Biddle or Elliot Richardson who recognizes that he is an officer of the court as well as a member of the Cabinet, and that his client is the Nation as well as the President, will have sufficient fidelity to both his professional and his public obligations to resist improper White House intrusion without any change in the existing statutory or institutional arrangement."[22] Ford's attorney general, Edward Levi, believed that the primary method of insulating Justice personnel from improper conduct was "their own moral conscience and the collective morality of the Department of Justice." Levi also recommended additional statutory safeguards, such as the office of a special prosecutor available on an ad hoc basis.[23] Confirmation hearings should focus, then, on the caliber of the nominee, with a recognition that higher expectations of performance and independence are justified because of the nature of the office.

This conception of abuse, that it stems primarily from the character of the individual attorney general, makes the normative question of which model is preferable seem even more salient. The comments of post-Watergate reformers reflect the view that many people continue to hold: that if the office cannot be depoliticized, then the law officer himself should be nonpolitical. Advocacy traits and abuse of the office have been so linked in the public mind that the Neutral law officer appears to be the only legitimate choice for a president to make. But this conclusion, tempting because of its simplicity, is premised on certain misunderstandings.

First of all, the Advocate does not by definition abuse his office. In fact, many of the law officers who are rated the highest by legal historians and attorneys have been the closest—politically and personally—to the person in the Oval Office. Herbert Brownell and Robert Kennedy are often on such lists, credited with running "very good offices with efficiency and decency." Caleb Cushing in the nineteenth century and Robert Jackson in the early twentieth also are considered excellent attorneys general.[24] While some may be perceived as embroiled in politics, the average Advocate does not seem to continue his party/political activity while in office. Kennedy, for example, avoided politicking during his tenure and required his staff to do so as well.[25]

The Advocate type has resurfaced in part because it has certain advantages. If the Neutral is able to inspire public trust, the Advocate engenders presidential trust. A close relationship between president and law officer may be essential when an administration is developing policies in the justice area, especially in such a sensitive field as civil rights. As an example, Harold Tyler, while an assistant attorney general of the civil rights division in 1960, recounted a telephone call from President Eisenhower supporting his division's efforts to enforce school desegregation in New Orleans. Brownell was then attorney general. "It seems to me unlikely that a President would be able or willing to do this if he did not have a close political tie with his Attorney General and the Department of Justice."[26] Cooper of the OLC notes the benefits of a longstanding close relationship between president and attorney general. "A president trusts the attorney general's judgments more, and knows it is intellectually honest advice, that he is not simply telling the president what he wants to hear."[27] A Neutral in office risks being bypassed altogether in administration policy-making if he is not trusted to share the president's view.

Presidents generally prefer Advocate officers, and there is long-standing consensus that presidents are entitled to the advisers of their choice. A president usually selects a law officer who is "most likely to hold views consistent with those forming the basis for the President's election."[28] Federal courts recognized that a president has a right to his choice in a 1963 case that upheld the Kennedy administration's right to replace a subordinate assistant attorney general from the Eisenhower years.[29] The Senate also defers to this convention, rarely rejecting a Cabinet nominee. Senator Hruska explained why during the confirmation hearings of Edward Levi: "It was for the President to appoint, and if the person had certain basic and fundamental attributes of honesty and integrity and good faith and good will and loyalty to the country and had the confidence of the President, the President was entitled to the approval of the candidate."[30]

A political career may even be something of an advantage to an attorney general. It could provide him with an outside base of support that would permit him to act more independently than a nonconnected Neutral. In their study of protest resignations, Edward Weisband and Thomas Franck found that advisers who have their own political clout are able to check presidential discretion more effectively. They write that most of the few officials "who have braved the sanctions against quitting the cabinet and going public have . . . been scrappy politicians. Historically, it is the politician who has the training, will, motive, and innate courage to speak up . . . , persons with roots in their own political turf."[31] An attorney general with a base of support separate from the president may be able to stand his ground by threatening resignation. As Elliot Richardson discovered during his trying five months in the office, an attorney general is not without options, which range from attempting to dissuade the president to resigning.[32] A politically astute attorney general, moreover, may be more sensitive to public opinion, aware of how his actions will appear to his constituents, and therefore less inclined to engage in questionable activity. One critic of Watergate wrote, "The fact of the matter is a lot of the problems [Nixon's] Administration had with its appointees is that they weren't public men. They didn't understand the requirements of public morality. One of Mitchell's failings was he didn't care what people said about him."[33]

Perhaps the most significant point to weigh in assessing the characteristics of attorneys general is the relationship between law and politics in the American political system. As Homer Cummings speculated more than fifty years ago, "Law and government are probably thought of too much as if they were opposites or as if the body social had two organs, one political and one legal." Instead, administration "is both law and government in action."[34] Perhaps for this reason, the depoliticization of the attorney generalship may not be possible; in no other office are law and politics so entwined. The notion that they can be severed is erroneous, and every incumbent experiences the symbiotic relationship between the two. Ronald Dworkin, writing about the American judiciary, posits that "law is a political enterprise" and that legal philosophy includes some "substantive claims about social goals and principles of justice." Dworkin defends the political nature of legal interpretation: "Reliance on political theory is not a corruption of interpretation but part of what interpretation means."[35] The choice of a legal philosophy is itself political.

Also, an attorney general is not needed to address legal questions that are clearly black and white. The issues he examines seldom have just one conceivable interpretation; they admit to diverse viewpoints on which lawyers might honestly disagree. Referring to a similar phenomenon in the courts, H. L. A. Hart found that there is no discoverable "right" way to interpret a law. "In the vast majority of cases that trouble the courts, neither statutes nor precedents . . . allow of only one result. . . . All rules have a penumbra of uncertainty where the judge must choose between alternatives."[36] The process of choosing—for either judge or attorney general—necessarily involves some notion of substantive good. This holds true of the Neutral officer as well, although he may not be conscious of making substantive choices and may—perhaps unintentionally—cloak his underlying values. In fact, as mentioned in chapter five, even his procedural decisions are not value neutral. They too involve political choice, even if it is a reaffirmation of the status quo.

In sum, no attorney general can act with total political neutrality. While a Neutral law officer may avoid overt political decisions, he still must engage in setting departmental priorities, drafting and promoting relevant legislation, and giving legal advice in murky areas of statutory and constitutional law. Political choices are inherent in most of the decisions he must make, especially "when one considers that many of the legal assignments of the Attorney General and the Department have broad national policy and political aspects."[37] There are occasions when policy direction from the president is essential, when there are solid legal arguments on both sides of an issue and the president must decide. Archibald Cox, in rejecting the idea that Justice should be independent of the White House, has argued, "The close relationship between law and policy, and between the Attorney General as lawyer and the President as client, make it unwise, if not impossible, to give independent status to the Attorney General and the Department of Justice."[38] Among the issues considered legitimately subject to policy direction are civil rights, antitrust, and internal security laws, according to the head of the civil rights division from 1961 to 1965, Burke Marshall.

> It seems right, not wrong, to me that an administration give policy direction on such matters as busing, employment quotas, school district consolidations, and private discrimination . . . as much as I disagree with the policy established by the present administration in most of these areas. . . . It seems to me that under our political system, Presidential candidates are entitled to run and, more important, the Nation's voters are entitled to vote for candidates on the basis of such issues.[39]

This democratic argument was used by William Rehnquist as well, when he was a member of the Mitchell Justice Department. Defending the change in the department's priorities under Nixon, he wrote, "If the two-party system in this country is to offer the voters any real choice between programs, it is surely not unreasonable to expect that there will be some changes in administration policy when a President of one party succeeds a President of another."[40] Richardson also notes the legitimacy of the party process, adding that "the more we 'purify' government by insulating it from the people who make the two-party system work and maintain its strength, the harder it becomes for any chief executive to accomplish the changes of policy which he was elected to carry out."[41]

Politics is an inescapable element in any attorney general's tenure, beginning with his nomination. Presidents and congressmen are well aware of the political repercussions inherent in the selection of either model. The Advocate is the choice not simply of presidents—who could be expected to seek advisers with whom they share political sympathies—but also of members of Congress of the president's party. A congressman's preference for an Advocate or a Neutral seems to depend largely on which party controls the White House. Opposition party members lament the politicization of the department when an Advocate is named. Their concern is that he will use the office to promote the president's policy agenda. Congressmen of the president's party then assert his right to have an adviser he trusts. They, of course, would like to see the implementation of that agenda. An illustration of the shifting positions of congressmen may be found in Meese's nomination battle in 1984. Some Republican senators who had opposed Griffin Bell's nomination six years earlier—because he was too close to the president—suddenly discovered that trait did not automatically disqualify a nominee. Some Democrats who frowned on Meese's intimacy with Reagan were reminded of their arguments in support of Bell. For example, both Robert Dole and Paul Laxalt, Republican senators, reminded Democratic colleagues of Bell's close relationship to Jimmy Carter. Dole, who did not support Bell because of this relationship, recanted that decision and argued against the notion that "a nominee for Attorney General [who] has had a personal and political relationship with a President . . . constitutes a sufficient basis for opposing confirmation." He then quoted a remark by Edward Kennedy during Bell's hearings that a president should have latitude in choosing his cabinet.[42] The political effects of an appointment sometimes preoccupy both sides in a confirmation hearing, despite the rhetoric with which they clothe these concerns. They practice what Dworkin accused conservative lawyers of doing in adopting the doctrine of original intent: hiding "the role their political convictions played in their choice"[43] of an ideal type.

The normative debate is incomplete without an exploration of an overarching principle embodied in each type. The typology attributes to the Neutral a primary commitment to rule of law and to the Advocate a primary commitment to majoritarian rule. Such a distinction is useful in terms of characterizing the underlying loyalty expressed by each. But it may be a distortion as well. First of all, such commitments are a matter of emphasis only; neither type rejects outright the other value. Secondly, the distinction is not totally accurate. In regard to majority rule, for example, the Neutral may appear less committed because he is not as responsive to the agenda of an elected chief executive. But in fact the practical effect of his neutrality may be to increase congressional impact on policy at the expense of the executive branch. After all, Congress creates the general procedures that the Neutral seeks to follow. By pursuing procedure over substance, the Neutral may shift power away from the executive branch toward the legislative. In this way, the majoritarian principle is respected by the Neutral.

The Advocate law officer in contrast fulfills the majoritarian principle as it is embodied in the president. Because of his emphasis on substantive values, the Advocate may be perceived by Congress as a threat to its participation in policy-making, especially if it is dominated by the opposition political party. One even might argue that the Neutral serves the majoritarian principle better than the Advocate by acceding to the legislature's substantive ends. Legal scholar David Lyons argues that the responsibility for choosing substantive end values belongs with legislators, not administrators. A well-designed law, from a legislative viewpoint, is one that requires little reference to end values when it is administered. "An official who is charged with applying the criminal law should generally be preoccupied with fidelity to its rules and should not attempt to deal with cases by seeking to serve the values that the rules are designed to serve." He adds that "officials who apply the rules must generally take care not to confuse their roles with that of the legislator."[44] Deciding which branch has a singular responsibility for end values is subject to much debate and will not be addressed here. However, there are some who believe that the executive branch may have usurped a legislative role, and this belief may have an impact on which type of attorney general seems preferable.

An analysis of the rule of law, the defining principle of the Neutral, also is instructive. F. A. Hayek defines rule of law as the state where "government in all its actions is bound by rules fixed and announced beforehand."[45] Government itself must be under the law. This principle permits us to predict government sanctions and to plan our futures accordingly. The more a law conforms to rule of law, the better it is able to guide human behavior; laws without rule of law cannot serve this basic purpose. Rule of law, then, is essential if we are to have a "stable and secure framework" for our lives, scholar Joseph Raz writes.[46] More than any other officer in the executive branch, the attorney general is responsible for ensuring adherence to rule of law. Legislators and judges also must respect certain set principles in writing and reviewing laws, but the attorney general has a special duty to see that the administration of the law is not perverted.[47] Yet with so much left to the law officer's discretion, it is unclear what mechanisms are in place to ensure that this principle is served. On the whole, Neutral attorneys general have exhibited a greater sensitivity to the requirements of rule of law in exercising their discretion than have Advocates, although some Advocates also have recognized the importance of the principle. Others, such as Palmer and Mitchell, have shown a marked indifference that has damaged rule of law in their administrations and consequently has shaken public confidence.

Rule of law, however, is not the only value of a legal system. It does not guarantee good law or justice, nor is it synonymous with democracy, equality, human rights, or respect for human dignity. In fact, as Raz notes, complete conformity is not only impossible, given the inescapable vagueness of legislation, but it is also undesirable. Limited administrative discretion is needed to adjust to the unique circumstances of each case.[48] A balance between rule of law and other competing values is both preferable and unavoidable in our political and judicial systems. Samuel Beer writes, "We have constitutionalism and we also have personalism, meaning by this the existence of wide opportunities for judgments which do not follow strictly from existing rules, but which serve justice by considering exceptional circumstances."[49]

Rule of law and the majoritarian principle are not mutually exclusive. Much of the time they operate in tandem, and an attorney general feels little conflict between the two ideals. The majority passed the laws that he executes. However, a tension can surface between the two principles. "Where laws are passed at the instance of a small group or where public sentiment changes, executive officers of the law are placed in the uncomfortable predicament of choosing between the law which they are sworn to execute and the democracy which they serve."[50] In a sense, the attorney general personifies the system's oscillation between rule of law and rule of man. His ideal characteristics, then, would accommodate the demands of both principles. Normatively, the Advocate model seems to be the better choice under ordinary circumstances. He has the necessary attribute of presidential trust; without that, an attorney general risks being ignored by a president who looks increasingly to his internal White House counsel for legal guidance. The Advocate's own previous political activity may give him a power base outside of the administration and sensitize him to the importance of appearances and public opinion. His political qualities should not disqualify him from the top law office, but, given recent experience, the burden of proof may be on him to convince senators at his confirmation hearings that he is capable of exercising independent judgment.

But the office does place special demands on the incumbent, and to satisfy those demands, the attorney general must exhibit a genuine commitment to the rule of law and understand his obligation to it. His Advocate features must be tempered with this important Neutral trait. Although difficult to find in everyday life, these combined Advocate/ Neutral qualities are not mutually exclusive. They represent the ideal to- ward which we should move in selecting future attorneys general. Other traits, such as administrative and public relations skills, may be beneficial if an attorney general is to successfully manage his depart- ment. They are not, however, part of our concern here. Griffin Bell makes a persuasive case for one final attribute that is worth mentioning: courage, in dealing with Congress as well as the president. An attorney general should be "an ethical lawyer and a person with backbone who will stand up and do what is right."[51] This type of person may be either an Advocate or a Neutral.

The qualities we should expect of an attorney general are strict when compared with those of other executive officers. But these expec- tations are justified because of the unique role that the attorney general plays in uniting the legal and political aspects of government. An officer of the court as well as an executive officer, he may be, as some have sug- gested, "the keeper of the executive conscience."[52] That is no small re- sponsibility.

Appendix

United States Attorneys General

Attorney General	State	Term	President
Edmund Randolph	Va.	1790–1794	Washington
William Bradford	Pa.	1794–1795	Washington
Charles Lee	Va.	1795–1801	Washington/Adams
Levi Lincoln	Mass.	1801–1805	Jefferson
John Breckenridge	Ky.	1805–1806	Jefferson
Ceasar Rodney	Del.	1807–1811	Jefferson/Madison
William Pinkney	Md.	1811–1814	Madison
Richard Rush	Pa.	1814–1817	Madison
William Wirt	Va.	1817–1829	Monroe/Adams
John Berrien	Ga.	1829–1831	Jackson
Roger Taney	Md.	1831–1833	Jackson
Benjamin Butler	N.Y.	1833–1838	Jackson/Van Buren
Felix Grundy	Tenn.	1838–1839	Van Buren
Henry Gilpin	Pa.	1840–1841	Van Buren
John Crittenden	Ky.	1841	Harrison/Tyler
Hugh Legare	S.C.	1841–1843	Tyler
John Nelson	Md.	1843–1845	Tyler
John Mason	Va.	1845–1846	Polk
Nathan Clifford	Maine	1846–1848	Polk
Isaac Toucey	Conn.	1848–1849	Polk
Reverdy Johnson	Md.	1849–1850	Taylor
John Crittenden	Ky.	1850–1853	Fillmore
Caleb Cushing	Mass.	1853–1857	Pierce
Jeremiah Black	Pa.	1857–1860	Buchanan
Edwin Stanton	Ohio	1860–1861	Buchanan
Edward Bates	Mo.	1861–1864	Lincoln
James Speed	Ky.	1864–1866	Lincoln/Johnson
Henry Stanberry	Ohio	1866–1868	Johnson
William Evarts	N.Y.	1868–1869	Johnson
Ebenezer Hoar	Mass.	1869–1870	Grant
Amos Akerman	Ga.	1870–1872	Grant

181

Attorney General	State	Term	President
George Williams	Oreg.	1872–1875	Grant
Edwards Pierrepont	N.Y.	1875–1876	Grant
Alphonso Taft	Ohio	1876–1877	Grant
Charles Devens	Mass.	1877–1881	Hayes
Wayne MacVeagh	Pa.	1881	Garfield
Benjamin Brewster	Pa.	1881–1885	Arthur
Augustus Garland	Ark.	1885–1889	Cleveland
William Miller	Ind.	1889–1893	Harrison
Richard Olney	Mass.	1893–1895	Cleveland
Judson Harmon	Ohio	1895–1897	Cleveland
Joseph McKenna	Calif.	1897–1898	McKinley
John Griggs	N.J.	1898–1901	McKinley
Philander Knox	Pa.	1901–1904	McKinley
William Moody	Mass.	1904–1906	Roosevelt
Charles Bonaparte	Md.	1906–1909	Roosevelt
George Wickersham	N.Y.	1909–1913	Taft
James McReynolds	Tenn.	1913–1914	Wilson
Thomas Gregory	Tex.	1914–1919	Wilson
A. Mitchell Palmer	Pa.	1919–1921	Wilson
Harry Daugherty	Ohio	1921–1924	Harding
Harlan F. Stone	N.Y.	1924–1925	Coolidge
John Sargent	Vt.	1925–1929	Coolidge
William Mitchell	Minn.	1929–1933	Hoover
Homer Cummings	Conn.	1933–1939	Roosevelt
Frank Murphy	Mich.	1939–1940	Roosevelt
Robert Jackson	N.Y.	1940–1941	Roosevelt
Francis Biddle	Pa.	1941–1945	Roosevelt
Tom Clark	Tex.	1945–1949	Truman
Howard McGrath	R.I.	1949–1952	Truman
James McGranery	Pa.	1952–1953	Truman
Herbert Brownell	N.Y.	1953–1957	Eisenhower
William Rogers	Md.	1957–1961	Eisenhower
Robert Kennedy	Mass.	1961–1964	Kennedy/Johnson
Nicholas Katzenbach	Ill.	1965–1966	Johnson
Ramsey Clark	Tex.	1967–1969	Johnson
John Mitchell	N.Y.	1969–1972	Nixon
Richard Kleindienst	Ariz.	1972–1973	Nixon
Elliot Richardson	Mass.	1973	Nixon
William Saxbe	Ohio	1974–1975	Nixon
Edward Levi	Ill.	1975–1977	Ford
Griffin Bell	Ga.	1977–1980	Carter
Benjamin Civiletti	Md.	1980–1981	Carter
William French Smith	Calif.	1981–1985	Reagan
Edwin Meese	Calif.	1985–1988	Reagan
Richard Thornburgh	Pa.	1988–1991	Reagan/Bush

Notes

Chapter One. The Attorney General of the United States

1. As of 1991. There have been seventy-six appointments though, because John J. Crittenden of Kentucky was appointed twice—in 1841 and again in 1850. In eight other cases (at least), an attorney general served in two consecutive administrations.

2. The Department of Justice is composed of the offices of the attorney general, deputy attorney general, associate attorney general, the solicitor general, the Office of Legal Counsel, the six legal divisions of the department (Tax, Civil, Antitrust, Criminal, Civil Rights, and Land and Natural Resources), and the offices of the ninety-five U.S. attorneys around the country. In addition, the attorney general oversees the Federal Bureau of Investigation, the Drug Enforcement Administration, the Bureau of Prisons, the Immigration and Naturalization Service, the Community Relations Service, the U.S. marshals, and another nine boards, commissions, and offices. Daniel J. Meador, *The President, the Attorney General, and the Department of Justice* (White Burkett Miller Center of Public Affairs, Charlottesville: University of Virginia, 1980), 15–24.

3. Judiciary Act of 1789, 1 Stat. 73, Section 35.

4. Even ordinary attorneys-at-law are considered officers of the court with public as well as private obligations. Among the many cases defining this are *State v. Babin*, 50 So.825, 826, 124 La. 1005, 18 Ann. Cas. 837; In re Holland's Estate, 97 N.Y.S. 202, 203, 110 App. Div. 799; *Langen v. Borkowski*, 206 N.W. 181, 190, 188 Wis. 277, 43 A.L.R. 622; *City of Pittsburgh v. O'Brien*, 86 A. 651, 652, 239 Pa. 60; *Schlitz v. Meyer*, 21 N.W. 243, 244, 61 Wis. 418; In re Mains, 80 N.W. 714, 716, 121 Mich. 603; *State v. Holding*, S.C. 1 McCord, 379, 380. For further listings, see *Words and Phrases*, Vol. 4A (St. Paul, Minn.: West Publishing Co., 1969), 528–529.

5. Meador, *The President, the Attorney General*, 26.

6. Ibid., 26–27.

7. Robert Palmer, "The Confrontation of the Legislative and Executive Branches: An Examination of the Constitutional Balance of Powers and the Role of the Attorney General," *Pepperdine Law Review* 11 (Jan. 1984): 349.

8. Whitney North Seymour, Jr., *United States Attorney: An Inside View of "Justice" in America under the Nixon Administration* (New York: William Morrow & Co., 1975), 228–229. While a U.S. attorney, Seymour experienced the conflict firsthand as two attorneys general under whom he served were convicted of serious crimes. "To me fell the unpleasant duty of supervising the investigation and indictment of one of those attorneys general for perjury and conspiracy to obstruct justice" (p. 11).

9. Sorensen testimony, U.S. Congress, Senate, *Hearings on S. 2803 and S. 2978 before the Subcommittee on the Separation of Powers of the Senate Committee on the Judiciary on Removing Politics from the Administration of Justice*, 93d Cong., 2d sess. (Washington, D.C.: Government Printing Office, 1974), 26.

10. Byrd comments, Senate Judiciary Committee, *Hearings on the Nomination of Edward H. Levi to Be Attorney General*, 94th Cong., 1st sess. (Washington, D.C.: Government Printing Office, 1975), 21. Byrd said during Levi's confirmation hearings that attorneys general have a "dual capacity as appointees of the President and part of an elected administration team, on the one hand, and prosecutors bound to investigate crimes . . . in the executive branch, on the other."

11. Maeva Marcus, *Truman and the Steel Seizure Case: The Limits of Presidential Power* (New York: Columbia University Press, 1977), 187.

12. Levi testimony, *Hearings on the Nomination of Edward H. Levi*, 39.

13. Edward Bates, quoted by Arthur S. Miller, "Justice without Politics," *Progressive* (Apr. 1974).

14. Homer Cummings and Carl McFarland, *Federal Justice: Chapters in the History of Justice and the Federal Executive* (New York: Macmillan, 1937), 204.

15. Bates argued from these grounds when the cabinet considered the provisioning of Fort Sumter and the handling of the *Trent* affair with Great Britain. Frederic Bancroft, *The Life of William H. Seward*, (New York: Harper & Bros., 1900), 2: 105–106, 235–236.

16. Cummings and McFarland, *Federal Justice*, 189–191. Taney did write an opinion on the illegality of the suspension and sent it to Lincoln, *Ex parte Merryman*.

17. 10 Opinions of the Attorney General 74–92 (5 July 1861) (the official published opinions, hereafter referred to as OAG). Bates argued that the president has the lawful discretionary power to arrest and hold persons who deal with insurgents (on probable cause), in a "time of great and dangerous insurrection." His duty to "preserve, protect, and defend" the Constitution exceeds that of other officials who are sworn only to "support" it. The president also may refuse to obey a writ of habeas corpus issued by a judge because their branches are coequal; the president cannot be forced to submit to the judge's judgment. The relevant part of the Constitution reads: "The privilege of the writ of habeas corpus shall not be suspended, unless when in cases of rebellion or invasion the public safety may require it" (Article I, Sec. 9(2)). While situated in the article dealing with Congress, the provision contains no explicit reference to either president or Congress, and Bates's interpretation is not without defenders.

18. Corwin notes their similarity also. See Edward S. Corwin, *The Presi-*

dent: Office and Powers 1787–1957, 4th ed. (New York: New York University Press, 1957), 145.

19. Alexis de Tocqueville, *Democracy in America*, ed. J. P. Mayer (Garden City, N.Y.: Anchor Books, 1969), 269–270.

20. Cummings and McFarland, *Federal Justice*, 511. For a related discussion, see Robert Toepfer, "Some Legal Aspects of the Duty of the Attorney General to Advise," *University of Cincinnati Law Review* 19 (1950): 201–202.

21. An attorney general's opinion differs from a court ruling in that it may deal with broader legal issues and interrelationships, at least when rendered at a presidential request. Opinions may be rendered in a variety of ways to many people, formally and informally. Peter E. Heiser, Jr., "The Opinion Writing Function of Attorneys General," *Idaho Law Review* 18 (Winter 1982): 9, 41. Furthermore, they are issued before the event, rather than *ex post facto*. David R. Deener, *The United States Attorneys General and International Law* (The Hague: Martinus Nijhoff, 1957), 70–71. There also is a distinction between an opinion and a brief. The former is prepared by an attorney for a client, embodying his understanding of the law as it applies to a given set of facts. The latter is prepared by an attorney arguing a case in court and includes an "argument of how the law applies to the facts supporting counsel's position." Henry Campbell Black, *Black's Law Dictionary*, 4th ed. revised (St. Paul, Minn.: West Publishing Co., 1968).

22. Griffin B. Bell, "The Attorney General: The Federal Government's Chief Lawyer and Chief Litigator, or One among Many?" *Fordham Law Review* 46 (May 1978): 1064–1065.

23. Edward Levi, *An Introduction to Legal Reasoning* (Chicago: University of Chicago Press, 1949), 6.

24. Corwin, *The President*, 119.

25. Caleb Cushing, "Office and Duties of the Attorney General," *American Law Register* (Dec. 1856): 72. Also in 6 OAG 326 (1856). Cushing, who served from 1853 to 1857, greatly contributed to the institutionalization of the office. See chapters two and three.

26. Dee Ashley Akers, "The Advisory Opinion Function of the Attorney General," *Kentucky Law Journal* 38 (1950): 561.

27. John A. Fairlie, "The United States Department of Justice," *Michigan Law Review* 3 (1905): 353. For similar assertions, see Albert Langeluttig, *The Department of Justice of the United States* (Baltimore: Johns Hopkins University Press, 1927), 145; Heiser, "The Opinion Writing Function," 15; and Toepfer, "Some Legal Aspects," 207. Also see 6 OAG 346 (1856).

28. Cushing, "Office and Duties," 72–74.

29. Akers, "The Advisory Opinion Function," 562, 570–571. Akers and most other scholars in the field disagree with Cushing and consider the courtroom role also quasi-judicial.

30. Terry Eastland, interview with the author, Washington, D.C., 19 Oct. 1987. Eastland was the director of the Office of Public Affairs, Department of Justice, and chief spokesman of Edwin Meese III, attorney general during Ronald Reagan's second term. Eastland explained the litigation-oriented ap-

proach of Meese, who sought to affect policy by rigorously pursuing cases that would overturn existing precedent.

31. Elliot Richardson, interview with the author, Washington, D.C., 20 Oct. 1987. Richardson had been attorney general for five months at the height of Watergate. His case is something of an anomaly, because he was "virtually foreclosed" from the legal advice role by Watergate. "When [Nixon] asked me to be attorney general, I thought maybe I could be a real help in giving him advice," he said. But when he realized how awkward that would be in light of his own responsibility in the investigation and prosecution of Watergate crimes, Richardson suggested that the president use White House attorneys instead.

32. Henry James, *Richard Olney and His Public Service* (Boston and New York: Houghton Mifflin Co., 1923), 3, 80.

33. Thomas Kauper, interview with the author, Ann Arbor, 30 Mar. 1988. Now a law professor at the University of Michigan Law School, Kauper served as an attorney in the Office of Legal Counsel and assistant attorney general in the Antitrust Division in the Nixon and Ford administrations.

34. J. Woodford Howard, Jr., *Mr. Justice Murphy: A Political Biography* (Princeton, N.J.: Princeton University Press, 1968), 213. Murphy's argument rested on political as much as legal grounds. He convinced the president that "it would be politically dangerous to flout the will of Congress, irrespective of legalities."

35. 8 OAG 436 (1853) and 10 OAG 455 (1860), both cited in Deener, *International Law*, 143f. Also see Cummings and McFarland, *Federal Justice*, 201. Bates's opposition to the creation of West Virginia seemed to rest less on constitutional grounds than on an interest in preserving his native Virginia.

36. Harold L. Ickes, *The Secret Diary of Harold L. Ickes* (New York: Simon and Schuster, 1954), 2: 566, 604.

37. Among the opinions later overruled by the Supreme Court were four by A. Mitchell Palmer (31 OAG 411, 31 OAG 475, 32 OAG 225, and 32 OAG 332), two by Harry Daugherty (33 OAG 327 and 33 OAG 562), and one by Harlan F. Stone (34 OAG 275). Arthur J. Dodge, *Origin and Development of the Office of the Attorney General*, H.R. Doc. 510, 70th Cong., 2d sess. (Washington, D.C.: Government Printing Office, 1929), 33–34.

38. *McGrath v. Kristensen* (1950), 340 U.S. 162. The attorney general opinion is 39 OAG 504. Also, *Youngstown Sheet & Tube Co. v. Sawyer* (1952), to be discussed later.

39. *State ex rel. Adams v. Cadwalader*, 227 Md. 21, 174 A.2d 786, 787 (1961), cited in Heiser, "The Opinion Writing Function," 20. Also see *American Jurisprudence*, 2d ed., vol. 7 (Rochester, N.Y.: Lawyers Cooperative Publishing Co., 1980), 10–12.

40. Dodge, "Origin and Development," 17; Corwin, *The President*, 120; Heiser, "The Opinion Writing Function," 36.

41. *Harrison v. Vose*, 9 How. 372 (1850).

42. 37 OAG 562 (1934).

43. Langeluttig, *The Department of Justice*, 151–154.

44. "A Discourse on the Professional Character and Virtues of the Late William Wirt, Delivered in the Hall of the House of Representatives, March 18,

1834, by Samuel L. Southard," reproduced in John P. Kennedy, *Memoirs of the Life of William Wirt* (Philadelphia: Lea and Blanchard, 1850), 2: 56.

45. Heiser, "The Opinion Writing Function," 31.

46. *Congressional Globe*, 41st Cong., 2d sess. (27 Apr. 1870), 3036. Jenckes added, "The head of a Department may act according to his own judgment, with or without the advice of his solicitor, and contrary to the advice of the Attorney General. If he does, he is responsible to the President of the United States . . . and to nobody else. But we propose that if he takes advice at all, . . . then he shall go to the fountainhead and receive the opinion of the chief law officer of the Government, and then act upon it or not, upon his own responsibility. This bill . . . will have that effect, which we deem will be highly beneficial."

47. 5 OAG 97 (8 May 1849); Dodge, "Origin and Development," 21. Johnson also reminded the secretary of the advantages of uniformity of legal opinions.

48. 9 OAG 33 (1857) in an opinion addressed to the secretary of the navy.

49. Langeluttig, *The Department of Justice*, 151–154. Rita Nealon, "The Opinion Function of the Attorney General," *New York University Law Review* 25 (1950): 840.

50. 746 U.S. 388 (1918).

51. Sewall Key, "The Legal Work of the Federal Government," *Virginia Law Review* 25 (1938): 187–188. Irwin S. Rhodes, "Opinions of the Attorney General, Revived," *American Bar Association Journal* 64 (Sept. 1978): 1375. Key writes, "This attitude [that opinions are binding] . . . was concurred in by the Supreme Court, which treated in no gentle manner an auditor of the Canal Zone who had refused to follow the Attorney General's ruling."

52. On the state level, courts generally have held that the recipient of advice from the state attorney general is not bound to its terms, although the advice is due great respect. Heiser, "The Opinion Writing Function," 24–26, 30. Toepfer, "Some Legal Aspects," 215–216.

53. Correspondence of Andrew Jackson, reproduced in Deener, *International Law*, 102. In this instance, of course, Jackson agreed with Attorney General Taney's advice on the controversial issue of removing federal funds from the Bank of the United States. The Treasury secretary to whom he wrote was less than convinced of the legality of such an act.

54. Deener, *International Law*, 102–103. Also see Langeluttig, *The Department of Justice*, 154, and Key, "The Legal Work of the Federal Government," 190f.

55. Deener, *International Law*, 101. Toepfer, "Some Legal Aspects," 216–217, 220, 225. According to Toepfer, there are no cases in which the attorney general has been held liable in damages for mistaken legal advice.

56. Thomas Kauper, interview with the author.

57. Heiser, "The Opinion Writing Function," 29, 31.

58. Thomas Kauper, interview with the author.

59. Langeluttig, *The Department of Justice*, 154. Specific instances of modern day conflicts may be found in later chapters.

60. Akers, "The Advisory Opinion Function," 583.

61. Ibid., 584, 595.

62. Deener, *International Law*, 73. Ross L. Malone, Jr., "The Department of Justice: The World's Largest Law Office," *American Bar Association Journal* 39 (1953): 382. The attorney general was allowed to delegate the opinion writing function to subordinates with the Act of 1870. After World War I, the solicitor general drafted many opinions. Then the Office of Legal Counsel (OLC), originally called the Executive Adjudications Division, was created.

63. Charles Cooper, interview with the author, Washington, D.C., 19 Oct. 1987. He served as assistant attorney general for the OLC, Department of Justice, in the Reagan administration. The OLC may research questions that arise in the cabinet at the request of the attorney general, who may want to strengthen his own policy position in cabinet discussions. Occasionally, such "cabinet advice" is later drafted as an official opinion, as in 40 OAG 41 (1941). The OLC also reviews for form and legality all proposed executive orders and proclamations and assists in preparing and organizing testimony to Congress on behalf of both the Department of Justice and the administration, although strictly speaking this is not considered rendering advice. It also assists other divisions in the department in preparing briefs related to constitutional or statutory issues. Deener, *International Law*, 75–76. Harold R. Tyler, Jr., "The Attorney General of the United States: Counsel to the President or to the Government?" *Albany Law Review* 45 (Fall 1980): 4–5. Luther A. Huston, *The Department of Justice* (New York: Frederick A. Praeger Publishers, 1967), 60–61.

64. "Office of Legal Counsel," *Annual Report of the Attorney General of the United States* (1975): 44–45. The question on the ownership of papers came up 6 Sept. 1974, shortly after Richard Nixon resigned.

65. Thomas Kauper, interview with author.

66. Cummings and McFarland, *Federal Justice*, 20f.

67. Deener, *International Law*, 12–13.

68. Senate, *Hearings before the Subcommittee of the Committee on Appropriations*, 83d Cong., 1st sess. (Washington, D.C.: Government Printing Office, 1954), 1011.

69. Thomas Kauper, interview with author.

70. Joseph Pois, *Watchdog on the Potomac* (Washington, D.C.: University Press of America, 1979), 250–251, 260. The Findlay Amendment to the Department of Agriculture's appropriation act banned the sale of agricultural commodities to any country then transporting goods to North Vietnam, which would have included Yugoslavia. The attorney general ruled that this case did not violate the ban, while the GAO ruled that it may have.

71. Testimony of Comptroller General Elmer Staats, Senate, Judiciary Committee, *Hearings before the Subcommittee on the Separation of Powers, The Philadelphia Plan*, 91st Cong., 1st sess. (Washington, D.C.: Government Printing Office, 1969), 147. Pois, *Watchdog on the Potomac*, 252–255.

72. *Contractors Assn. of Eastern Pa. v. Secretary of Labor*, 311 F.Supp. 1002 (E.D. Pa. 1970); *Contractors Assn. of Eastern Pa. v. Secretary of Labor*, 442 F.2d 159 (3d Cir. 1971).

73. Frankfurter letter to a mutual friend, Charles Burlingame (5 Jan. 1953), in Bruce Allen Murphy, *The Brandeis/Frankfurter Connection* (Garden City, N.Y.: Anchor Press/Doubleday, 1983), 325–326.

74. Griffin Bell, *Taking Care of the Law* (New York: Morrow, 1982), 35.
75. Ibid., 37–38, 42–43. These instances will be discussed in chapter five.
76. See chapter five. To a lesser extent, one might also include the role played by Counsel Lloyd Cutler when the Carter administration sought legal options in dealing with Iran after the embassy takeover.
77. Elliot Richardson, interview with author.
78. Terry Eastland, interview with author.
79. Charles Cooper, interview with author.
80. Sorensen testimony, *Hearings on Removing Politics*, 24. Sorensen served in the White House from 1961 to 1964.
81. Nicholas Katzenbach, recorded interview with Paige E. Mulhollan, 12 Nov. 1968, Oral History Program, Lyndon Baines Johnson Library.
82. Cummings and McFarland, *Federal Justice*, 513.
83. Robert H. Jackson, "A Presidential Legal Opinion," *Harvard Law Review* 66 (June 1953): 1353–1361.
84. Huston, *Department of Justice*, 8.
85. "Letter from the Attorney General in Reply to an Order by the House of Representatives of the United States, Wirt to Henry Clay, Speaker of the House," House Doc. 68 (3 Feb. 1820).
86. 10 OAG 164 (1861).
87. 10 OAG 50 (1861) and 10 OAG 220 (1862). Also see Cummings and McFarland, *Federal Justice*, 515. Langeluttig writes that a question of law arises when the head of a department is in doubt about the construction to be placed on an act of Congress that he must apply. Administrative rules that the department promulgates are not considered questions of law. Attorneys general also refrain from providing officials with advice for their private information. Langeluttig, *The Department of Justice*, 130.
88. 10 OAG 458 (1863).
89. 10 OAG 122 (1861); 34 OAG 31; 42 OAG 127 (1962).
90. Cummings and McFarland, *Federal Justice*, 515. Langeluttig, *The Department of Justice*, 132.
91. 42 OAG 43, in response to a question on the Hawaii Statehood Act posed during the Eisenhower administration.
92. 42 OAG 301 (1965).
93. Akers, "The Advisory Opinion Function," 579.
94. Don Fehrenbacher, *The Dred Scott Case: Its Significance in American Law and Politics* (New York: Oxford University Press, 1978), 69–70. Wirt was not enlightened in his earlier opinion and in fact had issued a number of opinions supporting racist practices, especially on the issue of citizenship for free blacks. But these state laws, he felt, infringed on the federal government's authority over interstate commerce and over foreign relations (since black British seamen also were detained).
95. 40 OAG 158 (1942). Biddle cites these earlier opinions on the subject: 38 OAG 252, 253 (1935) and 39 OAG 11 (1937). Another attorney general under Roosevelt, Homer Cummings, wrote a long memo advising the president that "it has been the practice of Attorneys General to refrain from rendering opinions as to the constitutionality of enactments of the Congress after their ap-

proval or disapproval by the President." "An opinion to the President, March 26, 1937," *Selected Papers of Homer Cummings*, ed. Carl Brent Swisher (New York: Charles Scribner's Sons, 1939), 274.

96. 31 OAG 475, 476 (1919). Palmer was Woodrow Wilson's attorney general.

97. See chapter two.

98. Cummings and McFarland, *Federal Justice*, 515-516.

99. See chapter four.

100. Luther A. Huston, "History of the Office of the Attorney General," in Huston et al., *Roles of the Attorney General of the United States* (Washington, D.C.: American Enterprise Institute, 1968), 33.

101. Cummings and McFarland, *Federal Justice*, 20-21. His bill did not pass, and the justice system remained largely unchanged until 1869.

102. Francis Biddle, *In Brief Authority* (Garden City, N.Y.: Doubleday & Co., 1962), 185.

103. Case studies in chapters three and five will document these points.

104. Meador, *The President, the Attorney General*, 48.

105. Moncure Daniel Conway, *Omitted Chapters of History Disclosed in the Life and Papers of Edmund Randolph* (New York: G. P. Putnam's Sons, Knickerbocker Press, 1888), 148-149. Washington considered Jefferson too partisan toward France to render an opinion. For a more detailed treatment of these and related incidents, see chapter two.

106. Richard G. Head, Frisco W. Short, and Robert McFarlane, *Crisis Resolution: Presidential Decision Making in the Mayaguez and Korean Confrontation* (Boulder, Colo.: Westview Press, 1978), 59.

107. Unlike some later incumbents, he did not engage in political campaigning. The nature of presidential elections differed in the days before political party and broad franchise.

108. Gary McDowell, interview with the author, Washington, D.C., July 1987. McDowell served in the Public Affairs Office of the Meese Justice Department.

109. Moorfield Storey and Edward Emerson, *Ebenezer Rockwood Hoar: A Memoir* (New York: Houghton Mifflin Co., 1911), 175-177, 179. Much later, Hoar was named one of five U.S. commissioners to a Joint High Commission with England to resolve the *Alabama* dispute. Their work—the Treaty of Washington of 1871—was considered a diplomatic triumph for the United States. See pp. 222-226.

110. James, *Richard Olney*, 30-33, 80-86, 91. Because the Treasury secretary was not communicating adequately with Wall Street, Olney opened channels to the business community himself, soliciting advice from New England bankers and businessmen. About the same time, Cleveland had a secret operation for cancer of the jaw, so Olney helped draft the president's message on the silver purchase bill. He also influenced Cleveland's response to the crisis in Hawaii and helped to draft the president's Special Hawaiian Message to Congress of 18 Dec. 1893.

111. Leonard D. White, *The Jeffersonians: A Study in Administrative History, 1801-1829* (New York: Macmillan, 1951), 343. Lincoln, a Jeffersonian Republi-

can, was called "the first important party leader to become Attorney General." Cummings and McFarland, *Federal Justice*, 52.

112. Fletcher Pratt, *Stanton: Lincoln's Secretary of War*, (New York: W. W. Norton & Co., 1953), 68. For his other cabinet appointments, Buchanan followed the advice of party bosses, but Black was his own choice.

113. Two of his other attorneys general, Frank Murphy and Robert Jackson, worked hard for FDR's 1932 victory. James A. Farley, *Behind the Ballots: The Personal History of a Politician* (New York: Harcourt, Brace & Co., 1938), 93, 98, 208. Howard, *Mr. Justice Murphy*, 56. Also see Frank M. Tuerkheimer, "The Executive Investigates Itself," *California Law Review* 65 (1977): 597, 601.

114. Harold F. Gosnell, *Truman's Crises: A Political Biography of Harry S Truman* (Westport, Conn.: Greenwood Press, 1980), 291.

115. The men selected were Charles Bonaparte, A. Mitchell Palmer, Edwin Meese, and Charles Beecher Warren, respectively.

116. It remains to be seen if this pattern will continue in the current Bush administration. For more information on politically active law officers, see chapter three.

117. Tuerkheimer, "The Executive," 599.

118. Tyler, "The Attorney General," 11. Judge Tyler is a former deputy attorney general and assistant attorney general in the civil rights division.

119. Huston, *Department of Justice*, 38. He lists only fourteen to the Senate and nine to the State House. Since 1968, former senator William Saxbe and former governor Richard Thornburgh have served.

120. William Wirt ran (albeit reluctantly) against Andrew Jackson. Mitchell Palmer and Robert Jackson also were considered presidential hopefuls. Robert Kennedy was assassinated during his bid for the office.

121. There might have been one instance of an attorney general becoming president if Polk had accepted President Pierce's offer of the post, ten years before Polk himself was elected president. One solicitor general—Taft—did go on to the presidency.

122. Randolph became Washington's secretary of State, as did Olney in the Cleveland administration. For a time, Benjamin Butler served concurrently as Jackson's attorney general and secretary of War. Stanton, who had served as attorney general under Buchanan, was Lincoln's secretary of War. Katzenbach became Lyndon Johnson's undersecretary of State. Richardson had been Nixon's secretary of Health, Education, and Welfare and then Defense before becoming attorney general during the Watergate crisis; he later was named Commerce secretary in the Ford administration.

123. They were Frank Murphy, Robert Jackson, and Tom C. Clark. The fourth, Francis Biddle, did not want to join the bench. Roger Brooke Taney, Edwin Stanton (who died after confirmation), James McReynolds, and Harlan Fiske Stone also were Supreme Court justices. Those failing to receive Senate confirmation were George Williams, Caleb Cushing, and Ebenezer Hoar, the latter two among the outstanding men of the times.

124. "UN Report of the International Law Commission," *American Journal of International Law*, Supplement—Official Documents, 44 (1950): 121.

125. Heiser, "The Opinion Writing Function," 17.

126. Palmer, "The Confrontation of the Legislative and Executive Branches," 351.

127. *Congressional Globe*, 39th Cong., 1st sess. (23 April 1866): 2115–2117.

128. Ibid., 41st Cong., 2d sess. (27 April 1870): 3036.

129. Among the writers who consider this a historic incident are Victor S. Navasky, "The Politics of Justice," *New York Times Magazine* (5 May 1974), 18–19, and Griffin Bell, "Office of Attorney General's Client Relationship," *Business Lawyer* 36 (Mar. 1981): 792. Corwin calls Taney "very compliant." Corwin, *The President*, 121. Cummings and McFarland also mention the story, but they question its veracity, *Federal Justice*, 109–110, as does Deener, *International Law*, 139.

130. Charles W. Smith, Jr., *Roger B. Taney: Jacksonian Jurist* (Chapel Hill: University of North Carolina Press, 1936), 10–11.

131. The case was *Etting v. Bank of the United States*. Walker Lewis, *Without Fear or Favor: A Biography of Chief Justice Roger Brooke Taney* (Boston: Houghton Mifflin Co., 1965), 85–88.

132. Reverdy Johnson, "Proceedings of the Bench and Bar of the Supreme Court of the United States on the Occasion of the Death of Roger Brooke Taney: Memorial on December 6, 1864," *Memorials of the Justices of the Supreme Court of the United States*, ed. Roger F. Jacobs (Littleton, Colo.: Fred B. Rothman & Co., 1981), 5: 136–137. This view seems supported by the research done by Cummings and McFarland, who write that Taney was the primary advocate of the plan to remove deposits. Cummings and McFarland, *Federal Justice*, 109.

133. Nor do I believe that the famous conversation occurred between Jackson and his first attorney general, John Berrien. Berrien shared Jackson's doubts about the bank's constitutionality. More cautious than Taney, he advised against Jackson's early challenge of the bank, five years before its charter was to expire, because emotions would be stirred up unnecessarily. The bank did not become a major issue during Berrien's seventeen-month tenure. He was removed not because of his bank stand, but as part of a general cabinet reshuffling orchestrated by Martin Van Buren. Cummings and McFarland, *Federal Justice*, 99–100.

134. Johnson, "Proceedings of the Bench and Bar of the Supreme Court," 137.

135. Sam J. Ervin, Jr., *The Whole Truth: The Watergate Conspiracy* (New York: Random House, 1980), 118–119.

136. Bell, *Taking Care of the Law*, 185.

137. Letter, Judge Charles Fahy, former solicitor general, to David Deener, 21 Mar. 1951, reproduced in Deener, *International Law*, 81.

138. Martin Sheffer, "The Attorney General and Presidential Power," *Presidential Studies Quarterly* 12 (Winter 1982): 54–65. The opinion is 39 OAG 484 (27 Aug. 1940).

139. 40 OAG 58 (23 May 1941). This was before American entry into the war, and neutrality legislation still applied.

140. 40 OAG 69 (3 June 1941).

141. 40 OAG 312 (22 Apr. 1944). He rested his opinion on the War Labor Disputes Act (57 Stat. 163) and the president's powers as chief executive and commander in chief. The Court later upheld this view.

142. Biddle, *In Brief Authority*, 308–324.

143. 42 OAG 347 (25 Feb. 1967). Clark was acting attorney general at the time, becoming permanent the next week. This is an interesting foreshadowing of an issue that a few years later erupted in an angry confrontation between Congress and President Nixon.

144. Those opinions are 3 OAG 738 (1841) and 5 OAG 92 (1849).

145. For example, Brewster advised the president that he did not have the power to take testimony from foreign prisoners in the United States without a treaty (17 OAG 565), nor did he have the authority to adopt the seventy-fifth meridian for Washington without legislation, because it would change the time in the capital by 8 minutes and 12 seconds (17 OAG 619). Brewster also advised that President Arthur could not set aside a sentence of court martial (17 OAG 297).

146. 33 OAG 358, 33 OAG 288, 33 OAG 570, 38 OAG 362, and 38 OAG 474.

147. Louis Fisher, *American Constitutional Law* (New York: McGraw-Hill, 1990), 222–223, 251–253. Fisher mentions sixteen such opinions rendered during the nineteenth century, and he includes in his book one by Caleb Cushing that clarified the different duties imposed on an executive official: ministerial (where the official owes his duty to the law), and discretionary (where the official owes his duty to the president). 6 OAG 326 (1854). In fulfilling his ministerial functions, assigned to him by statute, an executive official is not subject to presidential control. Fisher notes that this distinction was first drawn by the courts in *Marbury v. Madison* in 1803.

148. 23 OAG 589, 594.

149. 24 OAG 144 (25 Oct. 1902). Dodge, *Origin and Development of the Office of Attorney General*, 30.

150. Cummings and McFarland, *Federal Justice*, 515; Deener, *International Law*, 141.

151. 9 OAG 516, 523 (20 Nov. 1860).

152. Pratt, *Stanton*, 99–100, 105–107.

153. Meador, *The President, the Attorney General*, 47.

154. Sorensen testimony, *Hearings on Removing Politics*, 17.

155. Elliot Richardson, interview with author.

156. Deener, *International Law*, 132.

157. *Hearings on Removing Politics*, 2, 6.

158. Tyler, "The Attorney General," 1, 5.

159. Meador, *The President, the Attorney General*, 2.

160. Deener, *International Law*, 9.

161. Palmer, "The Confrontation of the Legislative and Executive Branches," 372.

162. Pratt, *Stanton*, 113.

163. Cushing was in no position to criticize; some called him "triplex" for his own changeability.

164. Benjamin Thomas and Harold Hyman, *Stanton: The Life and Times of Lincoln's Secretary of War* (New York: Alfred A. Knopf, 1962), 98–99, 112, 115.

165. Stuart Eizenstat, "White House and Justice Department after Watergate," *American Bar Association Journal* 68 (Feb. 1982): 176. Eizenstat was the chief domestic policy adviser in the White House.

166. Terry Eastland, interview with author. Also see the 1971 confirmation hearings of William Rehnquist to be associate justice, when Rehnquist had the following exchange with Sen. Edward Kennedy:

Kennedy: I thought that your client was the public as well.
Rehnquist: My client, in my position as the assistant attorney general for the Office of Legal Counsel, is the attorney general and the president.
Kennedy: Where does that put the rest of the Constitution?
Rehnquist: Well, that puts the rest of the Constitution in the position of having someone advising them as to what his interpretation of the Constitution is.

Senate, Committee on the Judiciary, *Hearings on the Nomination of William H. Rehnquist and Lewis F. Powell Jr. to be Associate Justices of the Supreme Court,* 92nd Cong., 1st sess. (Washington, D.C.: Government Printing Office, 1971), 48.

167. Cox testimony, *Hearings on Removing Politics,* 199. Cox served as solicitor general from 1961 to 1965.

168. Miller, "Justice without Politics," 378–379.

169. Cummings, *Selected Papers,* 9. Cummings seems to use the phrase "the United States" to connote the federal government. Others use the phrase to imply "the people."

170. Ronald Keller, "The Applicability and Scope of the Attorney-Client Privilege in the Executive Branch of the Federal Government," *Boston University Law Review* 62 (July 1982): 1008–1013. He cites *United States v. AT&T Co.,* 86 F.R.D. 603, 616–618 (D.D.C. 1979); *Coastal States Gas Corp. v. Dept. of Energy,* 617 F.2d 854 (D.C. Cir. 1980); and *Sterling Inc. v. Harris,* 488 F.Supp. 1019, 1025 (S.D.N.Y. 1980). Griffin Bell, although he answers the question differently when it is posed in regard to the attorney general himself, impressed on his departmental attorneys that their clients were the agencies they represented. Bell, "Attorney General's Client Relationship," 793.

171. Seymour, *United States Attorney,* 47. By this he may be referring to the sentiment inscribed on walls at the Justice Department: "The government wins when justice is done."

172. Thomas Kauper, interview with author.

173. Tom C. Clark, "The Office of the Attorney General," *Tennessee Law Review* 19 (1946): 155–156. Clark had just joined Truman's cabinet.

174. Elliot Richardson, interview with author.

175. Bell, "The Attorney General," 1069. Also, Griffin Bell, interview with author.

176. Mathias (R.-Md.) comments, Senate, Committee on the Judiciary, *Hearings on the Nomination of Edwin Meese III to Be Attorney General,* 98th Cong., 2d sess. (Washington D.C.: Government Printing Office, 1985), 4. In his opening statement, Mathias said that "the important issue to be determined at a confirmation hearing for Attorney General is exactly what the lawyer-client relationship is going to be; to nail down at the outset who the client is."

177. Palmer, "The Confrontation of the Legislative and Executive Branches," 373. One statute he cites is 28 U.S.C. 517 (1976), which reads in part,

"the Attorney General, or his delegate, shall attend to the interests of the 'United States.'" It is unclear if Palmer means the national government or the American people in this phrase. Palmer concedes that the U.S. attorney general, unlike his counterpart on the state level, has no independent authority from the common law to represent the public interest. A creation of statutory law, the office may still oversee the public interest, but it has no positive grant of power to do so. See 352, 355, 388.

178. Cranston (D.-Calif.) comments, *Hearings on Removing Politics*, 6.

179. Bell comments, Senate, Committee on the Judiciary, *Hearings on Griffin Bell, Attorney General Designate*, 95th Cong., 1st sess. (Washington, D.C.: Government Printing Office, 1977), 144.

180. Sorensen testimony, *Hearings on Removing Politics*, 16.

181. Marcus, *Truman and the Steel Seizure Case*, 161, 171.

182. 343 U.S. at 647 (1952). Current Chief Justice William Rehnquist, who was Jackson's law clerk at the time, recalled that a similar one occurred involving Justice Tom Clark, who had been Truman's attorney general before joining the Court. Rehnquist did not elaborate on the Tom Clark incident. *Hearings on the Nomination of William H. Rehnquist*, 20.

183. Marcus, *Truman and the Steel Seizure Case*, 172.

184. Elliot Richardson, interview with author.

185. See for example Michael Banton, *Roles* (London: Tavistock Publications, 1965), 151–171.

186. Judiciary Act of 1789, 1 Stat. 73, Section 35.

187. This incident is described further in chapter two.

188. Independence became an issue before Watergate, when John Mitchell's role as Nixon's campaign manager raised questions during his 1969 confirmation hearings.

189. After independence, these four issues were the most popular with the Senate. Even so, they were raised by only three senators. See *Hearings on the Nomination of Edward H. Levi*.

190. Cummings and McFarland, *Federal Justice*, 499–500. President Grover Cleveland issued such an order, as did Attorney General Sargent under Coolidge.

191. Guidelines issued to cabinet members before 1976 race. Memo, James E. Connor to the cabinet, 7 Jan. 1976, and Memo, James E. Connor to the cabinet, 19 July 1976, folder "FG 10 Exec. 1/1/76–1/20/77," Box 72, The Cabinet FG 10/FG 10-1, Gerald R. Ford Library.

192. Griffin Bell, interview with author.

193. Edward Weisband and Thomas Franck, *Resignation in Protest: Political and Ethical Choices between Loyalty to Team and Loyalty to Conscience in American Public Life* (New York: Grossman, 1975), 121. The result, they conclude, tends to be a cabinet of yea-sayers.

194. Richard F. Fenno, Jr., *The President's Cabinet: An Analysis in the Period from Wilson to Eisenhower* (Cambridge, Mass.: Harvard University Press, 1959), 5.

195. Biddle, *In Brief Authority*, 4–5. Biddle as a young boy had first met the older Franklin at Groton, where Franklin was "a magnificent but distant deity"

to the shy newcomer. One senses in Biddle's writings that this feeling of awe (although tempered somewhat) continued into their adult relations.

196. In fact, he had some success in protecting speech that criticized the president or the war, despite Roosevelt's pressure that he do something to stop "the scurrilous attacks" and "anti-war talk." Biddle refused to proceed with federal prosecution for sedition unless the speech or writing directly affected the war effort, a policy that FDR considered too soft. This was the only time that Roosevelt pressured him, according to Biddle. In the case of the wartime internment, the responsibility for implementation did not rest with the attorney general, so FDR did not need his cooperation. Biddle, *In Brief Authority*, 234–238.

197. Peter Irons, *Justice at War* (Oxford: Oxford University Press, 1983), 7–8, 17. About 120,000 people were interned, 77,000 of them American citizens. The last camp was not closed until January 1946, five months after the end of the war, and the issue was not finally resolved until 10 August 1988, with Reagan's signature on a bill apologizing for the forced relocation and establishing a trust fund of $1.25 billion to pay reparations. *New York Times*, 11 Aug. 1988, 1, 8. The federal judiciary reexamined the issues raised by the relocation, including the role of the Department of Justice in the original lawsuits, in the cases of *Korematsu v. United States*, 584 F.Supp. 1406 (N.D. Cal. 1984) and *Hirabayashi v. United States*, 828 F.2d 591 (9th Cir. 1987).

198. Irons, *Justice at War*, 17, 32. Biddle, *In Brief Authority*, 205–226. There is no record of an official attorney general opinion on the internment plan, so FDR may not have sent the executive order to Biddle for approval.

199. Biddle, *In Brief Authority*, 331.

200. Columnist Joseph Kraft, misusing Walter Bagehot's distinction between "dignified" and "effective" officers, once set up a typology similar to mine to describe two types of attorney general. He identified the "dignified" officer as "an upright man, learned in the law, . . . who acts less as a player on the Government team than as an umpire exerting a legal check." In contrast, he characterized the "effective" officer as one who is politically close to his president, sometimes to the detriment of the law. He continued the conventional wisdom that the ideal law officer is of the "dignified" type. Navasky, "The Politics of Justice," 18–19.

201. *Black's Law Dictionary*, 4th ed., 75.

202. Ibid., 1193.

Chapter Two. The Emergence of the Modern Law Officer

1. James Norton-Kyshe, *The Law and Privileges Relating to Colonial Attorneys General and to the Office Corresponding to the Attorney General of England in the United States* (London: Stevens & Haynes, 1900), 75. See also John A. Fairlie, "The United States Department of Justice," *Michigan Law Review* 3 (1905): 352, and Sewall Key, "The Legal Work of the Federal Government," *Virginia Law Review* 25 (1938): 165–166.

2. John Ll. J. Edwards, *The Law Officers of the Crown* (London: Sweet and Maxwell, 1964), 15.

3. Hugh C. Bellot, "The Origin of the Attorney General," *Law Quarterly Review* 25 (1909): 403. Key "The Legal Work," 166. James Hightower, "From 'Attornatus' to the Department of Justice," Library of Congress, Legislative Reference Service, 17 Aug. 1966, cited in Senate, the Subcommittee on Separation of Powers of the Senate Committee on the Judiciary, *Hearings on S. 2803 and S. 2978 on Removing Politics from the Administration of Justice*, 93d Cong., 2d sess. (Washington, D.C.: Government Printing Office, 1974), 405.

4. W. S. Holdsworth, "The Early History of the Attorney and Solicitor General," *Illinois Law Review* 13 (1919): 612–614.

5. Ibid., 606.

6. George W. Keeton, "The Office of Attorney General," *Juridical Review* 58 (1946): 108.

7. Bellot, "The Origin," 410. Keeton, "The Office," 108–109. Edwards, *The Law Officers*, 27. Hightower, "From 'Attornatus,'" 406. The issue in question was highly sensitive, involving the claim to the throne of Edward IV (when he was still the Duke of York).

8. Holdsworth, "The Early History," 602, 606, 615–617. Key, "The Legal Work," 167. National Association of Attorneys General, *The Report on the Office of the Attorney General* (Feb. 1971), 14.

9. Keeton, "The Office," 111–112.

10. Rita W. Cooley, "Predecessors of the Federal Attorney General: The Attorney General in England and the American Colonies," *American Journal of Legal History* 2 (1958): 306–307.

11. Key, "The Legal Work," 166. Hightower, "From 'Attornatus,'" 407.

12. Hightower, "From 'Attornatus,'" 407.

13. NAAG, *The Report on the Office*, 15.

14. Edwards, *The Law Officers*, 9. Abraham Goldstein, "Prosecution: History of the Public Prosecutor," *Encyclopedia of Crime and Justice*, ed. Sanford Kadish (New York: Free Press, 1983), 3: 1287. Originally, the colonies adopted the British system, but this method required too much effort and expense on the part of individual victims. More and more criminal cases were settled out of court, which deprived colonial courts of the revenue anticipated from fines. In order to make prosecution more evenhanded and remunerative for colonial governments, attorneys general began to prosecute routine criminal cases as well as those of interest to the state.

15. Norton-Kyshe, *The Law and Privileges*, 111.

16. Lewis W. Morse, "Historical Outline and Bibliography of Attorneys General Reports and Opinions," *Law Library Journal* 30 (Apr. 1937): 102, 195, 200, 226–227. Oliver W. Hammonds, "The Attorney General in the American Colonies," in *Anglo-American Legal History*, Ser. 5.1, no. 3 (New York: New York University School of Law, 1939), 3, 13, 15, 20, 22. Georgia was not established until 1733 and named its first attorney general in 1752.

17. Hammonds, "The Attorney General," 4, 9, 12, 14, 17, 18, 21. Trott commission reprinted from *South Carolina Historical Society Collection*, (1858), 1: 143.

18. Hammonds, "The Attorney General," 9.

19. Homer Cummings and Carl McFarland, *Federal Justice: Chapters in the*

History of Justice and the Federal Executive (1937; reprint, New York: Da Capo Press, 1970), 12.

20. Calendar of State Papers (1699), 210-211, and (1701), 15, cited in Hammonds, "The Attorney General," 8.

21. Cummings and McFarland, *Federal Justice,* 9-10. Key, "The Legal Work," 173. Hammonds, "The Attorney General," 8, 21-22.

22. Key, "The Legal Work," 172.

23. Cummings and McFarland, *Federal Justice,* 10-11.

24. Ibid., 11.

25. Ibid., 10-11. It was John Randolph's son and Peyton Randolph's nephew, Edmund, who was to serve as the first U.S. attorney general.

26. Arch. of Maryland XLII, cited in Hammonds, "The Attorney General," 4.

27. Edmund Randolph, *History of Virginia* (Charlottesville: Virginia Historical Society, University Press of Virginia, 1970), 161-162, 183. Also see Hammonds, "The Attorney General," 9-10, 35.

28. Hammonds, "The Attorney General," 10, 35. Because the state law officer has certain common law responsibilities to the public, he may be in a different position than the national law officer, who does not.

29. Ibid., 22. Cummings and McFarland, *Federal Justice,* 11, 15. Cooley, "Predecessors of the Federal Attorney General," 311-312. Goldstein, "Prosecution," 1287.

30. U.S. Congress, *Journals of the Continental Congress,* vol. 19 (1781), ed. Gaillard Hunt (Washington, D.C.: Government Printing Office, 1912), 155-156.

31. Ibid., 190.

32. *Journals of the Continental Congress* (23 Jan. 1781), 75, 354.

33. Hightower, "From 'Attornatus,'" 408-409.

34. Ibid., 409-410.

35. Ibid., 411.

36. U.S. Constitution, Article II, Section 3.

37. Ibid., Section 2.

38. Caleb Cushing, "Office and Duties of the Attorney General," *American Law Register* 5 (December 1856): 65.

39. Charles Warren, "New Light on the History of the Federal Judiciary Act of 1789," *Harvard Law Review* 37 (1923): 108-109, quoting Sen. William Maclay of Pennsylvania.

40. Warren, "New Light," 54-56.

41. Hightower, "From 'Attornatus,'" 411. Warren, "New Light," 57.

42. Warren, "New Light," 58.

43. Hightower, "From 'Attornatus,'" 412. The vote was fourteen to six.

44. Warren, "New Light," 130-131.

45. Act of Jan. 19, 1886, 24 Stat. 1.

46. Judiciary Act of 1789, 1 Stat. 73, Section 35.

47. Hammonds, "The Attorney General," 24.

48. Henry Barrett Learned, *The President's Cabinet* (New Haven, Conn.: Yale University Press, 1912), 159.

49. Luther A. Huston, *The Department of Justice* (New York: Frederick A. Praeger Publishers, 1967), 6–7.

50. Warren, "New Light," 109f. Hightower, "From 'Attornatus,'" 412, citing a letter from Christopher Gore to Sen. Rufus King of 22 Aug. 1789.

51. Hightower, "From 'Attornatus,'" 412.

52. *The Report on the Office*, 19–20. Hammonds, "The Attorney General," 5, 6, 20. Morse, "Historical Outline," 22.

53. Warren, "New Light," 53–54.

54. Judiciary Act of 1789, 1 Stat. 73, Section 35.

55. Key, "The Legal Work," 175.

56. Ibid.

57. Moncure Daniel Conway, *Omitted Chapters of History Disclosed in the Life and Papers of Edmund Randolph* (New York: G. P. Putnam's Sons, Knickerbocker Press, 1888), 129.

58. Arthur Shaffer, "Introduction," in Randolph, *History of Virginia*, xi–xii.

59. Conway, *Omitted Chapters*, 130, 133. Cummings and McFarland, *Federal Justice*, 19–20.

60. Cummings and McFarland, *Federal Justice*, 19.

61. Shaffer, "Introduction," xiii–xiv. Conway, *Omitted Chapters*, 125, 193–194. Leonard D. White, *The Federalists* (1948; reprint, Westport, Conn.: Greenwood Press, 1978), 169–170. White referred to it as "his deep-seated capacity for vacillation."

62. Conway, *Omitted Chapters*, 133, 138.

63. Key, "The Legal Work," 176.

64. Letter, 1790, reproduced in Conway, *Omitted Chapters*, 135.

65. Letter to Washington, (26 Dec. 1791), U.S. Congress, *American State Papers*, 1789–1809, Misc., (Gales & Seaton, 1834), 1: 45–46.

66. Cummings and McFarland, *Federal Justice*, 24. Huston, *The Department of Justice*, 6–7.

67. Cummings and McFarland, *Federal Justice*, 20, 22, 49.

68. White, *The Federalists*, 166–167.

69. Conway, *Omitted Chapters*, 148.

70. Ibid., 148–151. Cummings and McFarland, *Federal Justice*, 36–39.

71. Cummings and McFarland, *Federal Justice*, 24–25.

72. Conway, *Omitted Chapters*, 154–155. Cummings and McFarland, *Federal Justice*, 32–35.

73. Cummings and McFarland, *Federal Justice*, 22–24.

74. Ibid., 32.

75. Conway, *Omitted Chapters*, 151–152.

76. Ibid., 154–155. He did not write a history of the administration.

77. Cummings and McFarland, *Federal Justice*, 25. White, *The Federalists*, 166.

78. Conway, *Omitted Chapters*, 139, 198. Also see Shaffer, "Introduction," xv.

79. Letter, Jefferson to Judge Tucker (11 Aug. 1793), reproduced in Conway, *Omitted Chapters*, 190–191.

80. White, *The Federalists*, 172.

81. Conway, *Omitted Chapters*, 186, 191. Cummings and McFarland, *Federal Justice*, 26, 39, 40.

82. Letter (11 Aug. 1793), reproduced in Conway, *Omitted Chapters*, 190–191.

83. Cummings and McFarland, *The Federalists*, 512.

84. Letter (19 Apr. 1794), reproduced in Conway, *Omitted Chapters*, 218–219.

85. Shaffer, "Introduction," xiv.

86. "Letter from Mr. Monroe to Mr. Lowndes, Chairman of the House Committee of Ways and Means," *American State Papers 1801–1823*, Misc., (1834), 2: 419. Also in U.S. Congress, *Annals of Congress*, 14th Cong., 2d sess. (1816–1817), 699–700.

87. On the flyleaf of earliest record book in the Department of Justice, 13 Nov. 1817, reproduced in Albert Langeluttig, *The Department of Justice of the United States* (Baltimore: Johns Hopkins University Press, 1927), 4.

88. Letter, Wirt to the Judiciary Committee, House of Representatives, 27 Mar. 1818. Reproduced in John P. Kennedy, *Memoirs of the Life of William Wirt* (Philadelphia: Lea and Blanchard, 1850), 2: 58–61.

89. Letter to William Pope, 18 Jan. 1818, reproduced in Kennedy, *Memoirs*, 2: 65.

90. Langellutig, *The Department of Justice*, 6. Learned, *The President's Cabinet*, 169, 178.

91. *Register of the Department of Justice*, 8th ed. (Washington, D.C.: Government Printing Office, 1886). The register indicates that Attorney General Augustus Garland's salary was $8,000 in 1886. The solicitor general received $7,000, and the chief justice of the Supreme Court, Morrison Waite, $10,500. The twelfth edition of the register (1898), when John Griggs was attorney general, reflects the same figures.

92. Leonard D. White, *The Jeffersonians: A Study in Administrative History, 1801–1829* (New York: Macmillan, 1951), 336.

93. Marvin Cain, "Claims, Contracts, and Customs: Public Accountability and a Department of Justice, 1789–1849," *Journal of the Early Republic* 4 (Spring 1984): 33–34.

94. Learned, *The President's Cabinet*, 162–163.

95. Letter to Mr. Lowndes in 1817, *American State Papers*, 418.

96. Kennedy, *Memoirs*, 2: 32, 53–54.

97. Learned, *The President's Cabinet*, 176–177.

98. Claude M. Fuess, *The Life of Caleb Cushing* (New York: Harcourt, Brace & Co., 1923), 2: 136–137.

99. Keeton, "The Office," 116. Sir Elwyn Jones, "The Office of Attorney-General," *Cambridge Law Journal* 27 (1969): 45–46.

100. Letter to his friend Judge Carr, 21 Jan. 1818, reproduced in Kennedy, *Memoirs*, Vol. 2: 67.

101. Cummings and McFarland, *Federal Justice*, 31, 62, 154–155. Kennedy, *Memoirs*, 2: 142. Out of office, they continued to participate in important cases. Edmund Randolph, for example, was retained as the senior defense counsel for Aaron Burr's conspiracy trial.

102. Benjamin Thomas and Harold Hyman, *Stanton: The Life and Times of Lincoln's Secretary of War* (New York: Alfred A. Knopf, 1962), 91, 137. After he left in 1862, his salary climbed to more than $50,000.

103. Letter to Mr. Lowndes in 1817, *American State Papers*, 418.

104. Letter, 13 Nov. 1817, reproduced in Kennedy, *Memoirs*, 2: 32.

105. Cushing, "Office and Duties," 92.

106. Learned, *The President's Cabinet*, 191, 195.

107. See, for example, the comment of Benjamin F. Butler in 1879, praising Cushing for raising the office to a government department, reproduced in Learned, *The President's Cabinet*, 180–181.

108. Cushing, "Office and Duties," 86–87.

109. Langeluttig, *The Department of Justice*, 6–8. Learned, *The President's Cabinet*, 178, 184–185.

110. Frederic Bancroft, *The Life of William H. Seward*, (New York: Harper & Bros., 1900), 2: 355–356.

111. Senate, *Register of Debates*, 26 Mar. 1830, 13 Apr. 1830, and 30 Apr. 1830, 276, 322–324, 404.

112. Key, "The Legal Work," 177–179.

113. Learned, *The President's Cabinet*, 188–189. Key, "The Legal Work," 176–180. Langeluttig, *The Department of Justice*, 3. Also see Huston, *The Department of Justice*, 9–13.

114. Griffin Bell, "The Attorney General: The Federal Government's Chief Lawyer and Chief Litigator, or One among Many?" *Fordham Law Review* 46 (May 1978): 1052.

115. *Congressional Globe*, 41st Cong., 2d sess. (27 Apr. 1870), 3034–3038.

116. Department of Justice Act of 20 June 1870, Section 17.

117. For more on the development of the solicitor general's office, see Lincoln Caplan, *The Tenth Justice: The Solicitor General and the Rule of Law* (New York: Alfred A. Knopf, 1987), 5, 8–9.

118. Act to establish the Department of Justice, 16 Stat. 162 (22 June 1870).

119. Huston, *The Department of Justice*, 36.

120. Cummings and McFarland, *Federal Justice*, 493.

121. Hightower, "From 'Attornatus,'" 419.

122. Cummings and McFarland, *Federal Justice*, 495–496. Also see Bell, "The Attorney General," 1054.

123. Key, "The Legal Work of the Federal Government," 183–185.

124. Bell, "The Attorney General," 1054.

125. Key, "The Legal Work," 188–195. Wilson's Executive Order No. 2877 (1918). See related discussion in chapter one.

126. Langeluttig, *The Department of Justice*, 13.

127. Bell "The Attorney General," 1056. Bell noted that the comparable figures in 1978 were 3,806 out of 15,740. This constitutes about 24 percent.

128. Entry of 11 Dec. 1934, Harold Ickes, *The Secret Diary of Harold L. Ickes* (New York: Simon and Schuster, 1953), 1: 243.

129. Key, "The Legal Work," 195–198. See also Franklin Roosevelt's Executive Order No. 6166, 10 June 1933.

130. 5 Wall. 370 (U.S. 1866). Also see Key, "The Legal Work," 185.

131. *U.S. v. San Jacinto Tin Co.* 125 U.S. 273 (1888).
132. Ickes, *The Secret Diary*, 1: 306–307.
133. Daniel Meador, *The President, the Attorney General, and the Department of Justice* (Charlottesville: White Burkett Miller Center of Public Affairs, University of Virginia, 1980), 44.

Chapter Three. The Advocate Attorney General

1. William Rehnquist, "The Old Order Changeth: The Department of Justice Under John Mitchell," *Arizona Law Review* 12 (1970): 251, 252. He was an assistant attorney general in the OLC when he made this address on 22 Apr. 1970.
2. Arthur S. Miller, "The Attorney General as the President's Lawyer," in *Roles of the Attorney General of the United States*, ed. Luther A. Huston, Arthur Miller, Samuel Krislov, and Robert Dixon (Washington, D.C.: American Enterprise Institute, 1968), 52.
3. Richard F. Fenno, Jr. *The President's Cabinet: An Analysis in the Period from Wilson to Eisenhower* (Cambridge, Mass.: Harvard University Press, 1959), 70. Richard Kleindienst, law officer under Richard Nixon, believed erroneously that his political background was unusual. "Whether for good or ill, I may be the only person to have attained the high position of Attorney General of the United States for no other reason than my involvement in the organizational politics of the Republican party." Richard Kleindienst, *Justice: The Memoirs of Attorney General Richard Kleindienst* (Ottawa, Ill.: Jameson Books, 1985), preface.
4. Theodore Sorensen, "Presidential Advisers," in *The Presidential Advisory System*, ed. Thomas Cronin and Sanford Greenberg (New York: Harper & Row, 1969), 7, 9–10.
5. John Anderson, *Eisenhower, Brownell, and the Congress: The Tangled Origins of the Civil Rights Bill of 1956–57* (Tuscaloosa: University of Alabama Press, 1964), 3–5, 27, 28, 39, 41, 43.
6. Charles W. Smith, Jr., *Roger B. Taney: Jacksonian Jurist* (Chapel Hill: University of North Carolina Press, 1936), 8, 10, 12.
7. Ibid., 13. Jackson, although a Jeffersonian Democrat, had argued in a letter dated 1816 that some Federalists were honorable men and should not be overlooked. The letter was revealed in 1824, in time for the election.
8. Roger B. Taney, "Letter to William M. Beall, April 13, 1824," *Roger B. Taney*, Carl Brent Swisher (New York: Macmillan, 1935), 121.
9. Walker Lewis, *Without Fear or Favor: A Biography of Chief Justice Roger Brooke Taney* (Boston: Houghton Mifflin Co., 1965), 122. Swisher, *Roger B. Taney*, 122–123.
10. Swisher, *Roger B. Taney*, 139.
11. Lewis, *Without Fear or Favor*, 122.
12. Ibid., 123–124.
13. Smith, *Roger B. Taney*, 13–14.
14. Swisher, *Roger B. Taney*, 302–303.
15. Quoted in Homer Cummings and Carl McFarland, *Federal Justice: Chap-*

ters in the History of Justice and the Federal Executive (New York: Macmillan, 1937), 103–104.

16. Lewis, *Without Fear or Favor,* 80–81.

17. Smith, *Roger B. Taney,* 16.

18. Lewis, *Without Fear or Favor,* 54.

19. Smith, *Roger B. Taney,* 16.

20. Ibid., 67–71. The bank did engage in manipulative and vindictive activities that affected the national economy. It spent large amounts of money on propaganda, it increased its loans right before the recharter deadline, it contracted its business drastically when Jackson vetoed the recharter in 1832, and it increased its holdings of species, which forced state banks to call in their paper money. See Smith, 71 n.18 and 74 n.24.

21. Don Fehrenbacher, *The Dred Scott Case: Its Significance in American Law and Politics* (New York: Oxford University Press, 1978), 70. The 1832 opinion was never officially published, so it had little public impact at the time.

22. Caleb Cushing, *Outlines of the Life and Public Services, Civil and Military, of William Henry Harrison* (Boston: Weeks, Jordan & Co., 1840).

23. Claude M. Fuess, *The Life of Caleb Cushing* (New York: Harcourt, Brace & Co., 1923), 2: 13–14.

24. Ibid., 23–26, 94, 106–109.

25. Ibid., 111–126.

26. Ibid., 131–136, 138.

27. Cummings and McFarland, *Federal Justice,* 149–150, 156.

28. Fuess, *The Life of Caleb Cushing,* 2: 137.

29. Ibid., 112.

30. Hermann von Holst, *The Constitutional and Political History of the United States* (Chicago: Callaghan & Co., 1885), 4: 263.

31. Fuess, *The Life of Caleb Cushing,* 2: 133.

32. Ibid., 160–161.

33. Ibid., 301–302.

34. Caleb Cushing, *The Treaty of Washington: Its Negotiation, Execution, and the Discussions Relating Thereto* (New York: Harper & Bros., 1873), 95. In the *Alabama* dispute, the United States charged that Britain had been the Confederacy's arsenal, navy yard, and treasury and that the war would not have been as long or bloody without British assistance to the South. Feelings ran high in both countries, making arbitration difficult. See 15, 22–26.

35. Fuess, *The Life of Caleb Cushing,* 2: 379.

36. Ibid., 151–152. Cushing wrote Pierce's Third Annual Message, 31 Dec. 1855, that recognized the legitimacy of the proslavery faction, and he supported the president's message to Congress the next month.

37. 6 OAG 220, 14 Nov. 1853. 6 OAG 302, 18 Feb. 1854. 6 OAG 466, 27 May 1854.

38. 7 OAG 571, 576. Fuess, *The Life of Caleb Cushing,* 2: 153–156. Fuess incorrectly dates the opinion November 1855.

39. Fuess, *The Life of Caleb Cushing,* 2: 203.

40. von Holst, *The Constitutional and Political History of the United States,* 4: 267.

41. Fuess, *The Life of Caleb Cushing*, 2: 411.
42. Ibid., 165, 356–357. Fuess also notes Cushing's influence on the Treaty of Washington which scholars recognize as another important development in the law of neutrals. See Gerhard von Glahn, *Law among Nations*, 2d ed. (London: Macmillan, 1970), 626.
43. Fuess, *The Life of Caleb Cushing*, 2: 176–177.
44. von Holst, *The Constitutional and Political History of the United States*, 262.
45. From a speech made by Benton, a candidate for governor, in St. Louis on 21 July 1856. von Holst, *The Constitutional and Political History of the United States*, 263n.
46. Fuess, *The Life of Caleb Cushing*, 2: 412.
47. Ibid., 413.
48. Ibid., 205–206, 224. There was some talk of a Davis/Cushing ticket for 1860.
49. Ibid., 363–373. He also made some blatant political mistakes, as when he sent a cordial letter to Jefferson Davis after Davis went south at the start of the war. The letter inconveniently reappeared during his confirmation hearings. Cummings and McFarland, *Federal Justice*, 157.
50. Carl Brent Swisher, ed., *Selected Papers of Homer Cummings* (New York: Charles Scribner's Sons, 1939), xi–xiii. Cummings was Roosevelt's second choice for the post; Thomas Walsh, the special prosecutor in the Teapot Dome scandal, had been selected but died before the inauguration. See Louis B. Wehle, *Hidden Threads of History: Wilson through Roosevelt* (New York: Macmillan, 1953), 124–125, 128.
51. Homer Cummings, *Liberty under Law and Administration* (New York: Charles Scribner's Sons, 1934), 53, 66.
52. Swisher, *Selected Papers of Homer Cummings*, 10–11. Radio address of 10 June 1933.
53. Swisher, *Selected Papers of Homer Cummings*, 146–154, for a selection of memos, letters, addresses by Cummings on the subject. Also see Harold Ickes, *The Secret Diary of Harold L. Ickes* (New York: Simon and Schuster, 1954), 2: 64, 75, 152, 177.
54. J. Woodford Howard, Jr., *Mr. Justice Murphy: A Political Biography* (Princeton, N.J.: Princeton University Press, 1968), 12, 53, 54, 56, 111, 118, 180. Also see Ickes, *The Secret Diary of Harold L. Ickes*, 2: 423, 505.
55. Howard, *Mr. Justice Murphy*, 187, 214–216, 219.
56. James A. Farley, *Behind the Ballots: The Personal History of a Politician* (New York: Harcourt, Brace & Co., 1938), 93, 98–99.
57. Ickes, *The Secret Diary of Harold L. Ickes*, 2: 395; 3: 108. Whitney North Seymour, "Introduction," in Charles Desmond, Paul Freund, Lord Hartley Shawcross, and Potter Stewart, *Mr. Justice Jackson: Four Lectures in His Honor*, (New York: Columbia University Press, 1969), 1–2.
58. Ickes, *The Secret Diary of Harold L. Ickes*, 2: 712; 3: 172–173, 466.
59. Bruce Allen Murphy, *The Brandeis/Frankfurter Connection* (Garden City, N.Y.: Anchor Press/Doubleday, 1983), 254–255. Justice Murphy was less successful getting through.

60. Howard, *Mr. Justice Murphy*, 225.

61. Ickes, *The Secret Diary of Harold L. Ickes*, 2: 232, 680. Ickes was worried that Jackson, growing restive while Murphy served as attorney general, might resign. While Murphy had accomplished a lot, "cleaning up the political mess that Homer Cummings left," he was not as good a lawyer as Jackson, according to Ickes. Ickes, *The Secret Diary of Harold L. Ickes*, 2: 628, 679.

62. Desmond et al., *Mr. Justice Jackson*, 9–10, 12, 18.

63. Jones, in Desmond et al., *Mr. Justice Jackson*, 128.

64. Quoted in Howard, *Mr. Justice Murphy*, 221.

65. Ickes, *The Secret Diary of Harold L. Ickes*, 3: 76–77, 119, 132.

66. Robert Dallek, *Franklin D. Roosevelt and American Foreign Policy, 1932–1945* (New York: Oxford University Press, 1979), 225.

67. 39 OAG 484, 494, 27 Aug. 1940.

68. Wehle, *Hidden Threads of History*, 216–218. Roosevelt had asked for a repeal of the laws' embargo provisions on 21 Sept. 1939, but Congress responded with a joint resolution that was even more restrictive.

69. Elliott Roosevelt, ed., *FDR: His Personal Letters 1928–1945* (New York: Duell, Sloan & Pearce, 1950), 2: 1036, 1050–1051. Technically, five bases were transferred in exchange for the fifty destroyers; the other two were considered gifts. See 1061.

70. Ibid., 1052. Ickes, *The Secret Diary of Harold L. Ickes*, 3: 270–271, 282–283.

71. Ickes, *The Secret Diary of Harold L. Ickes*, 3: 270–271, 304, 313. The deal still required the certification of the chief of Naval Operations that the ships were not needed for American defense, but Knox felt confident that he could secure that. Jackson was not the only one to have changed his mind as events worsened; Ickes also defended the decision to avoid Congress because of the urgency of the trade by then.

72. 39 OAG 484, 494–496.

73. Wehle, *Hidden Threads of History*, 228.

74. Herbert W. Briggs, "Neglected Aspects of the Destroyer Deal," *American Journal of International Law* 34 (1940): 569, 587.

75. Edward S. Corwin, *The President: Offices and Powers 1787–1957* (New York: New York University Press, 1957), 238. He also wrote that Roosevelt, in making the destroyer deal, "converted, as it were at the blast of a trumpet, the international status of the United States as a neutral to that of a quasi-belligerent in the war then raging in Europe" (202).

76. Quincy Wright, "Editorial Comment: The Transfer of Destroyers to Great Britain" and Edwin Borchard, "Editorial Comment: The Attorney General's Opinion on the Exchange of Destroyers for Naval Bases," in *American Journal of International Law* 34 (1940): 680, 685, 697.

77. Ickes, *The Secret Diary of Harold L. Ickes*, 1: 308. Diary entry of 3 Mar. 1935.

78. Richard Tanner Johnson, *Managing the White House: An Intimate Study of the Presidency* (New York: Harper & Row, 1974), 5–6, 19–20, 32.

79. Robert F. Kennedy, *The Pursuit of Justice*, ed. Theodore J. Lowi (New York: Harper & Row, 1964), 9–10.

80. Kennedy, *The Pursuit of Justice*, 93–94.

81. In one speech, RFK equated law and rights: "We know it is law which enables men to live together, that creates order out of chaos. We know that the law is the glue that holds civilization together. And, we know that if one man's rights are denied, the rights of all are endangered." Law Day Address at the University of Georgia Law School, 6 May 1961. On another occasion, he said, "In the last analysis, our every right is only worth what our lawyer makes it worth. Our profession is quasi-public in its interests and purposes." Address at Fordham University, 18 Nov. 1961, folder "Fordham University 11/18/61." Both speeches in Box 1, RFK Papers—Attorney General Files—Speeches 1961–64, John F. Kennedy Library.

82. Law Day Address to the Virginia State Bar, 1 May 1962. Folder "Law Day Virginia State Bar 5/1/62," Box 1, RFK Papers—Attorney General Files—Speeches 1961–64, Kennedy Library.

83. His focus on certain issues is evident in the topics on which he gave congressional testimony or made public speeches. For example, between 16 Jan. 1962 and 26 June 1964 he testified before Congress at least seven different times on civil rights issues, five times on poverty issues, and twice each on juvenile delinquency and organized crime. Of the more than one hundred speeches he delivered between 20 Apr. 1961 and 27 Aug. 1964, a quarter were on civil rights: voting, poll taxes, literacy tests, public accommodations, and school integration. Problems of youth and juvenile delinquency accounted for about 12 percent. The Cold War and communism was the topic in 15 percent.

84. Kennedy, *The Pursuit of Justice*, 3.

85. Theodore C. Sorenson, *Kennedy* (New York: Harper & Row, 1965), 35, 117. Sorensen was John Kennedy's closest adviser; he held the post of special counsel to the president from January 1961 to January 1964.

86. Sorensen, *Kennedy*, 257.

87. Robert Novak, "Brother Bobby: His Appointment Runs Big Political Risks, Including His Own Aggressive Personality," *Wall Street Journal*, 19 Dec. 1960. Liberals remembered Robert's disregard for civil liberties while chief counsel of the Senate rackets committee, especially his badgering of witnesses. Earlier he had worked for the McCarthy committee. Joseph McCarthy was a family friend and had even dated sister Pat. To his credit, Robert left when Roy Cohn was made staff director, and he subsequently criticized McCarthyism. Victor S. Navasky, *Kennedy Justice* (New York: Atheneum, 1971), xvi–xvii.

88. Navasky, *Kennedy Justice*, 441.

89. Clark Mollenhoff, "Presidents, Communication and the Public: The Kennedy and Nixon Administrations," in *Virginia Papers on the Presidency*, White Burkett Miller Center Forums, ed. Kenneth Thompson (Lanham, Md.: University Press of America, 1985), 20: 82.

90. Arthur M. Schlesinger, Jr., *Robert Kennedy and His Times* (Boston: Houghton Mifflin Co., 1978), 229.

91. Edwin Guthman and Jeffrey Shulman, *Robert Kennedy: In His Own Words* (New York: Bantam, 1988), 73. Oral history interviews conducted with Anthony Lewis in December 1964. Guthman was in RFK's Office of Public Information in the Department of Justice.

92. Quoted in Schlesinger, *Robert Kennedy and His Times*, 230.

93. Novak, "Brother Bobby," 12.

94. Navasky, *Kennedy Justice*, xiv.

95. Ibid., xii, 441. The department was, Schlesinger wrote, "brilliantly staffed" (*Robert Kennedy and His Times*, 237–239).

96. Norbert Schlei, assistant attorney general in the OLC, interview by John Francis Stewart, 20–21 Feb. 1968, 23, John F. Kennedy Library Oral History Program.

97. Schlesinger, *Robert Kennedy and His Times*, 368.

98. Letter, Seigenthaler to John McCray, 15 May 1961. Folder "Civil Rights, 1/1961–6/1961," Box 9, RFK General Correspondence—Attorney General, Kennedy Library. He did add that Kennedy was "deeply interested in matters involving civil rights," which was evidently the nature of McCray's initial correspondence.

99. Guthman and Shulman, *Robert Kennedy: In His Own Words*, 359. Congressman Keogh had lined up the New York delegation behind Kennedy in 1960, thereby helping him secure the nomination.

100. Frank M. Tuerkheimer, "The Executive Investigates Itself," *California Law Review* 65 (1977): 597, 606–607. The president even told Seigenthaler that he hoped that Robert would not indict Vincent Keogh. Schlesinger, *Robert Kennedy and His Times*, 382–383.

101. Navasky, *Kennedy Justice*, 372–377.

102. Ibid., 378–391.

103. Schlesinger, *Robert Kennedy and His Times*, 382–391.

104. Ibid., 369–371.

105. Letter, Robert F. Kennedy to John M. Bailey, 19 July 1961. Folder "Democratic National Committee, RFK Personal, 12/1960–12/1961 and undated," Box 12, RFK Papers—Attorney General's Correspondence—Personal 1961–1964, Kennedy Library.

106. Memos, Roy Reuther to RFK, 17 Feb. 1961, 20 Apr. 1962, and 2 Mar. 1963. Folder "Reuther," Box 48, RFK Papers—Attorney General's General Correspondence, Kennedy Library.

107. See, for example, Memo, Udall to RFK, 2 Feb. 1962; Letter, Udall to RFK, 16 May 1962; and Letter, Udall to RFK, 12 June 1962. All in folder "1962 Udall-Unruh," Box 6, RFK papers—Attorney General's Correspondence—Personal 1961–1964, Kennedy Library.

108. Material in folders "Democratic National Committee 6/1962–9/1962," and "Democratic National Committee 1964 Campaign, 1963," Box 12, RFK Papers—Attorney General's Correspondence—Personal 1961–1964, Kennedy Library.

109. One state party chair wrote to thank Robert Kennedy for speaking with Agriculture Secretary Orville Freeman on his behalf; Freeman had evidently assured him that he would have a job there when his term as state chair ended. Letter, Bob Crites, state chairman of the Democratic State Central Committee of Colorado, to RFK, 4 Feb. 1961, Folder "Crimins, John W.—Crosswhite," Box 14, RFK Papers—Attorney General's General Correspondence, Kennedy Library.

110. Memo, Kenneth O'Donnell to Robert F. Kennedy, 20 July 1961. Folder "Democratic National Committee, RFK Personal, 12/1960–12/1961 and undated," Box 12, RFK Papers—Attorney General's Correspondence—Personal 1961–1964, Kennedy Library. Robert also wrote to congratulate the newly-organized seventh ward Democratic Club of Buffalo, New York, 23 July 1962. Folder "Democratic Study Group—DeSimone," Box 15, RFK Papers—General Correspondence, Kennedy Library.

111. In May 1961 he sent letters to about 130 law school deans asking for their assistance in locating qualified black attorneys interested in working for Justice. Also see letters from John Wheeler to John Seigenthaler, 22 Mar. 1961, and from John Seigenthaler to Henry Bramwell, 27 Apr. 1961, in folder "Civil Rights, 1/1961–6/1961," Box 9, RFK Papers—Attorney General's Correspondence, Kennedy Library.

112. The Democratic National Committee was working closely with local party organizations in mounting black registration drives. Kennedy was kept apprised through Matthew Reese. See Memos, Reese to DNC chairman, cc: RFK, of 6 Sept., 12 Sept., 19 Sept., 3 Oct., 11 Oct., 16 Oct., and 1 Nov. 1963, and Memo, Reese to RFK, 12 Nov. 1963, Folder "Democratic National Committee: Voter Registration Drive, 1963-64," Box 15, RFK Papers—Attorney General's General Correspondence, Kennedy Library.

113. Navasky, *Kennedy Justice*, xx, 329–332.

114. Johnson, *Managing the White House*, 134.

115. Quoted in Schlesinger, *Robert Kennedy and His Times*, 232.

116. Schlesinger, *Robert Kennedy and His Times*, 599.

117. Mollenhoff, "Presidents, Communication and the Public," 84–85. Mollenhoff had traveled extensively in Ghana in 1960 and developed a negative opinion of Nkrumah; his subsequent opposition to finance the Volta Dam convinced Robert but not John. At the time, Nkrumah was considered by some to be a prophet; by others, a despot; and still others, including himself, a Marxist socialist.

118. Schlesinger, *Robert Kennedy and His Times*, 560. The attorney general is not one of the statutory members of the NSC. When Robert Kennedy attended meetings, he generally sat with NSC staff members along the wall, and not at the table with the statutory members.

119. Mollenhoff, "Presidents, Communication and the Public," 85.

120. Schlesinger, *Robert Kennedy and His Times*, 417.

121. Ibid., 459.

122. Ibid., 446–449. Other members were Allen Dulles and Adm. Arleigh Burke. Robert Kennedy took the lead in examining the witnesses, and so won General Taylor's respect.

123. Norbert Schlei, interview, 11, John F. Kennedy Library Oral History Program.

124. Navasky, *Kennedy Justice*, 333–338, 342–347. Schlesinger, *Robert Kennedy and His Times*, 469–470. His assistant attorney general in charge of antitrust, Lou Oberdorfer, headed an effort to trade pharmaceuticals for the prisoners.

125. Schlesinger, *Robert Kennedy and His Times*, 461, 465.

126. Kennedy, *Pursuit of Justice*, 146.

127. For example, at the end of a memo to the president, Chester Bowles, the undersecretary of State, wrote, "I hope that I may have an opportunity before long to talk to Bobby or others whom you might suggest about the intricacies of the development process in Asia, Africa, and Latin America." Memo, Bowles to John Kennedy, 16 Nov. 1962, Folder "Bowles, Chester 10/62–11/62," Box 5, RFK Papers—Attorney General's Correspondence, Kennedy Library. Even after he was made ambassador to India, Bowles continued to send Robert Kennedy proposals, Folder "Bowles, Chester 1/64–6/64," Box 6, RFK Papers—Attorney General's Correspondence, Kennedy Library.

128. Schlesinger, *Robert Kennedy and His Times*, 566. Japan's newly appointed ambassador, Edwin Reischauer, said that "if I really had something that I just had to get to the President, . . . I could always do it that way [through contacting Robert]. . . . It was the most important channel."

129. See the folders "India," and "Indonesia 6/1962–12/1962," both in Box 26, RFK Papers—General Correspondence, Kennedy Library. Also see folder "Korea," Box 31, RFK Papers—General Correspondence, Kennedy Library.

130. Letter, President H. Maga of the Republic of Dahomey, to RFK, 13 Jan. 1962, Folder "State Department 1/1962–6/1962," Box 58, RFK Papers—Attorney General's General Correspondence, Kennedy Library.

131. Schlesinger, *Robert Kennedy and His Times*, 562.

132. Ibid., 499–500.

133. Robert F. Kennedy, *Thirteen Days: A Memoir of the Cuban Missile Crisis* (New York: W. W. Norton & Co., 1969), 24–25, 27, 65–66, 106–110. Robert Kennedy, at the request of the president and the secretary of State, met privately with Dobrynin on 27 Oct., at the height of the crisis, to explain the president's position. Schlesinger notes that Khrushchev, in his autobiography, wrote that Robert Kennedy had been especially open and candid with the Soviets during the missile crisis. Schlesinger, *Robert Kennedy and His Times*, 522.

134. Airgram, Secretary of State to RFK, 29 Jan. 1962, Folder "State Department 1/1962–6/1962," Box 58, RFK Papers—Attorney General's General Correspondence, Kennedy Library.

135. Schlesinger, *Robert Kennedy and His Times*, 563–573.

136. "Program for Attorney General's Debriefing on His Round-the-World Trip," 28 Mar., 1962, Folder "State Department 1/1962–6/1962," Box 58, RFK Papers—Attorney General's General Correspondence, Kennedy Library. Memo, Robert Kennedy to John Kennedy, 30 Mar. 1962, Folder "FG 135 3/21/62–8/10/62," Box 145, WHCF—Subject File, Kennedy Library.

137. Kennedy, *Pursuit of Justice*, 142–148. Material in folder "Canal Zone Trip, 1963," Box 8, RFK Papers—Attorney General's Correspondence, Kennedy Library. Schlesinger, *Robert Kennedy and His Times*, 575, 581, 635.

138. The incidents really are dissimilar, despite the parallels drawn between them, because the bases exchange involved domestic law, while the blockade involved international law, which is largely customary.

139. Miller, *Roles of the Attorney General of the United States*, 59.

140. Griffin Bell, *Taking Care of the Law* (New York: Morrow, 1982), 185–186.

141. Museum, Kennedy Library. Although I found no documented link between this memo and the legal opinion, they were written just days apart.

142. Memo, Norbert A. Schlei to Robert F. Kennedy, 30 Aug. 1962, Folder "Cuban Missile Crisis," Box 14, RFK General Correspondence—Attorney General, Kennedy Library. Other suggestions in the August memo also surfaced during the actual crisis, including his advice that the United States rely on collective security, particularly the Organization of American States, for policy as well as legal reasons.

143. Norbert Schlei, interview, 10–11, John F. Kennedy Library Oral History Program.

144. "Interdiction of the Delivery of Offensive Weapons to Cuba by the President of the United States of America—A Proclamation," 23 Oct. 1962, Folder "Cuban Matters 10/1962–12/1962," Box 14, RFK General Correspondence—Attorney General, Kennedy Library. These later versions, however, deleted Schlei's mention of the Monroe Doctrine, because of the sensitivity in Latin America toward unilateral North American action.

145. von Glahn, Law among Nations, 509, 511. One must point out that the OAS did not meet until the day after the United States had announced its intentions. Nevertheless, the actual blockade was not implemented until the day after the OAS vote.

146. Sorensen, Kennedy, 687.

147. Kennedy, Thirteen Days, 121.

148. Ibid., 33, 48–50.

149. Ibid., 34–37.

150. Ibid., 37–38. Robert, on the other hand, did have an underlying agenda, but it was moral rather than political or legal. He opposed an air strike because, "I could not accept the idea that the United States would rain bombs on Cuba, killing thousands and thousands of civilians in a surprise attack. . . . America's traditions and history would not permit such a course of action. . . . a surprise attack by a very large nation against a very small one."

151. von Glahn, Law among Nations, 506–508, 512.

152. Robert S. McNamara, "Introduction," in Kennedy, Thirteen Days, 14–15.

153. Sorensen, Kennedy, 679.

154. Kennedy, Thirteen Days, 86–89, 93–95, 101–102.

155. Ibid., 86.

156. Schlesinger, Robert Kennedy and His Times, 596.

157. Johnson, Managing the White House, 134. Sorensen, Kennedy, 373–374.

158. Sorensen, Kennedy, 269.

159. Schlesinger, Robert Kennedy and His Times, 599.

160. Navasky, Kennedy Justice, 159–160.

161. Harold F. Gosnell, Truman's Crises: A Political Biography of Harry S Truman (Westport, Conn.: Greenwood Press, 1980), 420.

162. Andrew J. Dunar, The Truman Scandals and the Politics of Morality (Columbia: University of Missouri Press, 1984), 34–35, 97, 104, 106–119.

163. Jeff Stein, "The Forgotten Side of the 1960's Comes to the White House—Officer Ed Meese," New Republic, 7 Oct. 1981, 21.

164. John A. Jenkins, "Mr. Power: Attorney General Meese Is Reagan's Man to Lead the Conservative Charge," *New York Times Magazine*, 12 Oct. 1986, 96. Also see Senate, Committee on the Judiciary, *Hearings on the Nomination of Edwin Meese III to Be Attorney General*, 98th Cong., 2d sess. (Washington, D.C.: Government Printing Office, 1985), 1: 20.

165. *Hearings on Edwin Meese III*, 1: 92. Meese denied that he was involved in fundraising or budgeting and denied any connection to Reagan's political action committee other than serving voluntarily as its counsel. See 145–148.

166. Terrel Bell, *The Thirteenth Man: A Reagan Cabinet Memoir* (New York: Free Press/Macmillan, 1988), 3, 39, 44–45, 57.

167. Larry Speakes with Robert Pack, *Speaking Out: The Reagan Presidency from Inside the White House* (New York: Charles Scribner's Sons, 1988), 68, 70.

168. Fred I. Greenstein, "The Need for an Early Appraisal of the Reagan Presidency," in *The Reagan Presidency: An Early Assessment*, ed. Greenstein (Baltimore: Johns Hopkins University Press, 1983), 17.

169. Speakes, *Speaking Out*, 71.

170. Gary McDowell, interview with author, Washington, D.C., 30 July 1987. While in the Justice Department, he headed the staff that wrote the attorney general's speeches.

171. Donald T. Regan, *For the Record: From Wall Street to Washington* (San Diego: Harcourt Brace Jovanovich, 1988), 235, 238. Former Chief of Staff Regan writes that this was the first time the attorney general was a member of the NSC and not just an observer.

172. Paula Dwyer and Stan Crock, "Ed Meese's Conservative Crusade: How Far Will He Get?" *Business Week*, 4 Nov. 1985, 70, 73.

173. Jenkins, "Mr. Power," 19.

174. Burt Solomon, "Meese Sets Ambitious Agenda That Challenges Fundamental Legal Beliefs," *National Journal* 17: 2640.

175. *Hearings on Edwin Meese III*, 1: 149. He said, for example, "I would say I am a major policy adviser to the President, if you can distinguish that from being a political adviser." Also see 2: 107.

176. Lincoln Caplan, *The Tenth Justice: The Solicitor General and the Rule of Law* (New York: Alfred A. Knopf, 1987), 70. Jenkins, "Mr. Power," 89. Elder Witt, *A Different Justice: Reagan and the Supreme Court* (Washington, D.C.: Congressional Quarterly, 1986), 139–147.

177. This was the first time that the solicitor general "had asked the Supreme Court to decide that a right the Justices had previously found in the Constitution was no longer there." Caplan, *The Tenth Justice*, 126.

178. Jenkins, "Mr. Power," 92. Also see Richard Wiley and Laurence Bodine, "Q & A with the Attorney General," *American Bar Association Journal* 71 (July 1985): 44, 45. The exclusionary rule prohibits illegally gained evidence from being introduced at trial. It is intended to discourage police officers from violating the constitutional prohibition on illegal searches and seizures.

179. Caplan, *The Tenth Justice*, 126–127. As we shall see, this approach may have contributed to Iran-contra and other scandals.

180. Witt, *A Different Justice*, 135–136.

181. Solomon, "Meese Sets Ambitious Agenda," 2643. Also see Caplan,

The Tenth Justice, 121. Justice William Brennan also issued a scholarly rebuttal of Meese's philosophy.

182. Stephen Macedo, "The Endangered Branch: The Judiciary under Reagan," in *Assessing the Reagan Years*, ed. David Boaz (Washington, D.C.: Cato Institute, 1988), 355.

183. Dwyer and Crock, "Ed Meese's Conservative Crusade," *Business Week*, 4 Nov. 1985, 70.

184. Wiley and Bodine, "Q & A with the Attorney General," 46. Meese explained that his approach stressed "judges who are interpreters of the law, not makers of new law."

185. *Hearings on Edwin Meese III*, 1: 91, 94–95. Elliot Richardson, for example, writes that "it undermines the integrity of the law when the President tells legal officers how to handle a particular case." Elliot Richardson, *The Creative Balance* (New York: Holt, Rinehart & Winston, 1976), 27.

186. Speakes, *Speaking Out*, 82.

187. *Bob Jones University v. United States*, 461 U.S. 574 (1983).

188. Caplan, *The Tenth Justice*, 51–60.

189. 104 S.Ct. 1211 (1984). The only federal funds the school received were indirect, through student financial aid. Claiming to be independent of government control, the college refused to fill out the required federal forms. There were no allegations of racial or sex-based discrimination.

190. Bell, *The Thirteenth Man*, 101.

191. Ibid., 112–113.

192. Interviewed in Solomon, "Meese Sets Ambitious Agenda," 2640.

193. Caplan, *The Tenth Justice*, 119.

194. Ibid., 271.

195. Ruth Marcus, "Hours of Preparation Preceded Testimony: Meese Was Grilled by Staff," *Washington Post*, 29 July 1987. For example, he spent much of two weeks preparing for his testimony before the Iran-contra hearings. In addition, others in the Justice Department were preoccupied with photocopying documents that had been subpoenaed by the special prosecutor.

196. Editorial, "Mr. Meese's Pipelines," *New York Times*, 2 Feb. 1988. Later that week, another story reported "he must spend hours each week huddling with his small army of private lawyers." Philip Shenon, "Despite Meese's Woes, Agency Muddles Through," *New York Times*, 5 Feb. 1988.

197. *Hearings on Edwin Meese III*, 1: 25–27, 103–112.

198. Ibid., 2: 12–18, 102.

199. Clifford May, "Meese Tells Panel He Didn't Violate U.S. Law on Ethics," *New York Times*, 10 July 1987.

200. U.S. Senate, *Hearings before the Subcommittee on Oversight of Government Management of the Committee on Governmental Affairs*, 100th Cong., 1st sess. (Washington, D.C.: Government Printing Office, 1988), 27–28, 34, 41.

201. Philip Shenon, "Attorney General Denies Wrongdoing on Pipeline Plan," *New York Times*, 2 Feb. 1988. Jeff Gerth, "1985 Pipeline Memo to Meese Said Peres Party Would Profit," *New York Times*, 23 Feb. 1988. Meese's attorneys insisted that his role was passive and limited. Other government officials claimed that he had played "an important and sustained role in the project."

Jeff Gerth, "Baker Says Reagan Has No Plan to Ask for Meese's Resignation," *New York Times*, 1 Feb. 1988.

202. James C. McKay, "Report of Independent Counsel in Re Edwin Meese 3d," 5 July 1988, U.S. Court of Appeals for the District of Columbia Circuit.

203. Oliver North testimony, *The Iran-Contra Puzzle* (Washington, D.C.: Congressional Quarterly, 1987), C-78. "North Insists His Superiors Backed Iran-Contra Deals," *New York Times*, 8 July 1987. "North Contradicts the Testimony of Others on Contra Aid Efforts," *New York Times*, 9 July 1987.

204. *Report of the Congressional Committee Investigating the Iran-Contra Affair*, 100th Cong., 1st sess., H. Rept. No. 100-433, S. Rept. No. 100-216, (Washington, D.C.: Government Printing Office, 1987), 414, 418–419, 424.

205. William S. Cohen and George J. Mitchell, *Men of Zeal: A Candid Inside Story of the Iran-Contra Hearings* (New York: Viking, 1989), 223–227. Edwin Meese testimony, *The Iran-Contra Puzzle*, C-120–C-126.

206. David Rosenbaum, "North Says His Shredding Continued Despite Presence of Justice Department Aides," *New York Times*, 10 July 1987.

207. Cohen and Mitchell, *Men of Zeal*, 223.

208. *Iran-Contra Affair Report*, 305. Elaine Shannon, "The Resilient Loyalist," *Time*, 3 Aug. 1987. Oliver North testimony, *The Iran-Contra Puzzle*, C-77.

209. Cohen and Mitchell, *Men of Zeal*, 228–299.

210. Haynes Johnson, "Affable Witness Talks of Confusion," *Washington Post*, 29 July 1987.

211. Caplan, *The Tenth Justice*, 134.

212. Stephen Engelberg, "Panel on Iran-Contra Affair Did Not Get Pipeline Memo," *New York Times*, 24 Feb. 1988.

213. Speakes, *Speaking Out*, 83, 306.

214. Cohen and Mitchell, *Men of Zeal*, 221.

215. Philip Shenon, "High Justice Aides Quit amid Concern over Meese's Role," *New York Times*, 30 Mar. 1988. Philip Shenon, "More Justice Aides Expected to Resign," *New York Times*, 31 Mar. 1988. Fox Butterfield, "Ex-Justice Aide Deeply Troubled by Meese Role," *New York Times*, 31 Mar. 1988.

216. See, for example, Editorial, "For an Earlier Meese Exit," *Christian Science Monitor*, 5 Feb. 1988. Editorial, "The D p tme t of J st ce," *New York Times*, 31 Mar. 1988. "Meese Told He Is Hurting GOP and Bush Presidential Campaign," *New York Times*, 26 May 1988.

217. Julie Johnson, "Democrats Press Meese to Resign; He Vows to Stay," *New York Times*, 31 Mar. 1988.

218. Ruth Marcus, "The Justice Department Renders a Verdict on Ed Meese," *Washington Post National Weekly*, 23 Jan. 1989.

219. Speakes, *Speaking Out*, 88.

220. Lou Cannon, Bill McAllister, Ruth Marcus, "Exit Ed Meese." *Washington Post National Weekly*, 11 July 1988.

221. He had served as a U.S. attorney and headed the department's criminal division during the Ford administration. Thornburgh also taught a short while at Harvard University's Kennedy School of Government.

222. Philip Shenon, "Nominee Is Backed for Meese's Post," *New York*

Times, 11 Aug. 1988. Thornburgh's subsequent tenure suggests that he also may have an activist conception of the attorney general's office.

Chapter Four. The Danger of the Advocate: Abusing the Office

1. Victor Navasky, "The Greening of Griffin Bell," *New York Times Magazine*, 27 Feb. 1977, 41.
2. Elliot Richardson, *The Creative Balance* (New York: Holt, Rinehart & Winston, 1976), 27.
3. Charles E. Goodell testimony, Senate, Subcommittee on Separation of Powers of the Senate Committee on the Judiciary, *Hearings on S. 2803 and S. 2978 on Removing Politics from the Administration of Justice*, 93d Cong., 2d sess. (Washington, D.C.: Government Printing Office, 1974), 142.
4. Stanley Coben, *A. Mitchell Palmer: Politician* (New York: Columbia University Press, 1963), 9, 16, 17, 28, 39. For more biography, also see Donald Johnson, "The Political Career of A. Mitchell Palmer," *Pennsylvania History* 25 (October 1958): 345, 347–348.
5. Coben, *A. Mitchell Palmer*, 53–55, 57.
6. Ibid., 57, 59–62. For example, he was offered the vice-presidential slot by one candidate and was encouraged by another to seek the nomination himself.
7. Ibid., 67–70.
8. Ibid., 67–72. Actually, Wilson did offer Palmer the post of secretary of War, but Palmer, as a Quaker, felt that he had to turn it down.
9. Johnson, "The Political Career of A. Mitchell Palmer," 348.
10. Coben, *A. Mitchell Palmer*, 75, 79, 80, 83.
11. Ibid., 112–113, 125.
12. Ibid., 127–134. One such appointee was Homer Cummings, later head of the national party and then attorney general under FDR.
13. Johnson, "The Political Career of A. Mitchell Palmer," 350.
14. Coben, *A. Mitchell Palmer*, 150–152, 155–156, 171.
15. Johnson, "The Political Career of A. Mitchell Palmer," 352.
16. Coben, *A. Mitchell Palmer*, 196–197, 203.
17. Ibid., 235–236.
18. Ibid., 203–205, 208, 210–211.
19. Ibid., 219–221. Johnson, "The Political Career of A. Mitchell Palmer," 357.
20. Coben, *A. Mitchell Palmer*, 225–229. Johnson, "The Political Career of A. Mitchell Palmer," 358–361. R. G. Brown et al., *Illegal Practices of the Department of Justice* (1920; reprint, New York: Arno Press and *New York Times*, 1969), 11–29.
21. Coben, *A. Mitchell Palmer*, 230–237, 241.
22. R. G. Brown et al., *Illegal Practices*, 4–6, 8.
23. Senate, Judiciary Committee, *Hearings on the Charges of Illegal Practices*

of the Department of Justice Made by Committee of Lawyers on Behalf of National Popular Government League (Washington, D.C.: Government Printing Office, 1921).

24. Coben, *A. Mitchell Palmer*, 239.

25. Ibid., 239–240.

26. Ibid., 239–241.

27. Ibid., 230, 244.

28. Ibid., 224, 226–228. Hoover alone decided that membership in the Communist Labor party was a deportable offense. He also established the procedure of rounding up crowds of people and then matching them to arrest warrants.

29. Ibid., 229, 245.

30. House, Rules Committee, *Hearings on Attorney General A. Mitchell Palmer on Charges Made against the Department of Justice by Louis F. Post and Others* (Washington, D.C.: Government Printing Office, 1921).

31. Johnson, "The Political Career of A. Mitchell Palmer," 363, 365–368.

32. Coben, *A. Mitchell Palmer*, 263–265.

33. Ibid., 147, 149.

34. Ibid., 251.

35. Ibid., 266.

36. James Giglio, *H. M. Daugherty and the Politics of Expediency* (Kent, Ohio: Kent State University Press, 1978), ix, 6, 7, 13, 18, 19, 61.

37. Ibid., 7.

38. Francis Russell, *The Shadow of Blooming Grove: Warren G. Harding and His Times* (New York: McGraw-Hill, 1968), 111–112.

39. Giglio, *H. M. Daugherty*, 38, 39, 41–50. The client was not dying, and this deception dogged Daugherty's nomination to the attorney generalship in 1920-21.

40. Russell, *The Shadow of Blooming Grove*, 110.

41. Ibid., 108, 113. At the time they met, Daugherty, the rally's main speaker, was well known in Ohio. Yet Harding's demeanor impressed Daugherty, who invited him to make an impromptu speech that evening.

42. Giglio, *H. M. Daugherty*, 83.

43. Ibid., 40, 90–96, 109, 116, 119. While his friends were eventually jailed for embezzlement in the 1913 incident, Daugherty never faced charges because of insufficient evidence.

44. Ibid., 123. Robert K. Murray, *The Harding Era* (Minneapolis: University of Minnesota Press, 1969), 106. Russell, *The Shadow of Blooming Grove*, 434.

45. Russell, *The Shadow of Blooming Grove*, 448–449. Giglio, *H. M. Daugherty*, 141. Murray, *The Harding Era*, 421, 486.

46. Richard Fenno, *The President's Cabinet: An Analysis in the Period from Wilson to Eisenhower* (Cambridge, Mass.: Harvard University Press, 1959), 187–189. Fenno is among those who have characterized Daugherty as a political wire-puller with an important influence on Harding.

47. Harry M. Daugherty, with Thomas Dixon, *The Inside Story of the Harding Tragedy* (New York: Churchill Co., 1932). Dixon also authored the racist novels *Birth of a Nation* and *The Klansman*.

48. Giglio, *H. M. Daugherty*, 142–143. Daugherty's opinion was not with-

out foundation, however. After all, a peace treaty had already been signed with Germany, and Congress had enacted two joint resolutions providing for cessation of hostilities.

49. H. M. Daugherty, "Letter to Finley Peter Dunne, April, 1922," in ibid., 144.

50. Giglio, H. M. Daugherty, 144–145, 160. Hoover wrote in his memoirs that, because of Daugherty's character, "he should never have been in any government." Herbert Hoover, Memoirs (New York: Macmillan, 1952), 2: 53.

51. Giglio, H. M. Daugherty, 118, 124, 125.

52. Ibid., 130–131.

53. Ibid., 124–130, 135–137. Murray, The Harding Era, 432–433. Also see C. Vann Woodward, Responses of the Presidents to Charges of Misconduct (New York: Dell, 1974), 244–247.

54. Russell, The Shadow of Blooming Grove, 546–548. Giglio, H. M. Daugherty, 144, 146, 152, 154–155. Secretary of Commerce Hoover called Daugherty's injunction against the strikers illegal, a violation of the most rudimentary rights of shopmen. The injunction was the most sweeping and drastic ever issued and appalled both Hoover and Secretary of State Hughes. When they denounced the action in a cabinet meeting, Daugherty just mumbled that it had been approved by his department lawyers.

55. Giglio, H. M. Daugherty, 154–155, 160.

56. Ibid., 163–164. Murray, The Harding Era, 474–479, 484. Burl Noggle, Teapot Dome: Oil and Politics in the 1920's (Westport, Conn.: Greenwood Press, 1980), 80–81, 106, 117, 118, 126–128. For more on Coolidge, see chapter five.

57. Giglio, H. M. Daugherty, 53.

58. Senate, Hearings before the Select Committee on Investigation of Attorney General Harry M. Daugherty, 68th Cong., 1st sess. (Washington, D.C.: Government Printing Office, 1924). The hearings ran for two months and produced almost three thousand pages of testimony.

59. Giglio, H. M. Daugherty, 176, 181–193. Woodward, Responses of the Presidents, 244–247.

60. Frank M. Tuerkheimer, "The Executive Investigates Itself," California Law Review 65 (1977): 597, 603–604. The first jury was deadlocked 7–5 for conviction; the second 11–1 for conviction. Noggle incorrectly writes that Daugherty never faced court charges for the wrongs he committed as attorney general. Noggle, Teapot Dome, 128.

61. Giglio, H. M. Daugherty, 177, 179.

62. James A. Farley, Behind the Ballots: The Personal History of a Politician (New York: Harcourt, Brace & Co., 1938), 223.

63. Stephen Grover, "Cabinet Enigma: New Attorney General Poses Question Marks on Antitrust, Rights," Wall Street Journal, 17 Jan. 1969.

64. Theodore H. White, The Making of the President 1968 (New York: Atheneum, 1969), 45–46, 142. White dates their first meeting to 1947, but others place it in 1963, after Nixon's move to New York.

65. Louis Kohlmeier, "A Velvet Glove: Despite New Image, the Attorney General Still Wields Iron Fist," Wall Street Journal, 5 Aug. 1970.

66. Dan Rather and Gary Paul Gates, *The Palace Guard* (New York: Harper & Row, 1974), 26.

67. Kohlmeier, "A Velvet Glove."

68. Rather and Gates, *The Palace Guard*, 207.

69. Jack Landau, "Mitchell Recalled," *New Orleans Times Picayune*, 14 Nov. 1988. Landau had been Mitchell's press secretary when he first joined the Justice Department. Rather and Gates note that Mitchell was a determining factor in Nixon's decision to approve the offensive into Cambodia. Rather and Gates, *The Palace Guard*, 208.

70. Kohlmeier, "A Velvet Glove."

71. Rather and Gates, *The Palace Guard*, 26, 208, 214.

72. Eleanora W. Schoenebaum, ed., *Political Profiles: The Nixon/Ford Years* (New York: Facts on File, 1979), 443–444.

73. Magruder testimony in *The Watergate Hearings: Break-In and Cover-up: Proceedings of the Senate Select Committee on Presidential Campaign Activities*, ed. *New York Times* staff (New York: Bantam, 1973), 247–261. John Dean, who had attended the first two meetings, corroborated Magruder's account. Dean, former counsel to the president, had initially served in the Justice Department under Mitchell. James McCord, Jr., one of the burglars, also testified that Mitchell knew and approved of the plan, although his knowledge was only through hearsay. See 146, 147, 155–163, 271.

74. Mitchell testimony in *The Watergate Hearings*, 366–373, 389–390, 392. He testified just a few days before Alexander Butterfield revealed the existence of a secret White House tape recorder.

75. Richardson, *The Creative Balance*, 8–9.

76. *The Watergate Hearings*, 387–388.

77. Mitchell testimony, Senate, Committee on the Judiciary, *Hearings on the Nomination of Richard G. Kleindienst to be Attorney General*, 92d Cong., 2d sess. (Washington, D.C.: Government Printing Office, 1972), 608, 633.

78. *Watergate Special Prosecution Force Report* (Washington, D.C.: Government Printing Office, 1975), 52, 156. The cases were *Mitchell, et al., v. Sirica*, USCA D.C. Cir. No. 74-1492, 502 F.2d 373 (1974), and *U.S. v. Mitchell*, USCA D.C. Cir. No. 75-1384.

79. Schoenebaum, ed., *Political Profiles*, 445.

80. Whitney North Seymour, Jr., *United States Attorney: An Inside View of "Justice" in America under the Nixon Administration* (New York: William Morrow & Co., 1975), 72–73.

81. Seymour, *United States Attorney*, 70–71.

82. Landau, "Mitchell Recalled."

83. Conversation of 30 Apr. 1974 in *Submission of Recorded Presidential Conversations to the Committee on the Judiciary of the House of Representatives by President Richard Nixon* (Buffalo, N.Y.: William Hein & Co., 1974), 440, 450–455, 499, 503, 524, 527.

84. Conversation of 14 Apr. 1974 in *Submission of Recorded Presidential Conversations*, 535–536.

85. H. R. Haldeman, with Joseph DiMona, *The Ends of Power* (New York: Times Books, 1978), 126. Actually, James McCord, Jr., one of the Watergate bur-

glars, testified that he attempted to bug McGovern's office on two or three occasions but that the office was always occupied. McCord testimony, *The Watergate Hearings*, 161.

86. Sam J. Ervin, Jr., *The Whole Truth: The Watergate Conspiracy* (New York: Random House, 1980), vii.

Chapter Five. The Neutral Attorney General

1. John P. Kennedy, *Memoirs of the Life of William Wirt* (Philadelphia: Lea and Blanchard, 1850), 2: 79–80, 142. In Burr's treason trial, Wirt had been retained to assist the U.S. attorney in the prosecution.

2. F. W. Thomas, *John Randolph of Roanoke and Other Sketches of Character, Including William Wirt* (Philadelphia: A. Hart, late Carey & Hart, 1853), 36–37, 46.

3. Kennedy, *William Wirt*, 367, 369, 371.

4. George Dangerfield, *The Era of Good Feelings* (New York: Harcourt, Brace & Co., 1952), 295.

5. Charles Francis Adams, ed., *Memoirs of John Quincy Adams* (1874–77; reprint, New York: AMS Press, 1970), 4: 205–206 (entry of 1 Jan. 1819); 5: 367–369 (entry of 24 Oct. 1821); and 6: 380–382 (entries of 10 and 11 June 1824).

6. See, for example, ibid., 4: 37; 5: 366; 6: 217, 380–382.

7. William Penn Cresson, *James Monroe* (Chapel Hill: University of North Carolina Press, 1946), 290–292, 297, 348–349.

8. Kennedy, *William Wirt*, 55, 147–148. The so-called Era of Good Feelings, although it became synonymous with the entire Monroe administration, rightly applies only to 1817–1819, a period of one-party government when most conflicts centered on personalities and not policies or principles.

9. Wirt, "Letter to Monroe, May 5, 1823," in Kennedy, *William Wirt*, 133–137.

10. Wirt, "Letter to Judge Carr, August 27, 1824," in Kennedy, *William Wirt*, 149.

11. Wirt, "Letter to Pope, June 24, 1828," Kennedy, *William Wirt*, 217–218. He expressed this sentiment in letters to other friends as well.

12. Wirt, "Letter to Rev. John Rice, February 1, 1822," in Kennedy, *William Wirt*, 120.

13. Wirt, "Letter to Pope, March 22, 1829," in Kennedy, *William Wirt*, 228.

14. Monroe, "Letter to Wirt, October 24, 1828," in Kennedy, *William Wirt*, 221–222.

15. "Biographical Sketch," preface in William Wirt, *The Letters of the British Spy* (New York: Harper & Bros., 1835), 46, 52, 57, 62–64.

16. Kennedy, *William Wirt*, 53. At this time, the attorney general did not relinquish his private practice on assuming public office.

17. Dangerfield, *Era of Good Feelings*, 101.

18. Kennedy, *William Wirt*, 300–350.

19. The "stars" were asterisks designating frontier routes on post office publications. For a fuller description of the scandal, see George Frederick Howe, *Chester A. Arthur* (New York: Frederick Ungar Publishing Co., 1957), 180–191.

20. Eugene C. Savidge, *Life of Benjamin Harris Brewster* (Philadelphia: J. B. Lippincott, 1891), 119–122, 136–138.

21. Ibid., 139, 144–147.

22. The party was split over the pro-Grant and the pro-Garfield forces. Arthur was a pro-Grant Republican. Some newspapers even intimated that Arthur was involved in Garfield's assassination. Savidge, *Benjamin Harris Brewster*, 173–174.

23. Ibid., 148–149.

24. Howe, *Chester A. Arthur*, 181–182.

25. Savidge, *Benjamin Harris Brewster*, 62–65, 70, 94–95.

26. Ibid., 60–61, 70–71, 91, 101, 106, 109–110. He did finally serve two years as Pennsylvania attorney general, twenty-two years after he had first been considered for the post. He also worked for the federal government in 1846 as a commissioner to adjudicate the Cherokee claims against the United States.

27. Ibid., 176–177.

28. Ibid., 55.

29. Ibid., 150. This appointment had the added advantage of protecting the government from partisan attack if the prosecutions proved unsuccessful.

30. Brewster, "Letter to P. H. Woodward, Investigator of Star Route Frauds, January 2, 1885," in Savidge, *Benjamin Harris Brewster*, 168.

31. Ibid., 171.

32. Ibid., 119–122, 136.

33. Ibid., 150–154, 157, 162–165.

34. Howe, *Chester Arthur*, 192.

35. *Report of the House Springer Committee*, 48th Cong., 1st sess., cited in Howe, *Chester Arthur*, 192.

36. Howe, *Chester Arthur*, 179, 192. Also see Savidge, *Benjamin Harris Brewster*, 172.

37. Savidge, *Benjamin Harris Brewster*, 185–200.

38. Brewster, "Letter of June 23, 1882," in Savidge, *Benjamin Harris Brewster*, 200–201.

39. Ibid., 208.

40. Ibid., 210–211. Robert Goldman, "The 'Weakened Spring of Government' and the Executive Branch: The Department of Justice in the Late 19th Century," *Congress and the Presidency* 11 (Autumn 1984): 170.

41. Arthur had been part of the machine of Sen. Roscoe Conkling and had been named Garfield's running mate in part to placate the pro-Grant Conkling. Once president, Arthur surprised friend and foe alike by refusing patronage demands and vetoing substantial pork barrel measures, as well as by supporting his attorney general. See Arnold Rogow and Harold Lasswell, *Power, Corruption, and Rectitude* (Englewood Cliffs, N.J.: Prentice Hall, 1963), 36–37.

42. Savidge, *Benjamin Harris Brewster*, 117.

43. Ibid., 174. Arthur wrote Brewster a grateful letter dated 25 Aug. 1881, in reply to a sympathetic letter from Brewster. This was almost a month before Arthur assumed the presidency and almost four months before Brewster was confirmed as attorney general, so their relations clearly were cordial well before Brewster became attorney general.

44. Ibid., 184. Arthur had three Treasury secretaries and four postmasters general.

45. Goldman, "Weakened Spring of Government," 168. I disagree with Goldman's assessment of Brewster as typical of the pattern of political appointees. Such a conclusion rests on a superficial review of Brewster's past.

46. Savidge, *Benjamin Harris Brewster*, 53–54.

47. For a fuller description of Daugherty and Palmer, see chapter three.

48. James N. Giglio, *H. M. Daugherty and the Politics of Expediency* (Kent, Ohio: Kent State University Press, 1978), 163–164, 181–193. Robert K. Murray, *The Harding Era* (Minneapolis: University of Minnesota Press, 1969), 479.

49. Stone, "Letter to Alfred Lief, Feb. 17, 1944," in Alpheus Thomas Mason, *Harlan Fiske Stone: Pillar of the Law* (New York: Archon Books, 1968), 3.

50. Mason, *Harlan Fiske Stone*, 54.

51. Stone, "Letter to His Sons, March, 1929," in ibid., 262.

52. Mason, *Harlan Fiske Stone*, 82, 85, 89–90, 138. One of his pupils at Columbia was William O. Douglas.

53. Charles A. Beard, Prefatory Note, in Samuel J. Konefsky, *Chief Justice Stone and the Supreme Court* (New York: Macmillan 1946), xvii.

54. Mason, *Harlan Fiske Stone*, 87.

55. Ibid., 102, 112–114. Stone's concern with protecting minority rights is evident in his judicial opinions also, especially in his famous dissent in the first flag salute case (310 U.S. 586), which became the majority view three years later in *West Virginia Board of Education v. Barnette*, 319 U.S. 624; 63 S.Ct. 1178 (1943).

56. Mason, *Harlan Fiske Stone*, 143–144.

57. Ibid., 142, 144.

58. Editorial, "The New Attorney General," *New York Times*, 3 Apr. 1924. An editorial cartoon of 5 April in the Rochester, New York, *American* showed a workman (Coolidge) replacing the rubble of "Daughertyism" with the solid cornerstone of "Stone" in the Department of Justice building. See Mason, *Harlan Fiske Stone*, 145–146.

59. Mason, *Harlan Fiske Stone*, 149–150, 154–155. The old bureau was known for its corruption and use of political blackmail. Hoover had been a young attorney in the old bureau, in charge of helping execute Palmer's "Red Raids."

60. Ibid., 154.

61. Beard, in Konefsky, *Chief Justice Stone*, xviii.

62. Mason, *Harlan Fiske Stone*, 158, 162, 188–195. His refusal to drop an indictment against Sen. Burton Wheeler of Montana, who claimed the indictment was started by Daugherty to persecute him, held up his Supreme Court confirmation. Stone took the unprecedented step (at the time) of appearing before the Senate Judiciary Committee to answer questions on the Wheeler case.

63. Stone, "Letter to Sterling Carr, U.S. District Attorney in San Francisco, September 17, 1924," in Mason, *Harlan Fiske Stone*, 157–158.

64. "Proceedings before the Supreme Court of the United States, in Memory of Harlan Fiske Stone, March 31, 1948," in Roger Jacobs, ed., *Memorials of the Justices of the Supreme Court of the United States* (Littleton, Colo.: Fred B. Rothman & Co., 1981), 4: 255, 322.

65. Mason, *Harlan Fiske Stone*, 5.

66. Beard, in Konefsky, *Chief Justice Stone*, xix–xxi.

67. Mason, *Harlan Fiske Stone*, 182–183.

68. Donald McCoy, *Calvin Coolidge: The Quiet President* (1967; Lawrence: University Press of Kansas, 1988), 276.

69. Mason, *Harlan Fiske Stone*, 167–171. The first case was *McGrain v. Daugherty*, 273 U.S. 135 (1927). The Supreme Court agreed with Stone's 1924 argument in support of the Senate's power to compel testimony. The second case was *Ex parte Grossman*, 267 U.S. 87 (1925), an important separation of powers case dealing with the executive pardoning power of those held in contempt of court.

70. McCoy, *Calvin Coolidge*, 276, 282–284.

71. Murray, *The Harding Era*, 500, 504, 505. Also see Burl Noggle, *Teapot Dome: Oil and Politics in the 1920s* (Baton Rouge: Louisiana State University Press, 1962; Westport, Conn.: Greenwood Press, 1980), 97, and Francis Russell, *The Shadow of Blooming Grove: Warren G. Harding and His Times* (New York: McGraw-Hill, 1968), 617.

72. McCoy, *Calvin Coolidge*, 220; Noggle, *Teapot Dome*, 175. Other factors helped as well, including a business recovery.

73. That was Henry Stanberry, renominated as attorney general by Andrew Johnson, after he had left office to defend the president in the impeachment trial.

74. McCoy, *Calvin Coolidge*, 278–281.

75. Harlan Fiske Stone, "Harvard Conference on the Future of the Common Law," cited in Jacobs, ed., *Memorials of the Justices of the Supreme Court* 269.

76. Mason, *Harlan Fiske Stone*, 6–7, 96, 97–99, 120–121.

77. For more on Mitchell and Watergate, see chapter four.

78. Contempt of Congress is a misdemeanor aimed at those who withhold information. His sentence was suspended. As some have pointed out, Kleindienst did more than withhold information; he lied when he falsely denied any knowledge of White House pressure in the ITT case. Lying to Congress is a felony. Kleindienst was allowed to plea bargain for the misdemeanor charge.

79. Nixon appointed Richardson with an eye toward restoring credibility, according to Richard Kleindienst in his autobiography, *Justice: The Memoirs of Attorney General Richard Kleindienst* (Ottawa, Ill.: Jameson Books, 1985), 168–170. Richardson also was conscious of this responsibility, writing, "My first duty [is] to do what I can to eliminate the causes of distrust." Elliot Richardson, "Building a New Confidence," *New York State Bar Journal* 45 (1973): 455. He resigned in protest before the article was published.

80. Thomas E. Kauper, interview with author, University of Michigan Law School, Ann Arbor, 29 Mar. 1988. Kauper served in the antitrust division from June 1972 until July 1976. Before that time, he had served two years in the Office of Legal Counsel in the Mitchell Justice Department.

81. Mitchell C. Lynch, "Rebuilding Morale at Justice," *Wall Street Journal*, 24 Feb. 1975. Lynch reports that Solicitor General Robert Bork joked that one attorney general had arrived at the department by taxi and asked the cab driver to wait.

82. Comments of Donald Rumsfeld and Richard Cheney, *The Ford White House*, ed. staff of White Burkett Miller Center of Public Affairs, University of Virginia (Lanham, Md.: University Press of America, 1986), 4–5, 7. Rumsfeld was assistant to the president and later secretary of Defense, and Cheney served as White House chief of staff.

83. Ronald G. Carr, "Mr. Levi at Justice," *University of Chicago Law Review* 52 (Spring 1985): 304. Carr served as special assistant to the attorney general during the Ford administration.

84. "Justice Department Gets a Just Man," *Economist* 25 Jan. 1975, 45.

85. When he entered office, Ford told his cabinet members, including Saxbe, that he did not want their resignations. Memo, Haig to Ford, Cabinet Talking Points, 9 Aug. 1974, folder "FG 10 Executive 1/1/76–1/20/77," Box 72, The Cabinet FG 10/FG 10–1, Gerald R. Ford Library.

86. "Justice Department Gets a Just Man," 46.

87. Gerald R. Ford, "Attorney General Edward H. Levi," *University of Chicago Law Review* 52 (Spring 1985): 284.

88. Ibid., 284–285. Perhaps Ford was influenced in his choice in part by Solicitor General Robert Bork, who was a former student and friend of Levi.

89. Memo on the president's talking points at the swearing-in ceremony of Edward Levi, 7 Feb. 1975, Folder "FG 17/A 8/9/74–2/10/75," Box 88, FG 17/A— Department of Justice, Ford Library.

90. Senate, Committee on the Judiciary, *Hearings on the Nomination of Edward H. Levi to be Attorney General*, 94th Cong., 1st sess. (Washington, D.C.: Government Printing Office, 1975), 7.

91. Ibid., 2–3, 7.

92. Ibid., 23. Kennedy's question reflects congressional skepticism about presidents' motives: "Are you going to call each case on the basis of the legality of the situation, or are you going to try to look for justification in support of action taken by the White House?"

93. *Hearings on Edward H. Levi*, The questions asked illustrate the concerns of the time: five of the ten senators who cross-examined him raised the issue of independence. By comparison, four asked about domestic surveillance, including wiretapping of congressmen, and only three asked about law enforcement, the death penalty, or the extension of the Voting Rights Act.

94. Ibid., 59–61.

95. Ibid., 23–24.

96. Ibid., 39, 50–51.

97. "The Wrong Kind of Controversy," *Wall Street Journal*, 27 Dec. 1974.

98. Letter, John Chester to Ford, 8 Jan. 1975, and Letter, Ford to the Republican Executive Committee of Louisville, Ky., 7 Mar. 1975, folder, "FG 17/A 2/11/75–8/1/75," Box 88, FG 17/A Department of Justice, Ford Library. Also initially critical of the appointment because of Levi's presumed liberalism were Senators John Eastland and John Tower, according to a memo, Phillip Arreda to Ford, 6 Jan. 1975, folder "Edward H. Levi (1)," Box 9, William T. Kendall Files—Congressional Relations Office, Ford Library.

99. Exchange of remarks between the president and Levi, 7 Feb. 1975,

folder "FG 17/A 8/9/74–2/10/75," Box 88, FG 17/A Department of Justice, Ford Library.

100. According to a notation of political speaking engagements for various cabinet heads. Memo, John Guthrie to Dean Burch, 4 October 1974, folder "Political Affairs 9/15/74–10/11/74," Box 3, PL 8/9/74–10/31/74 (Exec.), Ford Library.

101. Memo, James E. Connor to the cabinet, 7 January 1976, and Memo, James E. Connor to the cabinet, 19 July 1976, folder "FG 10 Exec. 1/1/76–1/20/77," Box 72, The Cabinet FG 10/FG 10-1, Ford Library.

102. For example, he testified on wiretapping on 11 Nov. 1975, before the Senate Select Committee to Study Governmental Operations with Respect to Intelligence Activities.

103. Ford talking points, Cabinet Meeting on the Sequoia, 7 May 1975, folder "FG 10 Exec. 1/1/75–12/31/75," Box 72, The Cabinet FG 10/10-1, Ford Library.

104. Memo, 30 Apr. 1975, folder "FG 17 4/4/75–5/20/75," Box 87, FG 17 Department of Justice, Ford Library.

105. Thomas Kauper, interview with author.

106. Eleanora Schoenebaum, *Political Profiles: The Nixon/Ford Years* (New York: Facts on File, 1979), 84.

107. The range of issues that Buchen handled can be seen in a review of the Buchen files at the Ford Library.

108. Memo, William E. Timmons to Buchen, 31 Oct. 1974, folder "Buchen, Phil (1)," Box 126, Ron Nessen Papers—White House Memoranda, Ford Library.

109. Memo, Buchen to Scowcroft, 25 Feb. 1976, folder "FG 17 1/1/76–3/31/76," Box 87, FG 17 Department of Justice, Ford Library.

110. Memo, Buchen to Ford, 14 Apr. 1975, folder "FG 17 4/4/75–5/20/75," Box 87, FG 17 Department of Justice, Ford Library. When the Senate requested the text of all understandings relating to the 1973 Vietnam cease-fire agreement, Buchen suggested that they seek the legal advice of Levi before responding. Also see Memo, Buchen to Levi, 4 Dec. 1975, folder "FG 17 11/25/75–12/31/75," Box 87, FG 17 Department of Justice, Ford Library. Buchen asked for legal advice on past executive branch refusal to provide documents on the Concorde to a House committee.

111. See, for example, a letter from the department to Buchen, 6 Apr. 1976, dealing with San Antonio and the Voting Rights Act, and a memo to Buchen, 24 Mar. 1975, on the laws relating to the Arab League boycott of businesses involved with Israel, folder "FG 17 11/25/75–12/31/75," Box 87, FG 17 Department of Justice, Ford Library.

112. For example, Levi checked with Buchen before authorizing parole for a limited number of Laotians, Vietnamese, and Cambodians, to see if the proposal was consistent with the president's program. Memo, Buchen to Levi, 14 July 1975, folder "FG 17 7/1/75–8/31/75," Box 87, FG 17 Department of Justice, Ford Library.

113. Memo, Buchen to Nessen, 11 Feb. 1975, folder "Buchen, Phil (1)," Box 126, Ron Nessen Papers—White House Memoranda, Ford Library.

114. Letter from Buchen to Blanchard, 14 Mar. 1975, folder "FG 17 3/1/75–4/3/75," Box 87, FG 17 Department of Justice, Ford Library.

115. Letter, Buchen to Nina Totenberg of the *New Times*, 31 Mar. 1976, folder "FG 17 1/1/76–3/31/76," Box 87, FG 17 Department of Justice, Ford Library.

116. See, for example, Memo, Cannon to Ford, Status of Justice Department lawsuit on one-house veto, 27 Oct. 1976, folder "FG 17 9/1/76–1/20/77," and Memo, Rumsfeld to Cannon, Decisions pending for Justice Department, 22 Apr. 1975, folder "FG 17 4/4/75–5/20/75," both in Box 87, FG 17 Department of Justice. Also, Memo, Buchen to Nessen, Chronology leading to review of Boston school busing case, 19 May 1976, folder "Buchen, Phil (3)," Box 126, Ron Nessen Papers—White House Memos, Ford Library.

117. Letter, Gerald Ford to House Speaker Carl Albert, 15 May 1975, folder "Mayaguez—General," Box 14, General Subject File: Ron Nessen Papers, Ford Library.

118. Richard G. Head, Frisco W. Short, and Robert C. McFarland, *Crisis Resolution: Presidential Decision Making in the Mayaguez and Korean Confrontation* (Boulder, Colo.: Westview Press, 1978), 71, 108, 141, 240.

119. Evidence of the White House taking these legal questions into account may be found in several papers briefing the president on possible press questions, undated and dated May 13, 14, 17. See folder "Mayaguez—General," Box 14, Ron Nessen files, Ford Library.

120. Mayaguez Chronologies, folder "Mayaguez Chronologies," Box 14, General Subject File: Ron Nessen Papers, Ford Library.

121. Head, Short, and McFarlane, *Crisis Resolution*, 51, 56, 71, 109, 113, 115, 122. They list the key policy-makers as Vice-President Nelson Rockefeller, Kissinger, Schlesinger, Scowcroft, Marsh, William Colby of the CIA, and Gen. David Jones of the Joint Chiefs of Staff.

122. Memo, John Marsh to Donald Rumsfeld for the president, 4 Apr. 1975, folder "War Powers," Box 125, Ron Nessen Papers—Foreign Guidance, Ford Library. The opinion was produced jointly by the White House counsel's office working with attorneys at Defense and State. Attached was a draft letter to Congress, which Ford subsequently signed. The attorney general evidently was not involved in this opinion.

123. Memo, Joy Chiles to Ron Nessen, 14 May 1975, folder "Mayaguez Chronologies," Box 14, General Subject File: Ron Nessen Papers, Ford Library.

124. Comments of White House staff members Brent Scowcroft, James E. Connor, James H. Cavanaugh, and Donald Rumsfeld in *The Ford White House*, 21–23.

125. See, for example, the agenda for 26 Aug. 1974, folder "FG 10-1 Cabinet Meetings 8/9/74–10/31/74," Cabinet meeting background and talking points, 11 Oct. 1974, folder "FG 10 Exec. 1/1/76–1/20/77"; the agenda for 19 Feb. 1975, folder "FG 10-1 Cabinet Meetings 11/1/74–2/28/75"; the agenda for 12 Mar. 1975, folder "FG 10 Exec. 1/1/75–12/31/75," all in Box 72, The Cabinet FG 10/FG 10-1. Also, Memo, Connor to Cabinet, Talking Points on Supplemental Assistance for Cambodia and South Vietnam, 5 Feb. 1975, folder "Memoranda to Cabinet from Connor," Box 2, James E. Connor—Cabinet Secretary Subject File, Ford Library.

126. Letter, Coleman to Ford, 26 June 1975, folder "FG 10-1 5/1/75–8/31/75," Box 72, The Cabinet FG 10/10-1, Ford Library.

127. Ford comments, Minutes of special cabinet meeting, 26 Mar. 1975, folder "FG 10 Exec. 1/1/75–12/31/75," Box 72, The Cabinet FG 10/FG 10-1, Ford Library.

128. Comments of James E. Connor, *The Ford White House*, 23. Connor was secretary to the cabinet and staff secretary to the president, 1975–1977.

129. Comments of Rumsfeld, in *The Ford White House*, 26–27.

130. Compiled from eight monthly summaries, folder "Presidential Meetings with Cabinet Members—Monthly Summaries," Box 2, Cabinet Secretary James E. Connor Papers, Subject File, Ford Library. Connor noted that records of two of these months were not comprehensive.

131. Ford, "Edward H. Levi," 284, 288–289.

132. Comments of William Coleman, attached to a Memo, Buchen to Richard Cheney, Jim Cavanaugh, and Ron Nessen, 21 May 1976, folder "Buchen, Phil (3)," Box 126, Ron Nessen Papers—White House Memos, Ford Library.

133. Carr, "Mr. Levi at Justice," 323.

134. Griffin Bell, *Taking Care of the Law* (New York: Morrow, 1982), 24, 182–183.

135. Senate, Judiciary Committee, *Hearings on the Nomination of Griffin Bell to be Attorney General*, 95th Cong., 1st sess. (Washington, D.C.: Government Printing Office, 1977), 44–46, 142–144. Also see comments by Senators Mathias, Heinz, and Bayh, 10, 33, 137.

136. Griffin Bell, interview with author, Washington, D.C., 21 Oct. 1987.

137. *Hearings on Griffin Bell*, 7.

138. Ibid., 32–33. He noted in his book that "my part in the 1976 election campaign did not approach the central role that the Watergate special prosecutor had in mind when . . . he recommended against Presidents naming their campaign managers as attorneys general." Bell, *Taking Care of the Law*, 63.

139. *Hearings on Griffin Bell*, 612.

140. Address at the dedication ceremony of the Legal Research Center, Lewis and Clark Law School, Portland, Oreg., 2 Feb. 1978, folder "Bell, Griffin—Speeches [O/A 6468]," Box 4, Annie Gutierrez—Domestic Policy Staff, Civil Rights and Justice Cluster, Subject File, Jimmy Carter Library.

141. Victor Navasky, "The Greening of Griffin Bell," *New York Times Magazine*, 27 Feb. 1977, 41–50. In support of this contention, Navasky cites Bell's work with Vandiver and the Kennedy campaign, then offers as further evidence Bell's efforts to organize the first law review at Mercer Law School and his work on the federal bench mediating civil rights disputes. In my view, Navasky's examples do not support his broad assertion that Bell is primarily a politician.

142. Griffin Bell, interview with author. Coupled with these complaints about Bell's political and personal association with the new president were questions regarding his commitment to civil rights, due to his work with Governor Vandiver who was a segregationist, although not on par with George Wallace or Lester Maddox. Also, Bell initially expressed hesitation about resigning from some private clubs that excluded blacks. See Navasky, "Greening of Griffin Bell," 42, 44. In fairness to Bell, once he was confirmed, he selected black at-

torneys for top posts in the Department of Justice, including the solicitor general and the assistant attorney general for civil rights.

143. Bell, *Taking Care of the Law*, 19.

144. Eugene Patterson, *Washington Post*, 6 Jan. 1977. Patterson had been editor of the *Atlanta Constitution* and vice-chair of the U.S. Civil Rights Commission from 1964 to 1968.

145. *Hearings on Griffin Bell*, 45.

146. Navasky, "The Greening of Griffin Bell," 41–42.

147. *Hearings on Griffin Bell*, 10.

148. Griffin Bell, interview with author.

149. *Hearings on Griffin Bell*, 136–137.

150. Griffin Bell, interview with author.

151. Ibid.

152. *Hearings on Griffin Bell*, 20, 33. This is reminiscent of a similar statement by Levi during his confirmation hearings. Bell later wrote that he conceived of the idea of the neutral zone out of George Washington's efforts to find an attorney general who was "a skilled, neutral expounder of the law rather than a political advisor." See Griffin Bell, "Office of Attorney General's Client Relationship," *Business Lawyer* 36 (March 1981): 791.

153. Bell, *Taking Care of the Law*, 63.

154. Griffin Bell, interview with author.

155. Press release, remarks of the president at the swearing-in ceremony of Griffin Bell, 26 Jan. 1977, folder "Griffin Bell press release," White House Central File-Name File, Carter Library.

156. Jimmy Carter, "Law Day Address," University of Georgia School of Law, Athens, Ga., 4 May 1974.

157. John Kessel, "The Structure of the Carter White House," *American Journal of Political Science* 27 (August 1983): 461. Kessel focuses on the White House staff, but there is no evidence that Carter treated his cabinet officers any differently in this respect.

158. Bell, *Taking Care of the Law*, 46.

159. Ibid., 25–27. The court eventually supported the OLC's legal opinion. When his successor, Benjamin Civiletti, defended CETA funding in the Wisconsin church schools case, a U.S. District Court judge issued a nationwide injunction on use of CETA funds in religious schools. The U.S. Court of Appeals for the Seventh Circuit affirmed that ruling, and the Department of Justice decided not to appeal to the Supreme Court.

160. Griffin Bell, interview with author.

161. Bakke had been twice turned down by U.C. Davis Medical School. The California Supreme Court ruled that he was unconstitutionally discriminated against by a special admissions program for minorities. The case went to the Supreme Court as *Regents of the University of California v. Bakke*, 438 U.S. 265 (1978).

162. Bell, *Taking Care of the Law*, 31–32. Lincoln Caplan, *The Tenth Justice: The Solicitor General and the Rule of Law* (New York: Alfred A. Knopf, 1987), 45–47. Note the difference and similarity between this case (and the snail darter case) and the *Bob Jones University* incident examined in chapter three.

163. Bell, "Attorney General's Client Relationship," 794.
164. Bell, *Taking Care of the Law*, 32.
165. Ibid., 32–34.
166. Griffin Bell, interview with author.
167. Bell, *Taking Care of the Law*, 34. Also see Bell, "Attorney General's Client Relationship," 795–796.
168. Bell, *Taking Care of the Law*, 42.
169. Memo, Robert Lipshutz to President Carter, 11 Jan. 1978, folder "Tellico Dam Litigation 1/77–9/79," Box 47, White House Counsel—Lipshutz, Carter Library.
170. For a more complete discussion of this position, see Memo, Eizenstat, Lipshutz, McIntyre, et al., to President Carter, 9 Jan. 1978, folder "Tellico Dam Litigation 1/77–9/79," Box 47, White House Counsel—Lipshutz, Carter Library.
171. Griffin Bell, interview with author.
172. Memo, Griffin Bell to President Carter, undated, attached to Memo, Robert Lipshutz to Carter, 11 Jan. 1978, folder "Tellico Dam Litigation 1/77–9/79," Box 47, White House Counsel—Lipshutz, Carter Library.
173. Memo, John Harmon of the Office of Legal Counsel to Stuart Eizenstat, Margaret McKenna, and Robert Lipshutz, 20 Dec. 1977, folder "Tellico Dam Litigation 1/77–9/79," Box 47, White House Counsel—Lipshutz, Carter Library.
174. Memo, Eizenstat, Lipshutz, McIntyre, et al., to President Carter, 9 Jan. 1978, folder "Tellico Dam Litigation 1/77–9/79," Box 47, White House Counsel—Lipshutz, Carter Library. Bell sent a memo to Carter before the president's review of the issue, but White House staff failed to give it to him then. When Bell then asked to meet with the president, the staff had to give Carter the attorney general's memo. In a handwritten note to Lipshutz, Carter wrote, "OK, I'll meet the AG, & should have been given his memo." Also see Bell, *Taking Care of the Law*, 43.
175. Bell, *Taking Care of the Law*, 44. Complicating this case was the fact that the TVA has independent litigating authority and could continue without the concurrence of Justice. Bell argued that TVA's petition for review could restrict the Endangered Species Act more than the Justice Department's rather narrow petition.
176. According to the author's interview with Judge Bell, this dual brief did not please the justices, who wondered which position was the government's.
177. Bell, *Taking Care of the Law*, 44.
178. Civiletti, who had served as Bell's deputy attorney general and assistant attorney general of the criminal division, had been a trial lawyer with a prominent firm. He initially was recommended by Charles Kirbo, whom he had met on a few occasions. Civiletti was not personally known by Carter before he joined the department.
179. Memo, Civiletti to the president, 12 Nov. 1979, and Memo, Civiletti to Lloyd Cutler, 13 Nov. 1979, folder "Iran—Memos to the President 11/79–6/80," Box 92, WHCF—Staff Offices—Counsel to the President, [Lloyd] Cutler, Carter Library. Civiletti and his staff sometimes sent status reports to Carter on the implementation of immigration sanctions.

180. Stuart Eizenstat, "White House and Justice Department after Watergate," *American Bar Association Journal* 68 (February 1982): 176.

181. Memo, Civiletti to the president, 30 Apr. 1980, folder "Iran—Memos to the President 11/79–6/80," Box 92, WHCF—Staff Offices—Counsel to the President, [Lloyd] Cutler, Carter Library.

182. Memo, Civiletti to the president, 15 Nov. 1979, folder "Iran—Demonstrations," Box 87, WHCF—Staff Offices—Counsel to the President, [Lloyd] Cutler, Carter Library. He wrote that "it is my firm opinion that we cannot deny the right to persons, Iranian or American, who do not have some provable record of violence themselves, to demonstrate on federal properties in Washington."

183. Jimmy Carter, *Keeping Faith: Memoirs of a President* (Bantam: New York, 1982), 460.

184. Ibid., 461–469, 484–488, 506, 518. Key advisers were Vice-President Mondale, Secretary of Defense Brown, Secretary of State Vance, NSC Adviser Zbigniew Brzezinski, General David Jones of the Joint Chiefs of Staff, Director Stansfield Turner of the CIA, and Hamilton Jordan and Jody Powell of the White House. Carter used other advisers as well, including Rosalynn Carter, who suggested stopping U.S. purchases of Iranian oil. Jordan, because of his close relationship with Carter, was an important contact for both the Iranians and their Panamanian liaisons.

185. This is because many of the relevant files have been removed from the Carter Library circulation for national security reasons.

186. Memorandum of Law, Lloyd Cutler to the president, 25 Apr. 1980, folder "War Powers, 12/77–3/80," Box 115, WHCF—Staff Offices—Counsel to the President, [Lloyd] Cutler, Carter Library.

187. President's report to House Speaker Tip O'Neill and Senate President Pro Tem Warren Magnuson, 26 Apr. 1980, folder "War Powers, 12/77–3/80," Box 115, WHCF–Staff Offices—Counsel to the President, [Lloyd] Cutler, Carter Library.

188. Testimony of Warren Christopher on the rescue operation, May 1980, folder "War Powers 12/77–3/80," Box 115, WHCF–Staff Offices—Counsel to the President, [Lloyd] Cutler, Carter Library. Cutler also worked on legal questions related to attaching Iranian assets in the United States, interning Iranian diplomats in retaliation, and on other Iranian-related litigation, including the deportation of Iranian students and the prohibition on violent demonstrations near the White House. Memo, Lloyd Cutler and Joe Onek to the senior White House staff, 19 Nov. 1979, and other letters and memos dated December 1979, folder "Iran—Memos General 11/79–6/80," Box 92, WHCF—Staff Offices—Counsel to the President, [Lloyd] Cutler, Carter Library.

189. Bell, *Taking Care of the Law*, 44, 46–48. Also see Griffin Bell, "Cabinet Government: An Alternative for Organizing Policy-making," *Virginia Papers on the Presidency* 18 (1984): 42–46.

190. Memo, Bob Malson to Stuart Eizenstat, Bert Carp, and Annie Gutierrez, 24 Mar. 1977, folder "Justice [Dept. of]," Box 23, Annie Gutierrez—Domestic Policy Staff, Civil Rights and Justice Cluster, Subject File, Carter Library. Eizenstat was director, Carp was deputy director, and Gutierrez was associate

director of the Domestic Policy Staff. Malson was the assistant director of the Civil Rights and Justice Cluster.

191. Handwritten notes from a meeting (undated), folder "Justice Department—Relationship," Box 14, Frank White—Domestic Policy Staff, Civil Rights and Justice Cluster, Subject File, Carter Library. Such cases as *Bakke, Wolfish, Weber, Silva,* and *Doe v. Plyler* he called "administration *policy* decisions."

192. Memo, Frank White to Stuart Eizenstat, 4 Dec. 1978, folder "Justice Department—Relationship," Box 14, Frank White—Domestic Policy Staff, Civil Rights and Justice Cluster, Subject File, Carter Library.

193. Memo, White to Eizenstat, 4 Dec. 1978, folder "Justice Department—Relationship," Box 14, Frank White—Domestic Policy Staff, Civil Rights and Justice Cluster, Subject File, Carter Library.

194. Memo, Stu Eizenstat to the President, 19 July 1979, folder "Justice Department—Relationship," Box 14, Frank White—Domestic Policy Staff, Civil Rights and Justice Cluster, Subject File, Carter Library.

195. Bell, "Attorney General's Client Relationship," 791.

196. Bell, *Taking Care of the Law,* 35. As an example, Bell recounted an incident that occurred when Civiletti was attorney general. Civiletti and Cutler disagreed on the immediacy of the need to amend the 1978 Ethics in Government Act. Cutler announced to the press that the act should be amended. When Civiletti the next month outlined in detail the changes he felt were necessary, the impression made was that he was subservient to the White House counsel. See 37–38.

197. Griffin Bell, interview with author. Congress's final report did comment on the lack of legal advice.

198. This policy was continued under Bell's successor, Benjamin Civiletti. Memo, Civiletti to heads of offices, boards, bureaus, and divisions, 18 Oct. 1979, Box 14, Frank White—Domestic Policy Staff, Civil Rights and Justice Cluster, Carter Library. The policy illustrates Bell's concern with improper congressional contacts as well as improper executive branch contacts. Also see Bell, *Taking Care of the Law,* 65, 78.

199. Caplan, *The Tenth Justice,* 48–49.

200. Griffin Bell, interview with author. The issue became moot when a California newspaper printed the article.

201. Bell, *Taking Care of the Law,* 124.

202. Griffin Bell, interview with author.

203. *Hearings on Griffin Bell,* 136.

204. Bell, "Attorney General's Client Relationship," 796–797. He argued in his book that "we must return to government by directly accountable public officials." Bell, *Taking Care of the Law,* 51.

Chapter Six. In Conclusion

1. Senate, Committee on the Judiciary, *Hearings on the Nomination of Edward H. Levi to Be Attorney General,* 94th Cong., 1st sess. (Washington, D.C.: Government Printing Office, 1975), 13. The typical view is that of Sen. Charles

Percy, who expressed his dismay at Mitchell's campaigning: "I object strenuously when a member of my own party, John Mitchell, as we now learn, ran the re-election of the President committee while he was Attorney General. I felt it totally inappropriate." Eizenstat, who was Carter's chief domestic policy adviser, agreed that "the attorney general should remain out of the partisan political arena . . . [because his] judgments must not even appear to be influenced . . . by political considerations." Stuart Eizenstat, "White House and Justice Department after Watergate," *American Bar Association Journal* 68 (February 1982): 175, 177.

2. Victor Navasky, "The Politics of Justice," *New York Times Magazine*, 5 May 1974, 18.

3. Victor Navasky, *Kennedy Justice* (New York: Atheneum, 1971), xx.

4. Navasky, "The Politics of Justice."

5. *Watergate Special Prosecution Force Report* (Washington, D.C.: Government Printing Office, 1975), 136.

6. Mitchell Rogovin, "Reorganizing Politics out of the Department of Justice," *American Bar Association Journal* 64 (June 1978): 855, 856.

7. Senate, Committee on the Judiciary, *Hearings on the Nomination of Edwin Meese III to Be Attorney General*, 98th Cong., 2d sess. (Washington, D.C.: Government Printing Office, 1985), I: 2, 4, 7, 9, 11, 18.

8. Arthur J. Goldberg testimony, Senate, Subcommittee on Separation of Powers of the Committee on the Judiciary, *Hearings on S. 2803 and S. 2978 on Removing Politics from the Administration of Justice*, 93d Cong., 2d sess. (Washington D.C.: Government Printing Office, 1974), 61–63. This view is shared by other legal writers. See, for example, Richard J. Kutak, "A Commitment to Clients and the Law," *American Bar Association Journal* 68 (July 1982): 804.

9. Cox testimony, *Hearings on Removing Politics*, 198–199.

10. *Congressional Quarterly Almanac 1977* (Washington, D.C.: Congressional Quarterly, 1977), 581, 584.

11. Senate, *Hearings before the Select Committee on Investigation of Attorney General Harry M. Daughtery*, Part 9, 68th Cong., 1st sess. (Washington, D.C.: Government Printing Office, 1924), 2565.

12. Whitney North Seymour, Jr., testimony, *Hearings on Removing Politics*, 216.

13. Whitney North Seymour, Jr., *United States Attorney: An Inside View of "Justice" in America under the Nixon Administration* (New York: William Morrow & Co., 1975), 229–232.

14. Rogovin, "Reorganizing Politics," 857.

15. See chapter five.

16. Lincoln Caplan, *The Tenth Justice: The Solicitor General and the Rule of Law* (New York: Alfred A. Knopf, 1987), 50.

17. Charles Cooper, interview with the author, Washington, D.C., 19 Oct. 1987.

18. Senate, Committee of the Judiciary, *Hearings on the Nomination of William Saxbe to Be Attorney General*, 93d Cong., 1st sess. (Washington, D.C.: Government Printing Office, 1974), 70.

19. Roman Hruska comments, *Hearings on Edward Levi*, 79.

20. Elliot Richardson, *The Creative Balance* (New York: Holt, Rinehart & Winston, 1976), 80. Also note Daniel J. Meador, *The President, the Attorney General, and the Department of Justice* (Charlottesville: White Burkett Miller Center of Public Affairs, University of Virginia, 1980), 31.

21. Quoted in Owen Thomas, "Attorneys General under Fire," *Christian Science Monitor*, 17 May 1988, 3, 5.

22. Sorensen testimony, *Hearings on Removing Politics*, 16. This view is held by some non-American legal scholars as well. British legal historian John Edwards wrote, "No matter how entrenched constitutional safeguards may be, in the final analysis, it is the strength of character, of personal integrity and depth of commitment to the principle of independent and impartial representation of the public interest, on the part of the holders of the office of Attorney General, which is of supreme importance." John Ll. J. Edwards, *The Attorney General, Politics and the Public Interest* (London: Sweet and Maxwell, 1984), 67.

23. *Hearings on Edward Levi*, 21–22. Because the attorney general is responsible for triggering any investigation by an independent counsel, he continues to exercise an important discretionary power, according to the 1977 Ethics in Government Act.

24. Harold R. Tyler, Jr., "The Attorney General of the United States: Counsel to the President or to the Government?" *Albany Law Review* 45 (Fall 1980): 6. Robert Kennedy was also praised as having "remarkable energy and dedication" by Seymour, *United States Attorney*, 39. Sen. Philip Hart noted that the "Justice Department under Bob Kennedy . . . provided a very high standard for future administrations." Hart comments, *Hearings on Edward Levi*, 14.

25. Sorensen testimony, *Hearings on Removing Politics*, 18. As documented in chapter three, however, he did stay informed of political currents that would affect the administration and his brother's reelection.

26. Tyler, "The Attorney General," 8.

27. Charles Cooper, interview with the author.

28. Tyler, "The Attorney General," 7–8.

29. *Leonard v. Douglas*, 321 F.2d 749. The case reached the U.S. Court of Appeals for the District of Columbia. Cited in William Rehnquist, "The Old Order Changeth: The Department of Justice under John Mitchell," *Arizona Law Review* 12 (1970): 251, 253.

30. Roman Hruska comments, *Hearings on Edward Levi*, 12.

31. Edward Weisband and Thomas M. Franck, *Resignation in Protest: Political and Ethical Choices between Loyalty to Team and Loyalty to Conscience in American Public Life* (New York: Grossman, 1975), 126, 174–175. Admittedly, not all Advocates have their own clout (Daugherty, for example, was very dependent on Harding for his political fortunes), and not all Neutrals are without clout (although their clout may be in academic and legal circles).

32. Richardson, *The Creative Balance*, 32, 33, 35.

33. Navasky, "The Politics of Justice," 519.

34. Homer Cummings, *Liberty under Law and Administration* (New York: Charles Scribner's Sons, 1934), 114, 119.

35. Ronald Dworkin, "Law as Interpretation," *Texas Law Review* 60 (March 1982): 527, 543, 545, 549.

36. H. L. A. Hart, *The Concept of Law* (Oxford: Clarendon Press, 1961), 12.

37. See Tyler for more criticisms of an independent department. Tyler, "The Attorney General," 7–12.

38. Archibald Cox testimony, *Hearings on Removing Politics*, 203, 207, 208.

39. Burke Marshall testimony, *Hearings on Removing Politics*, 114–115.

40. Rehnquist, "The Old Order Changeth," 256.

41. Richardson, *The Creative Balance*, 29.

42. *Hearings on Edwin Meese*, 6, 219–220.

43. Dworkin, "Law as Interpretation," 549.

44. David Lyons, *Ethics and Rule of Law* (Cambridge: Cambridge University Press, 1984), 198–199.

45. F. A. Hayek, *The Road to Serfdom* (Chicago: University of Chicago Press, 1945), 72. Hayek's phrase, "in all its actions," is hyperbole; clearly there is a need for some discretionary decision-making in government, as long as it is consistent with the law.

46. Joseph Raz, "The Rule of Law and Its Virtue," *The Authority of Law: Essays on Law and Morality* (Oxford: Clarendon Press, 1979), 220, 224–226. Rule of law is the most important inherent value of laws.

47. Raz, "The Rule of Law," 218. Among his eight principles, Raz requires that the discretion of crime-related agencies should not be allowed to pervert the law. "The prosecution should not be allowed, for example, to decide not to prosecute for commission of certain crimes, or for crimes committed by certain classes of offenders."

48. Raz, "The Rule of Law," 210–211, 222.

49. Samuel Hutchison Beer, "Comment," in *Government under Law*, ed. Arthur E. Sutherland (New York: Da Capo Press, 1968), 548.

50. Homer Cummings and Carl McFarland, *Federal Justice* (New York: Macmillan, 1937), 511.

51. Griffin Bell, interview with the author, Washington, D.C., 21 Oct. 1987. In this, Bell echoes Arthur Goldberg. A subject for future research may be the incidence of congressional pressure on attorneys general, specifically attempts to influence the government's position on a pending case or the administration's selection of a U.S. attorney or marshal.

52. Navasky, "The Politics of Justice," 18.

Selected Bibliography

Books and Articles

Adams, Charles Francis, ed. *Memoirs of John Quincy Adams*. 1874; reprint, New York: AMS Press, 1970.

Akers, Dee Ashley. "The Advisory Opinion Function of the Attorney General." *Kentucky Law Journal* 38 (1950): 561–598.

American Jurisprudence. 2d ed. Rochester, N.Y.: Lawyers Cooperative Publishing Co., 1980.

Anderson, John. *Eisenhower, Brownell, and Congress: The Tangled Origins of the Civil Rights Bill of 1956–57*. Tuscaloosa: University of Alabama Press, 1964.

Bancroft, Frederic. *The Life of William H. Seward*. Vol. 2. New York: Harper & Bros., 1900.

Banton, Michael. *Roles*. London: Tavistock Publications, 1965.

Bell, Griffin. "The Attorney General: The Federal Government's Chief Lawyer and Chief Litigator, or One among Many?" *Fordham Law Review* 46 (May 1978): 1049–1070.

_____. "Cabinet Government: An Alternative for Organizing Policy-making." *Virginia Papers on the Presidency*, Vol. 18, part 3. Charlottesville: White Burkett Miller Center Forums, University of Virginia, 1984.

_____. "Office of Attorney General's Client Relationship." *Business Lawyer* 36 (Mar. 1981): 791–797.

_____. *Taking Care of the Law*. New York: Morrow, 1982.

Bell, Terrel H. *The Thirteenth Man: A Reagan Cabinet Memoir*. New York: Free Press/Macmillan, 1988.

Bellot, Hugh C. "The Origin of the Attorney General." *Law Quarterly Review* 25 (1909): 400–411.

Biddle, Francis. *In Brief Authority*. Garden City, N.Y.: Doubleday & Co., 1962.

Black, Henry Campbell, *Black's Law Dictionary*. 4th ed., revised. St. Paul, Minn.: West Publishing Co., 1968.

Boaz, David, ed. *Assessing the Reagan Years*. Washington, D.C.: Cato Institute, 1988.

Borchard, Edwin. "Editorial Comment: The Attorney General's Opinion on the

Exchange of Destroyers for Naval Bases." *American Journal of International Law* 34 (1940): 690–697.

Briggs, Herbert W. "Neglected Aspects of the Destroyer Deal." *American Journal of International Law* 34 (1940): 569–587.

Brown, R. G., Z. Chafee, Jr., F. Frankfurter, R. Pound, and E. Freund. *Illegal Practices of the Department of Justice.* 1920; reprint, New York: Arno Press and *New York Times,* 1969.

Cain, Marvin. "Claims, Contracts, and Customs: Public Accountability and a Department of Justice, 1789–1849." *Journal of the Early Republic* 4 (Spring 1984): 27–45.

Caplan, Lincoln. *The Tenth Justice: The Solicitor General and the Rule of Law.* New York: Alfred A. Knopf, 1987.

Carr, Ronald G. "Mr. Levi at Justice." *University of Chicago Law Review* 52 (Spring 1985): 300–323.

Carter, Jimmy. *Keeping Faith: Memoirs of a President.* New York: Bantam, 1982.

———. "Address on Law Day." University of Georgia School of Law, Athens, Ga., 4 May 1974.

Civiletti, Benjamin, Kenneth Wright, and Richard Allen. "Question and Answer with the New Attorney General." *American Bar Association Journal* 65 (Oct. 1979): 1497.

Clark, Ramsey. *Crime in America.* New York: Simon and Schuster, 1970.

Clark, Tom C. "The Office of the Attorney General." *Tennessee Law Review* 19 (1946): 150–159.

Coben, Stanley. *A. Mitchell Palmer: Politician.* 1963; reprint, New York: DaCapo Press, 1972.

Cohen, William S., and George J. Mitchell. *Men of Zeal: A Candid Inside Story of the Iran-Contra Hearings.* New York: Viking, 1988.

Conway, Moncure Daniel. *Omitted Chapters of History Disclosed in the Life and Papers of Edmund Randolph.* New York: G. P. Putnam's Sons, Knickerbocker Press, 1888.

Cooley, Rita W. "Predecessors of the Federal Attorney General: The Attorney General in England and the American Colonies." *American Journal of Legal History* 2 (1958): 304–312.

Corwin, Edward S. *The President: Office and Powers 1787–1957.* New York: New York University Press, 1957.

Cresson, William Penn. *James Monroe.* Chapel Hill: University of North Carolina Press, 1946.

Cronin, Thomas E., ed. *The State of the Presidency.* Boston: Little, Brown, 1980.

Cronin, Thomas E., and Sanford D. Greenberg, eds. *The Presidential Advisory System.* New York: Harper & Row, 1969.

Cummings, Homer. *Liberty under Law and Administration.* New York: Charles Scribner's Sons, 1934.

———. *Selected Addresses While Attorney General.* Washington, D.C.: Government Printing Office, 1939.

Cummings, Homer, and Carl McFarland. *Federal Justice: Chapters in the History of Justice and the Federal Executive.* 1937; reprint, New York: DaCapo Press, 1970.

Cushing, Caleb. "Office and Duties of the Attorney General." *American Law Register* 5 (December 1856): 5–94.

_____. *Outlines of the Life and Public Services, Civil and Military of William Henry Harrison.* Boston: Weeks, Jordan & Co., 1840.

_____. *The Treaty of Washington: Its Negotiation, Execution, and the Discussions Relating Thereto.* New York: Harper & Bros., 1873.

Dallek, Robert. *Franklin D. Roosevelt and American Foreign Policy, 1932–1945.* New York: Oxford University Press, 1979.

Dangerfield, George. *The Era of Good Feelings.* New York: Harcourt, Brace & Co., 1952.

Daugherty, Harry M., with Thomas Dixon. *The Inside Story of the Harding Tragedy.* New York: Churchill Co., 1932.

Deener, David R. *The United States Attorneys General and International Law.* The Hague: Martinus Nijhoff, 1957.

Desmond, Charles, Paul Freund, Potter Stewart, and Lord Hartley Shawcross. *Mr. Justice Jackson: Four Lectures in His Honor.* New York: Columbia University Press, 1969.

Dunar, Andrew J. *The Truman Scandals and the Politics of Morality.* Columbia: University of Missouri Press, 1984.

Dworkin, Ronald. "Law as Interpretation." *Texas Law Review* 60 (Mar. 1982): 527.

Easby-Smith, J. S. *The Department of Justice: Its History and Functions.* Washington, D.C.: W. H. Lowdermilk & Co., 1904.

Edwards, John Ll. J. *The Attorney General, Politics, and the Public Interest.* London: Sweet and Maxwell, 1984.

_____. *Law Officers of the Crown.* London: Sweet and Maxwell, 1964.

Eizenstat, Stuart. "White House and Justice Department after Watergate." *American Bar Association Journal* 68 (Feb. 1982): 175–177.

Ervin, Sam J., Jr. *The Whole Truth: The Watergate Conspiracy.* New York: Random House, 1980.

Fairlie, J. A. "The United States Department of Justice." *Michigan Law Review* 3 (1905): 352–359.

Farley, James A. *Behind the Ballots: The Personal History of a Politician.* New York: Harcourt, Brace & Co., 1938.

Fehrenbacher, Don. *The Dred Scott Case: Its Significance in American Law and Politics.* New York: Oxford University Press, 1978.

Fenno, Richard F. *The President's Cabinet: An Analysis in the Period from Wilson to Eisenhower.* Cambridge, Mass.: Harvard University Press, 1959.

Fisher, Louis. *American Constitutional Law.* New York: McGraw-Hill, 1990.

Ford, Gerald R. "Attorney General Edward H. Levi." *University of Chicago Law Review* 52 (Spring 1985): 284–289.

Ford, Paul L., ed. *Pamphlets on the Constitution of the United States.* Brooklyn, 1888.

Fuess, Claude M. *The Life of Caleb Cushing.* Vol. 2. New York: Harcourt, Brace & Co., 1923.

Giglio, James N. *H. M. Daugherty and the Politics of Expediency.* Kent, Ohio: Kent State University Press, 1978.

Goldman, Robert. "The 'Weakened Spring of Government' and the Executive

Branch: The Department of Justice in the Late 19th Century." *Congress and the Presidency* 11 (Autumn 1984): 165–177.

Goldstein, Abraham. "Prosecution: History of the Public Prosecutor." *Encyclopedia of Crime and Justice.* Vol. 3. Edited by Sanford Kadish. New York: Free Press, 1983.

Gosnell, Harold F. *Truman's Crises: A Political Biography of Harry S Truman.* Westport, Conn.: Greenwood Press, 1980.

Greenstein, Fred I., ed. *The Reagan Presidency: An Early Assessment.* Baltimore: Johns Hopkins University Press, 1983.

Guthman, Edwin and Jeffrey Shulman, eds. *Robert Kennedy: In His Own Words.* New York: Bantam, 1988.

Haldeman, H. R., with Joseph DiMona. *The Ends of Power.* New York: Times Books, 1978.

Hammonds, Oliver W. "The Attorney General in the American Colonies." *Anglo-American Legal History.* Series 5.1, no. 3. New York: New York University School of Law, 1939.

Harris, Richard. *Justice.* New York: E. P. Dutton Co., 1970.

Hart, H. L. A. *The Concept of Law.* Oxford: Clarendon Press, 1961.

Hayek, F. A. *The Road to Serfdom.* Chicago: University of Chicago Press, 1945.

Head, Richard, Frisco Short, and Robert C. McFarlane. *Crisis Resolution: Presidential Decision Making in the Mayaguez and Korean Confrontations.* Boulder, Colo.: Westview Press, 1978.

Heiser, Peter E., Jr. "The Opinion Writing Function of Attorneys General." *Idaho Law Review* 18 (Winter 1982): 9–41.

Holdsworth, William S. "The Early History of the Attorney and Solicitor General." *Illinois Law Review* 13 (1919): 602–619.

―――. *A History of English Law.* Boston: Little, Brown & Co., 1938.

Howard, J. Woodford, Jr. *Mr. Justice Murphy: A Political Biography.* Princeton, N.J: Princeton University Press, 1968.

Howe, George Frederick. *Chester A. Arthur.* New York: Frederick Ungar Publishing Co., 1957.

Huston, Luther A. *The Department of Justice.* New York: Frederick A. Praeger Publishers, 1967.

Huston, Luther A., Arthur Miller, Samuel Krislov, and Robert Dixon. *Roles of the Attorney General of the United States.* Washington, D.C.: American Enterprise Institute, 1968.

Ickes, Harold. *The Secret Diary of Harold L. Ickes.* 3 vols. New York: Simon and Schuster, 1953, 1954, 1955.

Irons, Peter. *Justice at War.* Oxford: Oxford University Press, 1983.

Jackson, Richard M. *The Machinery of Justice in England.* 7th ed. Cambridge: Cambridge University Press, 1977.

Jackson, Robert. "A Presidential Legal Opinion." *Harvard Law Review* 66 (June 1953): 1353–1361.

Jacobs, Roger, ed. *Memorials of the Justices of the Supreme Court of the United States.* Vol. 4 and 5. Littleton, Colo.: Fred B. Rothman & Co., 1981.

James, Henry. *Richard Olney and His Public Service.* Boston: Houghton Mifflin Co. 1923.

Johnson, Donald. "The Political Career of A. Mitchell Palmer." *Pennsylvania History* 25 (Oct. 1958): 345–370.

Johnson, Richard Tanner. *Managing the White House: An Intimate Study of the Presidency*. New York: Harper & Row, 1974.

Jones, Sir Elwyn. "The Office of Attorney-General." *Cambridge Law Journal* 27 (1969): 43–53.

"Justice Department Gets a Just Man." *Economist*, 25 Jan. 1975.

Keeton, George W. "The Office of Attorney General." *Juridical Review* 58 (1946): 107–231.

Keller, Ronald. "The Applicability and Scope of Attorney-Client Privilege in the Executive Branch of the Federal Government." *Boston University Law Review* 62 (July 1982): 1003–1027.

Kennedy, John P. *Memoirs of the Life of William Wirt*. Philadelphia: Lea and Blanchard, 1850.

Kennedy, Robert F. *The Pursuit of Justice*. Edited by Theodore J. Lowi. New York: Harper & Row, 1964.

———. *Thirteen Days: A Memoir of the Cuban Missile Crisis*. New York: W. W. Norton & Co., 1969.

Kessel, John. "The Structure of the Carter White House." *American Journal of Political Science* 27 (August 1983): 431.

Key, Sewall. "The Legal Work of the Federal Government." *Virginia Law Review* 25 (1938): 165–201.

Kleindienst, Richard. *Justice: The Memoirs of Attorney General Richard Kleindienst*. Ottawa, Ill.: Jameson Books, 1985.

Konefsky, Samuel. *Chief Justice Stone and the Supreme Court*. New York: Macmillan, 1946.

Kutak, Richard. "A Commitment to Clients and the Law." *American Bar Association Journal* 68 (July 1982): 804.

Langeluttig, Albert. *The Department of Justice of the United States*. Baltimore: Johns Hopkins University Press, 1927.

Learned, Henry B. "The Attorney-General and the Cabinet." *Political Science Quarterly* 24 (1909): 444–467.

———. *The President's Cabinet*. New Haven, Conn.: Yale University Press, 1912.

Levi, Edward H. "The Justice Department: Some Thoughts on Its Past, Present and Future." *Illinois Bar Journal* 64 (1975): 216.

———. *An Introduction to Legal Reasoning*. Chicago: University of Chicago Press, 1949.

———. "Law Day Address." *Nebraska Law Review* 55 (1975): 35–41.

Lewis, Walker. *Without Fear or Favor: A Biography of Chief Justice Roger Brooke Taney*. Boston: Houghton Mifflin Co., 1965.

Lyons, David. *Ethics and Rule of Law*. Cambridge: Cambridge University Press, 1984.

McCoy, Donald. *Calvin Coolidge: The Quiet President*. New York: Macmillan, 1967.

MacDermott, Lord John Clark. *Protection from Power under English Law*. London: Stevens & Sons, 1957.

Malone, R. L., Jr. "The Department of Justice: The World's Largest Law Office." *American Bar Association Journal* 39 (1953): 381.

Marcus, Maeva. *Truman and the Steel Seizure Case: The Limits of Presidential Power.* New York: Columbia University Press, 1977.

Mason, Alpheus T. *Harlan Fiske Stone: Pillar of the Law.* New York: Archon Books, 1968.

Meador, Daniel J. *The President, the Attorney General, and the Department of Justice.* Charlottesville: White Burkett Miller Center, University of Virginia, 1980.

Miller, Arthur S. "Justice without Politics." *Progressive* (April 1974): 34–36.

Mitchell, G. Duncan, ed. *A Dictionary of Sociology.* London: Routledge & Kegan Paul, 1968.

Mitchell, Richard Clare. *Chronicle of English Judges, Chancellors, Attorneys General and Solicitors General.* Oswego, N.Y.: W. P. Mitchell Printing Co., 1937.

Mollenhoff, Clark. "Presidents, Communication and the Public: The Kennedy and Nixon Administrations," in *Virginia Papers on the Presidency,* White Burkett Miller Center Forums, ed. Kenneth Thompson (Lanham, Md.: University Press of America, 1985) 20: 77–90.

Morse, Lewis W. "Historical Outline and Bibliography of Attorneys General Reports and Opinions." *Law Library Journal* 30 (April 1937): 226.

Murphy, Bruce Allen. *The Brandeis/Frankfurter Connection.* Garden City, N.Y.: Anchor Press/Doubleday, 1983.

Murray, Robert K. *The Harding Era.* Minneapolis: University of Minnesota Press, 1969.

National Association of Attorneys General. *The Report on the Office of the Attorney General.* February 1971.

Navasky, Victor. "The Greening of Griffin Bell." *New York Times Magazine,* 27 Feb. 1977, 41–50.

———. *Kennedy Justice.* New York: Atheneum, 1971.

———. "The Politics of Justice." *New York Times Magazine,* 5 May 1974, 18–19.

Nealon, Rita W. "The Opinion Function of the Attorney General." *New York University Law Review* 25 (1950): 825–843.

New York Times Staff, ed. *The Watergate Hearings: Break-in and Cover-up.* New York: Bantam, 1973.

———. *The White House Transcripts.* New York: Bantam Books, 1973.

Noggle, Burl. *Teapot Dome: Oil and Politics in the 1920's.* Westport, Conn.: Greenwood Press, 1980.

Norton-Kyshe, James. *The Law and Privileges Relating to Colonial Attorneys General and to the Office Corresponding to the Attorney General of England in the United States.* London: Stevens & Haynes, 1900.

Palmer, Robert. "The Confrontation of the Legislative and Executive Branches: An Examination of the Constitutional Balance of Powers and the Role of the Attorney General." *Pepperdine Law Review* 11 (Jan. 1984): 331.

Pois, Joseph. *Watchdog on the Potomac.* Washington, D.C.: University Press of America, 1979.

Polsby, Nelson W. "Presidential Cabinet Making: Lessons for the Political System." *Political Science Quarterly* 93 (Spring 1978): 15–25.

Pratt, Fletcher. *Stanton: Lincoln's Secretary of War*. New York: W. W. Norton & Co., 1953.

Randolph, Edmund. *History of Virginia*. Charlottesville: Virginia Historical Society, University Press of Virginia, 1970.

Rather, Dan, and Gary Paul Gates. *The Palace Guard*. New York: Harper & Row, 1974.

Raz, Joseph. *The Authority of Law: Essays on Law and Morality*. Oxford: Clarendon Press, 1979.

Regan, Donald T. *For the Record: From Wall Street to Washington*. San Diego: Harcourt, Brace Jovanovich 1988.

Rehnquist, William. "The Old Order Changeth: The Department of Justice under John Mitchell." *Arizona Law Review* 12 (1970): 251–259.

Rhodes, Irwin S. "Opinions of the Attorney General, Revived." *American Bar Association Journal* 64 (Sept. 1978): 1375–1376.

Richardson, Elliot L. "Building a New Confidence." *New York State Bar Journal* 45 (1973): 455–459.

_____. *The Creative Balance*. New York: Holt, Rinehart & Winston, 1976.

_____. "The Paradox: The Nixon Presidency." *Virginia Papers on the Presidency*, Vol. 13, Part 2. Charlottesville: White Burkett Miller Center, University of Virginia, 1983.

_____. "The Office of Attorney General: Continuity and Change." *Massachusetts Law Quarterly* 6 (March 1968): 5–22.

_____. "The Saturday Night Massacre." *Atlantic Monthly*, March 1976.

Robson, Robert. *The Attorney in Eighteenth Century England*. Cambridge: Cambridge University Press, 1959.

Rogovin, Mitchell. "Reorganizing Politics out of the Department of Justice." *American Bar Association Journal* 64 (June 1978): 855–858.

Rogow, Arnold and Harold Lasswell. *Power, Corruption, and Rectitude*. Englewood Cliffs, N.J.: Prentice Hall, 1963.

Roosevelt, Elliott, ed. *FDR: His Personal Letters 1928–1945*. New York: Duell, Sloan & Pearce, 1950.

Russell, Francis. *The Shadow of Blooming Grove: Warren G. Harding and His Times*. New York: McGraw-Hill, 1968.

Savidge, Eugene C. *Life of Benjamin Harris Brewster*. Philadelphia: J. B. Lippincott, 1891.

Schlesinger, Arthur M., Jr. *Robert Kennedy and His Times*. Boston: Houghton Mifflin Co., 1978.

Schoenebaum, Eleanora W., ed. *Political Profiles: The Nixon/Ford Years*. New York: Facts on File, 1979.

Seymour, Whitney North, Jr., *United States Attorney: An Inside View of "Justice" in America under the Nixon Administration*. New York: William Morrow & Co., 1975.

Sheffer, Martin S. "The Attorney General and Presidential Power." *Presidential Studies Quarterly* 12 (Winter 1982).

Smith, Charles W. Jr. *Roger B. Taney: Jacksonian Jurist*. Chapel Hill: University of North Carolina Press, 1936.

Solomon, Burt. "Meese Sets Ambitious Agenda That Challenges Fundamental Legal Beliefs." *National Journal* 17 (23 Nov. 1985): 2640–2646.

Sorensen, Theodore C. *Kennedy.* New York: Harper & Row, 1965.

Speakes, Larry, with Robert Pack. *Speaking Out: The Reagan Presidency from inside the White House.* New York: Charles Scribner's Sons, 1988.

Storey, Moorfield and Edward Emerson. *Ebenezer Rockwood Hoar: A Memoir.* New York: Houghton Mifflin Co., 1911.

Sutherland, Arthur, E., ed. *Government under Law.* New York: Da Capo Press, 1968.

Swisher, Carl Brent. "Federal Organization of Legal Functions." *American Political Science Review* 33 (1939): 973–1000.

———. *Roger B. Taney.* New York: Macmillan, 1935.

———. ed. *Selected Papers of Homer Cummings.* New York: Charles Scribner's Sons, 1939.

Thomas, Benjamin, and Harold Hyman. *Stanton: The Life and Times of Lincoln's Secretary of War.* New York: Alfred A. Knopf, 1962.

Thomas, Frederick W. *John Randolph of Roanoke and other Sketches of Character, Including William Wirt.* Philadelphia: A. Hart, 1853.

Tocqueville, Alexis de. *Democracy in America,* ed. J. P. Mayer. Garden City, N.Y.: Anchor Books, 1969.

Toepfer, Robert. "Some Legal Aspects of the Duty of the Attorney General to Advise." *University of Cincinnati Law Review* 19 (1950): 201–229.

Tuerkheimer, Frank M. "The Executive Investigates Itself." *California Law Review* 65 (1977): 597–635.

Tyler, Harold R., Jr. "The Attorney General of the United States: Counsel to the President or to the Government?" *Albany Law Review* 45 (Fall 1980): 1.

"United Nations Report of the International Law Commission, 2nd session, June 5–July 29, 1950." *American Journal of International Law* 44 (1950): 121. Supplement: Official Documents.

von Glahn, Gerhard. *Law among Nations.* 2nd ed. London: Macmillan, 1970.

von Holst, Hermann. *The Constitutional and Political History of the United States.* Chicago: Callaghan & Co., 1885.

Warren, Charles. "New Light on the History of the Federal Judiciary Act of 1789." *Harvard Law Review* 37 (1923): 49–132.

Wehle, Louis B. *Hidden Threads of History: Wilson through Roosevelt.* New York: Macmillan, 1953.

Weisband, Edward, and Thomas Franck. *Resignation in Protest: Political and Ethical Choices between Loyalty to Team and Loyalty to Conscience in American Public Life.* New York: Grossman, 1975.

White Burkett Miller Center Staff, eds. *The Ford White House.* Lanham, Md.: University Press of America, 1986.

White, Leonard D. *The Federalists.* 1948; reprint, Westport, Conn.: Greenwood Press, 1978.

———. *The Jeffersonians: A Study in Administrative History, 1801–1829.* New York: Macmillan, 1951.

White, Theodore H. *The Making of the President 1968.* New York: Atheneum, 1969.

Wiley, Richard, and Laurence Bodine. "Q and A with the Attorney General." *American Bar Association Journal* 71 (July 1985): 44–48.
Wilson, Henry, and J. S. Black. *Edwin M. Stanton: His Character and Public Services on the Eve of the Rebellion.* Easton, Pa.: Cole, Morowitz & Co., 1871.
Wirt, William. *The Letters of the British Spy.* 10th ed. New York: Harper & Bros., 1835.
_____. *Sketches of the Life and Character of Patrick Henry.* Philadelphia: James Webster, 1818.
Woodward, C. Vann. *Responses of the Presidents to Charges of Misconduct.* New York: Dell, 1974.
Wright, Quincy. "Editorial Comment: The Transfer of Destroyers to Great Britain." *American Journal of International Law* 34 (1940): 680–689.

Public Documents

American State Papers, 1789–1809. Misc. Vol. 1. Gales & Seaton, 1834.
American State Papers, 1801–1823. Misc. Vol. 2. Gales & Seaton, 1834.
Annals of the Congress of the United States. 14th Cong., 2d sess. (1816–1817).
Congressional Globe. 46 vols. Washington, D.C., 1834–73.
Dodge, Arthur. *Origin and Development of the Office of the Attorney General.* H.R. Doc. 510, 70th Cong., 2d sess. Washington, D.C.: Government Printing Office, 1929.
Journals of the Continental Congress, 1774–1789, Vol. 19. Edited by Gaillard Hunt. Washington, D.C.: Government Printing Office, 1912.
Key, Sewall, and Francis A. LeSourd. "The Struggle of the Attorney General to Retain His Powers." U.S. Department of Justice Speech, 1937, Library of Congress.
McKay, James C. *Report of Independent Counsel in re Edwin Meese III.* U.S. Court of Appeals for the District of Columbia Circuit. 5 July 1988.
Submission of Recorded Presidential Conversations to the Committee on the Judiciary of the House of Representatives by President Richard Nixon. 30 Apr. 1974. Buffalo, N.Y.: Reprinted by William Hein & Co., 1974.
U.S. Congress. *Register of Debates, 1829–1830.*
U.S. Congress. *Report of the Congressional Committees Investigating the Iran-Contra Affair.* 100th Cong., 1st sess. Washington, D.C.: Government Printing Office, 1987.
U.S. Congress. House. "Letter from the Attorney General in Reply to an Order by the House of Representatives of the United States, Wirt to Henry Clay, Speaker of the House." House Document No. 68. 16th Cong., 1st. sess., February 1820. Vol. 5.
U.S. Congress. House. Rules Committee. *Hearings on Attorney General A. Mitchell Palmer on Charges Made against the Department of Justice by Louis F. Post and others.* Washington, D.C.: Government Printing Office, 1921.
U.S. Congress. Senate. *Journal of the First Session of the Senate.* Gales & Seaton, 1820.

U.S. Congress. Senate. Committee on the Judiciary. *Hearings on Griffin B. Bell, Attorney General Designate*. 95th Cong., 1st sess. Washington, D.C.: Government Printing Office, 1977.

――――. *Executive Report No. 95-4 on Griffin B. Bell to Be Attorney General*. 95th Cong., 1st sess. Washington, D.C.: Government Printing Office, 1976.

――――. *Hearings on Benjamin R. Civiletti, Attorney General Designate*. 96th Cong., 1st sess. Washington, D.C.: Government Printing Office, 1980.

――――. *Hearings on the Charges of Illegal Practices of the Department of Justice made by Committee of Lawyers on Behalf of National Popular Government League*. Washington, D.C.: Government Printing Office, 1921.

――――. *Hearings on Nicholas Katzenbach, Attorney General Designate*. 89th Cong., 1st sess. Washington, D.C.: Government Printing Office, 1965.

――――. *Hearings on Richard G. Kleindienst, Attorney General Designate*. 92d Cong., 2d sess. Washington, D.C.: Government Printing Office, 1972.

――――. *Hearings on Edward H. Levi, Attorney General Designate*. 94th Cong., 1st sess. Washington, D.C.: Government Printing Office, 1975.

――――. *Hearings on Edwin Meese III, Attorney General Designate*. 98th Cong., 2d sess. Washington, D.C.: Government Printing Office, 1985.

――――. *Hearings on Edwin Meese III, Attorney General Designate*. 99th Cong., 1st sess. Washington, D.C.: Government Printing Office, 1985.

――――. *Hearings on John N. Mitchell, Attorney General Designate*. 91st Cong., 1st sess. Washington, D.C.: Government Printing Office, 1969.

――――. *Hearings on the Nomination of William H. Rehnquist and Lewis F. Powell Jr. to Be Associate Justices*. 92d Cong., 1st sess. Washington, D.C.: Government Printing Office, 1971.

――――. *Hearings on Elliot L. Richardson, Attorney General Designate*. 93d Cong., 1st sess. Washington, D.C.: Government Printing Office, 1973.

――――. *Hearings on William B. Saxbe, Attorney General Designate*. 93d Cong., 1st sess. Washington, D.C.: Government Printing Office, 1974.

――――. *Hearings on William French Smith, Attorney General Designate*. 97th Cong., 1st sess. Washington, D.C.: Government Printing Office, 1981.

U.S. Congress. Senate. Select Committee. *Hearings on the Investigation of Attorney General Harry M. Daugherty*. 68th Cong., 1st sess. Washington, D.C.: Government Printing Office, 1924.

U.S. Congress. Senate. Subcommittee on Oversight of Government Management of the Committee on Governmental Affairs. *Office of Government Ethics' Review of the Attorney General's Financial Disclosure*. 100th Cong., 1st sess. Washington, D.C.: Government Printing Office, 1988.

U.S. Congress. Senate. Subcommittee on Separation of Powers of the Committee on the Judiciary. *Hearings on S. 2803 and S. 2978 on Removing Politics from the Administration of Justice*. 93d Cong., 2d sess. Washington, D.C.: Government Printing Office, 1974.

U.S. Department of Justice. *Annual Report of the Attorney General*. Washington, D.C.: Government Printing Office, 1872 to date.

――――. *Attorneys General of the United States, 1789–1985*. Washington, D.C.: Government Printing Office, 1985.

――――. *Opinions of the Attorney General*.

_____. *Register of the Department of Justice*. 8th ed. Washington, D.C.: Government Printing Office, 1886.

Watergate Special Prosecution Force Report. Washington, D.C.: Government Printing Office, 1975.

Presidential Libraries

Cabinet Files. Gerald R. Ford Library. Ann Arbor, Mich.

Clark, Ramsey. Transcripts of Oral History Interviews. Oct. 1968, Feb., Mar., Apr., and June 1969. Lyndon Baines Johnson Library, Austin, Tex.

Connor, James E. Cabinet Secretary Files. Gerald R. Ford Library. Ann Arbor, Mich.

Department of Justice Files. Gerald R. Ford Library. Ann Arbor, Mich.

Katzenbach, Nicholas DeB. Transcripts of oral history interview. Nov. 1968. Lyndon Baines Johnson Library, Austin, Tex.

Kendall, William T. Files. Gerald R. Ford Library. Ann Arbor, Mich.

Kennedy, Robert F. General Correspondence. John F. Kennedy Library, Boston.

Kennedy, Robert F. Papers. John F. Kennedy Library, Boston.

Nesson, Ron. Papers. Gerald R. Ford Library. Ann Arbor, Mich.

Schlei, Norbert. Transcripts of oral history interview. February 1968. John F. Kennedy Library Oral History Program. John F. Kennedy Library, Boston.

Subject Files: Domestic Policy Staff. Jimmy Carter Library. Atlanta.

White House Central Files. Jimmy Carter Library. Atlanta.

White House Counsel Files. Jimmy Carter Library. Atlanta.

Interviews with the Author

Bell, Griffin. Washington, D.C. 21 Oct. 1987.

Cooper, Charles. Washington, D.C. 19 Oct. 1987.

Eastland, Terry. Washington, D.C. 19 Oct. 1987.

Kauper, Thomas E. Ann Arbor, Mich. 29 Mar. 1988.

McDowell, Gary. Washington, D.C. 7 July 1987.

Richardson, Elliot. Washington, D.C. 20 Oct. 1987.

Index